The Duke of Wellington
in 100
OBJECTS

The Duke of Wellington
in 100
OBJECTS

Gareth Glover

FRONTLINE
BOOKS

First published in Great Britain in 2020 by

Frontline Books
An imprint of
Pen & Sword Books Ltd
Yorkshire – Philadelphia

ISBN 978 1 52675 862 0

Printed and Bound in India by Replika Press Pvt. Ltd.

Pen & Sword Books Limited incorporates the imprints of Atlas, Archaeology,
Aviation, Discovery, Family History, Fiction, History, Maritime, Military, Military
Classics, Politics, Select, Transport, True Crime, Air World, Frontline Publishing,
Leo Cooper, Remember When, Seaforth Publishing, The Praetorian Press,
Wharncliffe Local History, Wharncliffe Transport, Wharncliffe True Crime and
White Owl.

For a complete list of Pen & Sword titles please contact

PEN & SWORD BOOKS LIMITED
47 Church Street, Barnsley, South Yorkshire, S70 2AS, England
E-mail: enquiries@pen-and-sword.co.uk
Website: www.pen-and-sword.co.uk

Or

PEN AND SWORD BOOKS
1950 Lawrence Rd, Havertown, PA 19083, USA
E-mail: Uspen-and-sword@casematepublishers.com
Website: www.penandswordbooks.com

Contents

Foreword   ix

1. Mornington House, 24 Upper Merrion
   Street, Dublin   1
2. Last Page of a Music Score for
   'Caractacus' by Garret Wesley dated
   1764   3
3. Sketch of Anne, Countess Mornington
   by Sir Thomas Lawrence in 1820   6
4. The Kildare Street Club   8
5. Eton College   10
6. Chateau Pignerolle built for the
   Marquis in 1776   12
7. Army List for 1787   14
8. Miniature Portrait of Richard Wellesley   16
9. Irish Masonic Painting circa 1800   19
10. Victorian Photograph of the Irish
    Parliament Buildings   21
11. Plate Depicting an Incident during the
    Battle of Boxtel   23
12. Shako of the Light Company 33rd
    Foot   25
13. English Violin circa 1790   27
14. Automaton Owned by Tipu Sultan   29
15. Button of the 19th Light Dragoons   33
16. Etching of General Sir David Baird   36
17. Indian Sword Captured at Assaye,
    Presented to Lieutenant General John
    Stuart   38
18. Gawilghur Fortress   43
19. The Briars Pavilion, St. Helena   45
20. Pencil Drawing of Kitty Pakenham in
    1814   47
21. Dress Coat Worn by Admiral Nelson
    at the Battle of Trafalgar   50
22. Deerfield, the Official Residence of
    the Secretary to the Lord Lieutenant
    of Ireland   53

23. Gerald's Sick Note Allowing Him to
    be Absent from his Parish dated 1842   56
24. Early Painting of Arthur and Kitty's
    Two Sons Carried by Arthur in the
    Peninsula   59
25. Walrus Tusk Carved with Image of the
    Bombardment of Copenhagen 1807   61
26. Permission Slip Granted to Carry
    Firearms, Signed by General Delaborde
    as Commander of Lisbon   66
27. Cartoon Lampooning the Convention
    of Cintra   70
28. Traditional Salt Boats at Aveiro   74
29. Monument to the Battle of Talavera on
    the Heights of Medellin   78
30. A Pair of Wellington's Glasses   81
31. The Wellington Monument in Somerset   83
32. Traditional Portuguese Tiled Mural
    depicting the Portuguese Victory,
    Busaco Palace   85
33. Metal-Cased Mysorean Rockets – Part
    of a Huge Batch Recently Discovered   89
34. Wellington's Headquarters at Pero
    Negro   91
35. Portuguese Print Commemorating the
    Victory at Porto 1809   95
36. Original Map of the Vicinity of Fuentes
    de Oñoro (north to the right)   98
37. French Model 1812 Lance   103
38. Ivory Miniature of Henry Wellesley   107
39. Cathedral Tower at Ciudad Rodrigo
    Still Showing the Marks Made by
    Cannon Balls   109
40. Arthur's Headquarters at Freineda for
    Extensive Periods in the Winters of
    1811 and 1812   112
41. La Torre, Residence of the Duque de
    Ciudad Rodrigo in Granada   115

42. Unexploded Shell Casing from Badajoz 117
43. Water Jug Celebrating the Victory at Salamanca 1812 122
44. Medal Struck to Commemorate the Battle of Salamanca and the Entry into Madrid 127
45. The Spanish Order of The Golden Fleece 130
46. Button of the Royal Sappers & Miners 132
47. Duke of Wellington's Necessaire or Travelling Case 136
48. Spanish Pigs Traditionally Reared in the Woods 138
49. Painting of an Indian Mahout and his Elephant 141
50. Drawing of Lady Anne Wellesley 144
51. Sabretache of Joseph 'Napoleon' Bonaparte Captured at the Battle of Vitoria 145
52. The Duke of Wellington's Peninsular Despatch Case 150
53. Marshal Jourdan's Baton 153
54. The Spanish Royal Collection at Apsley House 155
55. Dramatic Painting of Wellington and his Staff in the Pyrenees 157
56. Cartoon depicting Wellington as a Huntsman and Napoleon as the Fox 162
57. Silver Fork Plundered from San Sebastian on 31 August 1813 164
58. Contemporary View of the Mouth of the Bidassoa near Fontarrabie 169
59. La Rhune Mountain 171
60. The Church at Arcangues 173
61. Photograph of the Bridge of Orthez circa 1855 176
62. Arthur Wellesley, Duke of Wellington, with all his Regalia 180
63. Cartoon of Wellington Driving King Louis Back to his Throne 183

64. Bayonne Citadel 187
65. Hotel du Charost, Paris 190
66. Portrait of Giuseppina Grassini 194
67. Seals and Signatories of The Congress of Vienna 196
68. Cloak Worn by Wellington during the Waterloo Campaign 199
69. Saw and Bloodied Glove from the Amputation of Lord Uxbridge's Leg 203
70. Russian Miniature Commemorating the Victors of the Wars against Napoleon, the Russian Kutuzov, Wellington and Blücher 205
71. The Grave of General Miguel de Alava at Vitoria 208
72. The Gravestone of Copenhagen at Stratfield Saye 211
73. Pieces of the Prussian Service given to the Duke of Wellington 214
74. A French Cavalry Officer's An IX Pistol 216
75. Statue of Napoleon as Mars the Peacemaker by Canova 220
76. Apsley House, London 224
77. Ivory Coach Pass of William Wellesley-Pole 228
78. Stratfield Saye from the Garden 231
79. The Duke of Wellington's Annual Rent Flag 235
80. The Waterloo Shield 236
81. Cartoon of the Duke of Wellington as Master General of the Ordnance 238
82. The Wellington Tower, Kilcooney Abbey 241
83. A Pair of Arthur's Original Leather 'Wellington' Boots 244
84. A Print of Harriet Wilson 246
85. The Great Reform Act of 1832 249
86. The Catholic Emancipation Act 252
87. Contemporary Print of the Duke of Wellington's Duel with Earl Winchelsea 254

CONTENTS

88. Portrait of Kitty Wellesley in 1815   255
89. Photograph of Ewhurst Park, near Basingstoke circa 1908   257
90. Medal Commemorating Wellington becoming Chancellor of Oxford University   260
91. Replica of the Original *Rocket*   262
92. Painting of the Waterloo Gallery at Apsley House as it looked in 1852   265
93. Cartoon Depicting Arthur Acting in All the Posts of Government   267
94. Piece of Cake from Queen Victoria's Wedding, 10 February 1840   268
95. Colza Lamp at Stratfield Saye   272

96. Arthur with Four of his Grandchildren at Stratfield Saye   275
97. Wellington's Breguet Pocket Watch with a Portrait of Marianne Patterson Within   278
98. Death Mask of Arthur Wellesley, Duke of Wellington   282
99. An Invitation for Mrs Passmore to Attend the Duke of Wellington's Funeral at St Paul's   285
100. Pub Sign for The Duke of Wellington   289

Index   293

The Duke of Wellington by Sir Thomas Lawrence. Wellington believed that this was the best portrait of himself ever produced.

Foreword

This is the second volume of a pair published in 2019, to mark the 250th anniversary of two of the greatest men in world history. Both Napoleon Bonaparte and his greatest adversary, Arthur Welsey (later Wellesley), the Duke of Wellington, were born in the remarkable year of 1769. When I say remarkable, I do not mean because of particular world events, scientific discoveries or even life-changing social revolutions. What 1769 should be famous for is the incredible number of military men born this year, many of whom would certainly appear in a list of the world's top 100 military leaders of all time. Beyond Napoleon and Wellington, 1769 saw the birth of Marshals Ney, Soult and Lannes, Generals Decaen, Anson, Lumley, Arakcheyev, Malcolm, Belliard, Brock, Muhamad Ali, von Decken, Hope, Joubert, Markov, Thiebault, Wallmoden and Wittgenstein, not to mention Admiral Hardy (of 'Kiss me Hardy' fame), Sir Hudson Lowe (Napoleon's gaoler) and Sergeant Ewart (who captured an eagle at Waterloo), to name but a few. In fact, well over fifty major military figures were born this year, a truly remarkable total.

Arthur, Duke of Wellington did not become an emperor or a king, but in every other respect, his influence throughout Europe was just as great as Napoleon's. His renown was great before the Battle of Waterloo, but after his great victory, ably assisted by Marshal Blücher, he was feted everywhere as 'the conqueror of the conqueror of Europe'. After that stunning success, he could not walk into any function anywhere, without the band striking up the tune to the hymn 'See the Conquering Hero Comes'.

There however, almost all the similarities with Napoleon Bonaparte end, their characters,

Wellington bust.

backgrounds and careers being very different and fate only ever brought them together to meet across a battlefield on 18 June 1815.

Arthur Welsey (the family later changed the spelling to Wellesley), was born into minor aristocracy in Ireland and he did not show any great aptitude for anything, apart from playing the violin quite well. With his father dying whilst young, he went into the army, and rose in rank quickly thanks to his brother's financial support. However, the British Army he joined was at a low ebb and as he said himself, his early forays abroad taught him the valuable lesson of how not to do things. Arthur showed some early promise as a soldier, but he had yet to commit himself to the profession and he enjoyed a wayward life, which drew much criticism from friends and family. Unrequited love was to change all of this, for having fallen head over heels for the beautiful Kitty Pakenham, he sought her hand in marriage, but was refused by her family, as having no fortune and few prospects of ever attaining one. Being spurned was the turning point in Arthur's career, as he determined to make a serious effort to gain promotion and success within the army, so that he could return to finally gain Kitty's hand in marriage.

Arthur was sent to India with his regiment, where his elder brother was already installed as Governor General. This gave him the opportunity to command large armies of British and native Indian troops in government regiments and also work in coordination with various Indian princes with whom the British were allied. The experiences of marching through thick jungle, carrying everything needed in the way of supplies with them and engaging huge armies of ill-disciplined Indian troops with much smaller armies of highly disciplined soldiers using European methods, saw him win some incredible victories, such as the Battle of Assaye and the storming of Gawilghur Fortress. Returning home in 1805, the victor of numerous battles in India and, more importantly, rich, he now gained the hand of Kitty and his military career continued to burgeon.

Wellesley's great opportunity would come on the European stage, with Napoleon's ill-fated decision to invade Portugal and then to usurp the crown of Spain and give it to his brother. The British had a small army, but a huge navy which had already gained virtual control of the oceans and British manufacturing and trade meant that Britain had very deep pockets indeed. Whilst Napoleon's enemies were heavily subsidised, Arthur was sent with a small British army into Portugal and he quite quickly gained a high reputation, having defeated French armies in the field, something that was almost unknown in Europe these last ten years.

Wellington's organisational skills, strategic expertise and abilities in close command slowly moulded his British army into a superb fighting

THE DOUBLE DEALER.

Cartoon of Wellington as both soldier and politician.

force, whilst he also saw the Portuguese army brought up to the same standards and eventually became commander-in-chief of the Spanish forces as well. Despite never being able to put anywhere near comparative forces in the field, he fought in the Peninsula for six years, eventually driving the French out and even pushing his forces deep into Southern France, before Napoleon was forced to abdicate. Napoleon's overthrow was not down to Wellington alone, as Prussia, Austria and Russia fully participated in finally bringing him down, but Wellington's stunning victories often gave hope at a time when Napoleon was routinely crushing any opposition to his ambitions in Central Europe.

Wellington gained great honours and riches from all of the Allied sovereigns and he was sent to the Congress of Vienna to use his undoubted influence to gain concessions, particularly relating to Britain's attempts to garner support for the end of the slave trade.

However, his fame following his stunning victory at Waterloo eclipsed all that came before and he became one of the most famous individuals in the entire world and he was invited to almost everything. He was given command of the entire combined European army based in France for three years to oversee the re-establishment of the monarchy, whilst Napoleon was banished to St. Helena, where he saw out the rest of his life.

With the war finally over (Britain had been at war almost continuously for twenty-three years), Arthur was taken into the Cabinet and he soon became a leading politician. He eventually became Prime Minister in 1828 and saw through the Catholic Emancipation Act and helped the passage of the Great Reform Act, although he was not sure about it. His political career was not, however, as dazzling as his military career, but he was able to exert enormous influence on people and events and did so always in the belief that what he did, he did for the best for his country. He was always loyal to his sovereign and he was close to all three that reigned after he came home from the wars.

When he finally died in 1852, the entire country went into mourning and his funeral procession was one of the largest ever seen in Britain, with over one and a half million crowding the streets to glimpse the coffin as it passed.

Like every great, larger-than-life character, the legacy of the Duke of Wellington is huge but not everything he did is regarded well today and opinions are divided. As a historian I have attempted to take an impartial, balanced approach in describing the various aspects of his life and I leave it to the reader to make their own final judgement on him.

Arthur Wellesley was never a tyrant; indeed when the opportunity arrived to possibly be one, it never occurred to him to take it. Duty was his simple watchword. Duty to his monarch, duty to the country and duty to his family, and he often went against his better judgement in support of these simple principles. A caricature of the man has developed over the centuries, as that of a hard, indeed heartless, man, who was cold and aloof, and a reactionary who refused to move with the times. Like all such simple stereotypes there is an element of truth in them, but there is a great deal of evidence that shows a man who demanded much from his subordinates, but cared greatly for their welfare. He often showed great remorse and was actually seen to break down and cry on a number of occasions where his orders had led to the deaths of large numbers of his troops. He was also passionate and often to be seen walking with the lowest in society and happy to be alone in their company. His political career has often been criticised, but he tempered his zeal for the status quo by being pragmatic and bending when the winds of change were simply too strong to avoid being broken by them. By the end of his life he was feted as a truly great man and he is recognised as having had a greater effect on Britain in the last two centuries than anyone, perhaps with the exception of Winston Churchill. Today, he is seen as a lesser figure within Europe but at the time nobody eclipsed him; he was a true giant on the world stage.

How he rates alongside Napoleon, only the reader can decide, having viewed the achievements and failures of both, but have no doubt, that in the early decades of the nineteenth century, these two men were seen as two equal giants on the world stage.

It has been my honour to bring both of their superb legacies into perspective over these two volumes.

Gareth Glover 2019

The Duke of Wellington.

1: Mornington House, 24 Upper Merrion Street, Dublin

The date of birth of Arthur Wesley, later to become the Duke of Wellington, would, you might assume, be an established fact, but it is far from that. Even the location of his birth is not certain.

A written statement submitted by his father to the Irish House of Lords dated April 1779 and a letter believed to have been written by his mother in 1815[1] both state that Arthur was born on 1 May 1769 at their Dublin residence, Mornington House. This is further backed up by his entry in *Burke's Peerage* (which had been first published the year he was born) and in the family tree preserved by his elder brother Richard. All of this evidence would seem conclusive, added to which, Arthur consistently celebrated his birthday on 1 May throughout his life.

However, the historical evidence is far from as clear. The newspaper announcements are not helpful: the *Dublin Gazette* of 2 May states that the birth occurred 'a few days ago in Merrion Street', whilst the weekly *Dublin Mercury*, *Freeman's Journal* and *Pue's Occurrence* all announce the birth without stating its date.

However, the baptismal record from St Peter's Church, Church of Ireland, clearly shows that Arthur was baptised on 30 April 1769. Doubts have been raised over this record simply because the date does not sit comfortably with the family claims, but there is no reason to doubt its authenticity. Given that the Anglican tradition was often to baptise the child some days after the birth, to ensure it was likely to survive, it is highly likely that Arthur was born prior to

---

1. James Cuthbertson, a correspondent of *The Times* newspaper, claimed in 1815 to have written to Lady Mornington, Wellington's mother, and that she had replied by letter confirming the date of Arthur's birth as 1 May 1769, but unfortunately the letter has never been found.

30 April. Indeed, *Exshaw's Gentleman's Magazine* which published monthly, actually gave the date of birth as 29 April.

It is also interesting to note that the family had already named a previous son Arthur, who was born in 1761. Had this child survived, it is more than likely that the future Duke of Wellington would have been named Gerald Valerian, the name given to the next son.

The Reverend Gleig, a close friend of the Duke, later made claims that he had found a newspaper report stating that he was born on 3 April and that he even obtained a statement from the midwife that he was born on 6 March! However, no evidence has been found to corroborate these later claims and they can be discounted.

The place of birth has also been disputed, as the family had previously used a property in Grafton Street. Contemporary newspaper reports, however, generally agree that Arthur was born at the family residence in the city, Mornington House, 6 Merrion Street (since renamed and renumbered 24 Upper Merrion Street) in Dublin. The house, built in 1762 and probably designed by the architect Christopher Myers, was leased by the family. Other properties have been suggested,

as renovation works were underway at the house until the summer of 1769, but a Dublin birth is almost universally accepted by historians.

There is however some circumstantial evidence for the birth having occurred at the family's country house, Dangan Castle. This location was supported by *Burke's Peerage* and a Nurse Daly swore on oath at an enquiry in 1791 that she had attended the birth of Arthur at Dangan Castle. Many other claims for locations for the birth have been made, but none have any real substance. It is therefore quite possible that the birth occurred at Dangan Castle, but that the birth was then announced from Mornington House, where the family had transferred to.

All that can be said is that the most likely scenario is that Arthur Welsey was born at Dangan Castle during the last week of April 1769 and was soon transferred to Dublin, where the birth was announced and the baptism then occurred. Despite all of the family evidence, the birth date of 1 May cannot be correct, but it is unclear why this date was preferred.

Mornington House and the three adjoining properties were purchased in the 1990s and converted into the extremely prestigious five-star Merrion Hotel.

The ruins of Dangan Castle.

2: Last Page of a Music Score for 'Caractacus' by Garret Wesley dated 1764

Garret Colley Wesley, his father, rarely receives much coverage in biographies of the Duke of Wellington, largely because he died when Arthur was still a child and is therefore deemed not to have had much influence on the future Duke. This, however, is far from the truth, as he was undoubtedly a significant influence on Arthur's life-long love of music.

Garret was born at Dangan Castle in 1735, the first son of Richard Wesley, the 1st Baron Mornington. Educated at Trinity College, Dublin, he showed a real talent for playing the violin (just like his father) and became a composer, principally of 'glees' – short baroque songs often sung by three people without music – but also of more substantial works such as 'Caractacus'. He was a good-humoured and gregarious man. Money was only useful to Garret, one of his guests recorded, 'as … the means of making those about him happy'.

He was eventually to be elected as the first ever Professor of Music at Trinity, in 1764. Arthur grew up with an organ standing in the hall and a harpsicord played every morning at breakfast, music filled his early life and he also

Garret Colley Wesley.

showed talent in the violin in his youth and practised assiduously.

Garret also represented the constituency of Trim in the Irish Parliament for just one year in 1757–8, the seat being a 'rotten borough' in the pocket of the Wesleys. A year later, he became *Custos Rotulorum* for the County of Meath (the precursor to the Lord Lieutenant).

Garret initially tried for the hand of Louisa Lennox, the daughter of a duke, but apparently she preferred another suitor, not just because he was much wealthier but also because she 'had an insurmountable dislike' for Garret. On 6 February 1759, Garret married Anne Hill-Trevor, from whom no dowry was required, being the daughter of a one-time banker (who later became the 1st Viscount Dungannon on the death of his brother), a marriage that would be happy despite their financial worries.

In 1760, he was awarded the title of Viscount of Dangan Castle and 1st Earl of Mornington in the Irish peerage for his musical achievements and his charitable works. In 1776 he was also elected Grandmaster of the Grand Lodge of Irish Masons.

Unfortunately, despite all of these honours, Garret was a spendthrift, just like his father before him, spending fortunes which he did not have on improving Dangan. Due to pecuniary embarrassment, he eventually moved the family to London in 1774 and he ominously began to purchase large numbers of lottery tickets in the hope that they would solve his financial worries. His early death at the age of 45, when Arthur was only 12 years old – of an unknown cause – in London in 1781, left the family ruined financially and forced them to raise mortgages on much of their lands in Ireland.

3: Sketch of Anne, Countess Mornington by Sir Thomas Lawrence in 1820

Anne was born in London in 1742, the daughter of Anne Stafford of Brownstown and Arthur Hill-Trevor, a resonably successful banker, whose childless brother was the 1st Viscount Hilsborough.

Although not being his first choice, Anne married Garret Wesley on 6 February 1759 aged 16, being seven years younger than him. No dowry had been required by Garret's generous father. Instead he provided them with an income of £1,600 per annum and £500 a year for Anne's personal expenses, adding that if she had a dowry, that she could spend it on jewellery! His godmother's view of Anne at this time was also begrudgingly accepting, describing her as 'rather a little clumsy, but with [a] fine complexion, teeth and nails, with a great deal of modesty and good humour'.

The couple had a happy marriage, despite Garret's profligacy and Anne's apparent 'want of judgement'. They had nine children, Richard Colley born in 1760, Arthur born in 1761, William in 1763, Francis Seymour in 1765, Arthur in 1769, Gerald Valerian in 1770, Mary Elizabeth in 1772, Henry in 1773 and finally Anne in 1775. The first Arthur and Francis Seymour both unfortunately died very young and Mary died aged only 22 in 1794. As the children grew up, they showed a bent for debating and politics, but they were to get little of this debate at home, the eldest, Richard, later describing his parents disdainfully as 'frivolous and careless personages'.

Following Garret's death in 1781, Richard was forced to leave education to try to sort out the mess of the family finances and to gain

paid employment. By 1784, Anne was forced to move abroad to reduce the family expenses and she settled in Brussels, where Arthur joined her, having left Eton early. They lived there for a full year. However, Arthur's relationship with his mother was always strained and their relationship cannot be regarded as close. Following Garret's death, the joy seems to have left Anne's life and she was later described as formidable, being 'cold and severe'. Richard was

IN A VAULT BENEATH THE CHAPEL
LIE THE REMAINS OF
GARRET
1ST EARL OF MORNINGTON 1735-81
& OF ANNE HILL HIS WIFE 1740-1831
PARENTS OF
ARTHUR 1ST DUKE OF WELLINGTON

undoubtedly the 'golden child' and her favourite. As to Arthur, she expected little of the difficult boy, once famously declaring to a relative, 'I vow to God I don't know what I shall do with my awkward son Arthur'.

In 1795, she moved into a 'grace and favour' apartment, No. 12, at Hampton Court Palace, which was almost certainly down to Richard, where she had a private garden which was later named after her. One quiet spot in the sun was a favourite spot of hers, which Arthur named on his visits 'Purr Corner'. She was also later granted a government pension of £600 per annum. She lived here for a number of years before moving to No. 3 Henrietta Street, Cavendish Square, Covent Garden, where she died, aged 89, on 10 September 1831 and she was buried alongside Garret in Grosvenor Chapel, Mayfair.

A print of Anne in her official robes surrounded by busts of her famous sons.

4: The Kildare Street Club

The young Arthur Wesley and stories of his adventures in Dublin chime very discordantly with the serious, refined and gentlemanly elder statesman we think we know. Georgian Dublin, like London, was a seething mass of drunkenness and debauchery, far from the more straight-laced, prim and proper public life of Victorian Britain which slowly superseded it.

Arthur rented lodgings on Lower Ormond Quay in the house of a boot-maker and lived the life of a drunken, debauched rake, spiralling into heavy debt and even borrowing money from his landlord. He was addicted to gambling and would bet on almost anything, even such mundane events as betting 150 guineas on the time it might take him to walk from Cornelscourt to Leeson Street (on this occasion he won). What

else could be expected when the family consisted primarily of profligate spendthrifts? Drinking and carousing were everyday occurrences and there are accounts of Arthur being fined for breaking into a woman's house and for beating a Frenchman with a stick in a bawdy house.

He almost certainly frequented Daly's Club on Dame Street, which was rumoured to be linked by a tunnel to the Irish Houses of Parliament. He was certainly a member of the rival Kildare Street Club, which opened its doors in 1782 and was begun by a number of members barred from Daly's. Interestingly, many of its original members were against the Act of Union.

The old clubhouse at No. 6 was gutted by fire in 1860, destroying everything in the building including a fine library and in which three of

the maidservants were unfortunately killed, a fourth only surviving because she was in the club accountant's bedroom! The Italianate building shown in the picture at No. 1 Kildare Street was built to replace the original club building. The club has since merged with the University Club and has since moved again, although it is still in existence.

Arthur also sought to attract the ladies, but the loutish youth turned many away; one young lady to positively refused to attend a picnic until assured 'that mischievous boy' would not be there, whilst another lady grew so bored of him as her partner at a picnic that she departed in her carriage, leaving Arthur many miles from home without transport, apparently only getting home via a lift from the musicians. Arthur, it seems, was an innocent and fell in love at the drop of a hat, his friend Cradock recording that his 'propensity to fall in love, you are aware of'. Arthur confirmed to his friend Fremantle that he had been forced to take lodgings, because of his reputation for a roving eye, explaining that

'I wished to have a room in the house which you [had] inhabited but Dean Butler upon my applying for it, gave me to understand that he would do it if he could with propriety, but his wife & daughter were in the house. He certainly cannot think me such an irresistible man as Williams. I hinted to him that I would not touch his wife, if she would [even] let me & that I would do all I could to harden his daughter from falling in love with me. He would not hear of it, therefore I was obliged to take a lodging.'

When he had no money he would remain in his rooms and practise his beloved violin, until Kitty Pakenham came along.

No. 6 Kildare Street, the home of the original club, rebuilt as the Royal College of Physicians after a devastating fire.

5: Eton College

Arthur's schooling began at the Diocesan School in Trim and then at Samuel Whyte's Academy on Grafton Street, but with the family move to London, he was entered into Brown's establishment at Chelsea, but the education he received there was mediocre at best. Following the death of his father and despite the financial challenges of the family, when he was 12 years old he was sent to Eton in the autumn of 1781, where he remained until 1784. He later admitted to his biographer, Gleig, that he was singularly ill-equipped for going to Eton and that he was 'a dreamy, idle and shy lad', only excelling at mental arithmetic. Arthur suffered from indifferent health and never took part in school-yard games, but usually simply 'lounged' against a large walnut tree watching them play. If picked on, he was fully prepared to stand up and fight his corner, but then would simply return to his tree. Indeed young Arthur became distinctly 'combative'. He is recorded as having been the instigator of a number of fist fights, but whether he won or lost, he apparently never bore any ill will to his opponent. There

were no compulsory organised games at Eton and Arthur generally preferred playing in the grounds alone. He was undoubtedly lonely and withdrawn. Academically he was not particularly bright and he was soon outshone by his younger brother Gerald, who joined him there a year later. Eventually Richard, who had been forced to curtail his own academic life when his father died, saw no point in continuing to waste money on Arthur and removed him from Eton, using the funds released to continue the educations of the much more promising Gerald and Henry.

He left without regret, having little affection for the place and proceeded to join his mother in Brussels. Arthur did not, however, bear any grudges against the school, indeed he later sent both of his sons to Eton. He did not visit the school again until January 1818 when his sons were there, when he delighted in visiting his old room, the kitchen, garden and the maid's workroom, which he delighted in recalling was dubbed 'Virgin's Bower' by the boys. He visited once more whilst his sons were there and only on two other formal occasions during the rest

of his long life, once to attend the service for his brother Richard's funeral and once when escorting Queen Victoria and Louis Philippe King of France. Given his ambivalence for the place it is not particularly surprising that in 1841, when he was asked to make a contribution to the school for new buildings, he flatly refused.

Having seen that he had little real affection for his old alma mater it is therefore all the more surprising that he reputedly later said

'The Battle of Waterloo was won on the playing-fields of Eton.'

Except he never said it.

The famous phrase was never recorded during his lifetime and actually seems to have been invented later as an amalgamation of various comments made both by him and others.

In 1856, four years after his death, Charles de Montalembert recorded in a book written in French, that on returning to Eton late in life, Arthur had reputedly said 'It was there that the Battle of Waterloo was won!'. He provides no evidence for this claim and indeed these words would have had to have been said in front of Queen Victoria, an avid diarist, who does not mention a word of it. Twenty years later Sir Edward Creasy published a book entitled *Memoirs of Eminent Etonians*, in which it is recorded, that on some unspecified occasion, whilst riding past the playing fields of Eton, whilst a cricket match was under way, the Duke of Wellington had announced 'There grows the stuff that won Waterloo'. Later, these two phrases were combined by Sir William Fraser in 1889 in his book *Words on Wellington* into the immortal words that have passed down to us today.

When Arthur was at Eton, there were no organised games and therefore no playing fields. Indeed, he actively avoided team sports there, always remaining alone and withdrawn from any such games.

The phrase is very unlike Wellington, and given his experiences there, very unlikely to have ever been uttered by him, they are one of many Victorian inventions that surround him.

A nineteenth-century photograph of a classroom at Eton.

6: Chateau Pignerolle
built for the Marquis in 1776

After a year of doing little in Brussels, his mother deemed that Arthur was 'food for powder and little more' and with the financial support of his brother Richard, he was shipped off to The Royal Academy of Equitation at Angers, on the Loire, which was effectively a finishing school for gentlemen. It was one of four such *Ecoles d'Equitation* created by the king in 1764 at Metz, Douai, Besançon and Angers, each under the management of a general officer. The Director at Angers was the celebrated military engineer, the Marquis Marcel de Pignerolle, whose brother ran the excellent stable. Arthur arrived and was enrolled on 16 January 1786, arriving with two other Irish boys, a son of Lord Walsh and a son of Lord Powerscourt. Of the 334 pupils at the academy, some 108 were British when Arthur was there. The pupils wore a distinctive scarlet coat, with sky-blue facings on the collar and cuffs and yellow gold buttons (totally unlike the painting opposite). The Marquis was eventually to become a victim of 'Madame Guillotine' in 1794 during the French Revolution. The building housing the academy was apparently destroyed during a British bombing raid in 1944.

Here Arthur was taught the arts of, riding, fencing, dancing (a form of formalised exercise), deportment, mathematics, fortifications and literature. Arthur was to become an efficient rider, not a pretty one, but this equipped him well for the long hours in the saddle he endured in later years. It also helped him perfect his courtly French, which he later found of great use. However, Arthur learnt little else. His fellow student, Alexander Mackenzie of Fairburn, who eventually became a general himself, later recalled that Arthur was 'ailing and sickly, too much so to take much part in the bodily exercises, riding, fencing, etc, which, I believe, were the principal part of the instructions at this school. He passed most of the time on a sofa,

Chateau Brissac.

playing with a white terrier, which followed him everywhere.' What happened to the terrier named 'Vick' when Arthur returned to England in 1786 is not recorded, but he never mentioned it again.

Arthur was also introduced into the French *'Ancien regime'*, often attending dinners at Chateau Brissac, the home of the Duc de Brissac, although he was horrified to discover that the Duke regularly reserved the best food and wine for himself, serving lesser quality to his guests.

However, his experiences at Angers had clearly had some effect on the young man, as his mother was unusually impressed on first meeting him after his return from France. Despite initially greeting him testily with 'I do believe there is my ugly boy Arthur', she later stated that 'He really is a charming young man, never did I see such a change for the better in anyone'.

A Victorian painting of Arthur at Angers, when he was actually aged 16.

7: Army List for 1787

On his return to England in 1786, Arthur was clearly destined for the army, which was not then seen as an auspicious career, but rather 'as the last refuge of wastrels'. He was, however, totally dependent on his brother Richard's support, in terms of both money and influence, to gain a commission. Richard, now a junior Lord of the Treasury, reminded George Nugent-Temple-Grenville, 1st Marquess of Buckingham, then Lord Lieutenant of Ireland, that he had promised to help him gain a commission for Arthur, adding sardonically, 'He is here at the moment and perfectly idle. It is a matter of indifference to me what commission he gets, provided he gets it soon.'

Finally, he was gazetted to be an ensign in the 73rd Highland Regiment on 7 March 1787, although it is certain that he did not physically join the regiment, which was then serving in India. On Christmas Day 1787, he purchased the rank of lieutenant in the 76th Foot. In November 1787, he was appointed as aide-de-camp to the Lord Lieutenant of Ireland. His regiment was due imminently to sail for India and perhaps to avoid going with them, Arthur rapidly transferred again on 23 January 1788 to the 41st Foot and despite evidence in the muster rolls that he may have briefly joined the regiment at Hilsea Barracks, he was soon back at his post in Ireland. Arthur had been present with his regiments for literally a handful of days at most during his first two years of army service.

Fifteen months later Arthur was on the move again, transferring to the 12th (Prince of Wales's) Light Dragoons on 25 June 1789, a more prestigious regiment which presumably required him to pay another 'purchase' fee. There is again some limited evidence of Arthur's presence with

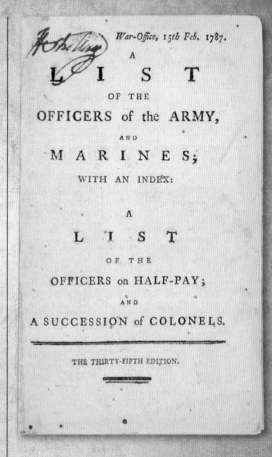

the regiment in Kilkenny, Ireland, but it is clear that he largely remained in Dublin, continuing in his role as aide-de-camp to the new Lord Lieutenant, Lord Westmorland.

Arthur finally gained promotion to captain by purchase in the 58th Foot on 30 June 1790, which was then based in Cork and Kinsale, but how much time he spent with them again is debatable, as the regimental musters show him at Dublin 'on recruiting service', which might well have been a cover to allow him to continue in his role as aide-de-camp. On 31 October 1792 he then transferred to the 18th Light Dragoons, an Irish regiment.

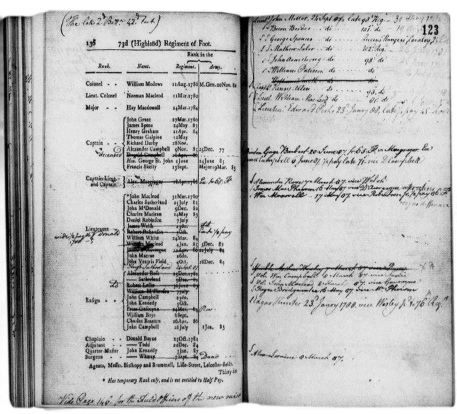

1787 Army List with Ensign Arthur Wesley 73rd Foot written in and already struck through as he had moved to the 76th Foot before the end of the year.

On 30 April 1793, Arthur purchased the position of major in the 33rd Foot and only five months later he purchased the rank of lieutenant colonel still within the 33rd Foot, giving him the command of a battalion in the field. This was a regiment which Arthur would continue to have close links with throughout his life.

Arthur's rapid promotion, from ensign to lieutenant colonel within five and a half years, was fuelled by his brother Richard's money. The standard fee to purchase a lieutenant colonelcy was £3,500, which with the additional provision of uniforms and horses was a very serious amount of money to outlay, equating in modern terms to around a third of a million pounds! Though quick, Arthur's rise in rank was not, however, seen as excessively so at the time, when the worst abuses of the 'purchase' system effectively allowed children still at school to command regiments! Two years later, the Duke of York instigated changes to the system and introduced minimum terms of service in each rank, meaning that the minimum required to become a lieutenant colonel was seven years' service, which was not a great deal longer than Arthur's apprenticeship, although far longer than he actually served with the regiments.

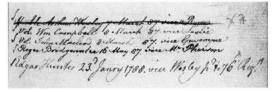

Close-up of 'Honourable Arthur Wesley 7 March '87 vice A. Ross' (followed in pencil – 76 Ft).

8: Miniature Portrait of Richard Wellesley

Arthur's elder brother was some nine years older and when their father died he had a very significant impact on his early military career.

Seen as a very bright young man and heir to the family estates, no expense was spared on Richard's education. He initially attended The Royal School at Armagh, one of four schools established by King James I in 1608 to educate the sons of the Protestant settlers who established the Ulster Plantation. When the family moved to London, he transferred to Harrow and then moved on to Eton before finally attending Christ Church College Oxford.

Richard had been elected to the Irish House of Commons in 1780 as the member for Trim, the traditional family seat, and he also became a Mason, to garner their votes. However, in 1781, everything was about to change radically for Richard, with the sudden death of their father. He immediately inherited the title of 2nd Earl of Mornington, which gave him a seat in the Irish House of Lords. However, he was soon to discover the parlous state of the family finances and Richard was forced to leave Oxford without completing his degree in order to apply all of his efforts to saving the family from ruin.

Richard also replaced his father as *Custos Rotulorum* of Meath, an office which was a precursor of the role of Lord Lieutenant of the county, and he was elected Grand Master of the Grand Lodge of Ireland in 1782, a position he held for the following year.

Richard began to take all necessary measures to relieve the family of the financial burden of their Irish estates, and would now seek his fortune in England. In 1784 he was elected to the House of Commons as the MP for Bere Alston, a rotten borough with two seats available to friends of the Duke of Northumberland, and was soon given a lucrative post as one of the Lords Commissioners of the Treasury by William Pitt the Younger. Mornington House in Dublin was sold to Lord Cloncurry in 1791 for a handsome £8,000 (it went for only £2,500 only ten years later) and Dangan Castle was also finally sold in 1793. This stabilised the family finances and allowed Richard to fund Arthur's early rise through the officer ranks of the army, but his influence on his younger brother was yet to be much greater than simply purchasing him his lieutenant colonelcy.

Whilst in Paris in the late 1780s, Richard had met Hyacinthe-Gabrielle Roland, a French actress (at a time when actresses were viewed

Richard Marquess Wellesley in 1833.

as little more than prostitutes), and they lived together for a number of years, having five illegitimate children together, before they eventually married in London on 29 November 1794. Richard also had two other illegitimate sons by Elizabeth Johnston, his mistress. Throughout his life Richard was prone to unexplained blackouts, which did occasionally interfere with his official duties, but he was not otherwise a sickly man.

In 1793, Richard had become a member of the Board of Control on India and having immersed himself in the detailed running of the subcontinent, he was offered the high office of Governor General of India in 1797. This move was of course highly fortuitous for Arthur, who had already sailed to India with his regiment in June 1796. Although Hyacinthe was now a Countess, she remained a social pariah, but despite this, she refused to travel to India with Richard and it soon became apparent that he had set up home there with a new mistress.

Mornington determined that he would use his time in India to consolidate British control and to negate French ambitions there, his brother soon becoming a useful ally in this cause. Arthur was able to gain immense military experience whilst carrying out his brother's policies, whilst their brother Henry was also persuaded to serve in India as Richard's secretary. Richard was raised to the peerage as Baron Wellesley – the family surname reverting to the West Country spelling, which the entire family adopted – and in 1799 he was made Marquess Wellesley in the Irish peerage. He remained as Governor General until July 1805, by which time British control of India was almost complete and French interests virtually eradicated. He was a very able administrator who also planned for the future, by founding Fort William College to train future administrators

and lightened trade restrictions between India and Britain, but his policies often brought him into conflict with the directors of the East India Company, tendering his resignation on a number of occasions before he finally left and a later attempt to impeach him in Parliament was defeated in 1808.

Having returned to Britain, Richard bought Apsley House and he and Hyacinthe lived there together for a short time, before they became estranged and he took another mistress. On his return, Richard refused to take office until all attempts to condemn his conduct in India had been defeated. In 1809, he then accepted the post as Ambassador to Spain, but he soon returned to Britain to become Foreign Secretary, which office he held until 1812, when he resigned largely because of the government's failure to support Arthur's forces in Portugal and Spain properly. He had separated formally from Hyacinthe in 1810, who died in 1812. Richard married again to the widowed Marianne Patterson (née Caton) in October 1825, despite Arthur's advice not to marry his brother because of his children, whom he called collectively 'The Parasites'.

Richard remained in the political wilderness until 1821, when he eventually accepted the post of Lord Lieutenant of Ireland and he strived hard for Catholic Emancipation, but felt he had to resign when Arthur became Prime Minister in 1828. He resumed the post in 1833, but soon fell ill and he retired from public life. He died on 26 September 1842.

Arthur had been estranged from his brother for a number of years when he died, their relationship always being a little brittle, perhaps not surprising when you had two such strong-willed characters, but at his brother's funeral Arthur openly wept and declared that he knew of no greater honour than being Richard's brother.

9: Irish Masonic Painting circa 1800

Garret Wesley had been a Mason and had served as Grand Master of the Grand Lodge of Ireland for a year, the standard term of office. Richard had in turn joined the Masons and he also rose to be Grand Master like his father.

Maintaining the family tradition, Arthur also became a Mason in the Trim Lodge (No. 494) on 7 December 1790 and he underwent the initiation ceremony and paid his admittance fee of £2 5s 6d. Despite his regular financial difficulties, Arthur managed to pay his dues

and in 1794 is even recorded as having paid 14 shillings and 1 pence in advance. His last payment appears in the records on 8 September 1795. In the February of that year he is also shown as a part purchaser of an English lottery ticket from the Lodge Treasurer but they did not win.

He resigned from the Lodge on sailing to India in 1806 and he never actively resumed his Masonic career. In a speech shortly after Wellington's death, Lord Combermere referred to his having been a Mason and claimed that

Arthur had regretted not progressing further in the lodge, but Arthur's words do not seem to support this claim.

When the troops arrived in Portugal, some officers held a Masonic meeting at Lisbon, following which they had paraded through the city in full regalia, when they were pelted with stones and nearly caused a riot. A number of Papal Bulls had been issued against the Masons and the Portuguese government complained to Arthur, as the Masons were banned in both Portugal and Spain. In 1810 he felt compelled to issue a General Order on 5 January requiring everyone in the army to refrain from overt Masonic activity, as it was 'an amusement which, however innocent in itself and allowed by the law of Great Britain, is a violation of this country, and very disagreeable to the people'.

In 1815, Marshal Ney, a renowned Mason was sentenced to death by firing squad and he appealed to Wellington as a 'brother', believing him to also be one. Ney was shot, but rumours that Wellington arranged for a mock execution and arranged for Ney to escape to America where he lived out his life as a schoolteacher abound to this day, although there is not a single shred of evidence to support them.

Throughout his life however, claims of his Masonic leanings continued to follow him, indeed, when in 1843 he was asked if his old lodge could rename themselves in his honour, he declined, stating that he 'perfectly recollects he was admitted to the lowest grade of Free Masonry in a Lodge which was fixed at Trim, in the County of Meath. His consent to give this Lodge his Name would be a ridiculous assumption of the reputation of being attached to Free Masonry; in addition to being a misrepresentation.'

As the rumours persisted, he went even further in a letter on 13 October 1851 when he replied: 'Field Marshal the Duke of Wellington presents his compliments to Mr Walsh. He has received his letter of 7th ult. The Duke has no recollection of having been admitted a Freemason. He has no knowledge of that association.'

10: Victorian Photograph of the Irish Parliament Buildings

When Arthur took up his role as secretary to the Lord Lieutenant, he found a Dublin which was blossoming, full of confidence and enterprise. A purpose-built parliament building imitating the British parliament with two chambers had begun construction in 1729. In 1782, following a series of constitutional reforms, Ireland's first independent parliament had sat, but the real seat of power still resided in Dublin Castle, the Irish nobility bound to the British rule by their titles, pensions, sinecures and employment. In fact, two-thirds of the parliament were firmly with the King's government for just these reasons, whom Wolfe Tone called 'the prostitutes of the King's Bench'.

The Wesleys traditionally held the seat of Trim in the Irish House of Commons, Richard had held the seat and William had succeeded him, but he now sought to transfer to the English House of Commons, leaving Trim to Arthur. Arthur sought his seat in March 1790 and established his claim by a concerted attack on the corporation, who sought to grant the freedom of the town on the nationalist leader Henry Grattan. He successfully defeated the attempt by highlighting that the only reason announced for granting the freedom was because Grattan 'was a respectable man'. Arthur rightly pointed out, that if respectability was all that was needed to be granted the freedom of the town, then soon the whole community would be freemen!

Arthur won the subsequent vote 47 to 29. He also became a Freemason, being initiated into the Trim Lodge (No. 494) to garner more votes. Having been elected for Trim, there was some talk of a petition against him as it was claimed that he was not fully 21, the legal requirement to sit, but it came to nothing. But, despite sitting in the Irish House of Commons for three years, he never spoke until in early 1793 he seconded an address deploring the imprisonment of King Louis XVI and the French invasion of Holland. The real reason for this sudden change was his hope of impressing the Pakenhams enough to allow him to marry Kitty. Unfortunately, Arthur was deemed to have an unpolished address and showed no real promise as a fledgling politician. It would seem that Arthur largely agreed with the assessment and as soon as he learnt that his regiment would be going on Lord Moira's expedition in mid-1793, he promptly resigned his seat.

The 1790 election was the last one for the Irish Parliament, the Act of Union of 1800 meaning that Irish Members of Parliament from now on sat at Westminster. Parliament House in Dublin was effectively redundant and the building was used at one time as a garrison and at another as an art gallery. Eventually it was sold to the brand-new Bank of Ireland in 1803 for £40,000 as their headquarters under the stipulation that it had to be so modified that it could never be used as a parliament building ever again. They retain it to this day, although there are regular calls for it to return to government use.

The Irish House of Commons sitting in 1780. This original domed structure burnt down in 1790 and was replaced by a less elaborate chamber without a dome.

11: Plate Depicting an Incident during the Battle of Boxtel

Prussia and Austria had declared war on Revolutionary France in 1792, but with the execution of King Louis XVI on 21 January 1793, Britain, Spain and Holland also joined the fight. Britain financed the coalition and as the French drove into Holland, a small force under the command of the Duke of York was sent to support the Allied efforts, the British hoping to regain Dunkirk. This small force landed on the Continent in February 1793 and Arthur tried everything to get his regiment involved, initially without success.

General Dumouriez, commanding the French forces, had seen early success, but with the arrival of significant Austrian reinforcements, the French were pushed out of Holland and Dumouriez promptly defected to the Allies, rather than face the guillotine for his failures. With the French forces demoralised, the Allies also drove them out of the Austrian Netherlands (modern-day Belgium) and began to besiege the French fortresses of Conde and Valenciennes, which both fell to the Allies in July 1793. Unfortunately, at this point the Allied army effectively broke up as each sought to further their own aims, giving the demoralised French time to regroup.

Further British reinforcements had been shipped over, allowing the Duke of York to turn to the blockade of Dunkirk, despite the fact that little preparation had been made and that he had no proper siege artillery. A French counter-attack soon broke the Hanoverian troops on York's left wing and forced the British to retire, abandoning the little equipment they had and soon both sides retired into winter quarters.

Arthur was keen to take his regiment to Flanders, but they were held ready to embark with a force of 10,000 men, under the command of Lord Moira, initially planned to land on the Normandy coast behind the French lines, but frustratingly it came to nothing. Finally, in the spring of 1794, Lord Moira's force was reallocated to reinforce the Duke of York in Flanders and in June 1794, he sailed from Cork to Ostend to command a brigade.

Events in Flanders did not go well, however, and Arthur suffered from a serious bilious complaint, which caused him to consider returning to Dublin to restore his health. During the retreat into Holland, Arthur was involved however in his first-ever action, at the tiny village of Boxtel on 15 September 1794.

The previous day, the French army under General Pichegru had captured the village and forced two Hessian battalions to capitulate. The Duke of York ordered two brigades of infantry, consisting of the Guards and Wellesley's 3rd

Brigade, which included the 33rd Foot, and ten squadrons of cavalry to drive the French out. During the advance, it was realised that they actually faced Pichegru's entire army and a hasty retreat was ordered, which under severe pressure from the French cavalry was in real danger of turning into a rout. This was prevented, by the swift action of Lieutenant Colonel Sherbrooke who commanded the 33rd in Arthur's absence as brigadier. The regiment deployed in line and drove off the French pursuit with controlled volleys, allowing an orderly retreat to continue. Arthur Wellesley gained much of the credit for this action as the brigadier.

The story that this short action is the source of the term 'Tommy Atkins' for a British soldier, is dubious to say the least. Arthur reputedly observed a mortally wounded soldier at this action and remembered his name and later used it in War Office documents he was preparing. This has no basis in fact, as the term was already in use as early as 1743.

The retreat in the harsh winter weather was terrible and eventually Holland was abandoned to French rule and the British troops were evacuated from German ports on the North Sea coast. The troops suffered appallingly, with inadequate shelter, equipment and provisions, it is therefore incongruous that the main reason why this disastrous campaign is remembered, is the children's nursery rhyme of 'The Grand Old Duke of York, who had ten thousand men', of which Arthur Wellesley was one.

Many years later, when asked about this campaign, he recalled that it had proven an invaluable lesson, as

'I learnt what one ought not to do, and that is always something.'

The Duke of York reviewing troops in Flanders in 1794.

12: Shako of the Light Company 33rd Foot

The 33rd Regiment of Foot has its origins as Huntingdon's Regiment, which was raised in 1702 and in 1782, Lord Cornwallis, colonel of the regiment, requested that the name of the regiment would officially become the 33rd (or the 1st West Yorkshire West Riding) Regiment of Foot, because 'the 33rd Regiment of infantry has always recruited in the West Riding of Yorkshire, and has a very good interest & the general good will of the people, in that part of the country'. The application was approved and the regiment's affiliation with Yorkshire has been retained throughout its various guises in subsequent years. Since 2004, it forms the third battalion of the Yorkshire Regiment and is based at Halifax. The regiment was known colloquially as 'The Havercakes' apparently from the habit of their recruiting sergeants carrying oatcakes on the tip of their swords to attract recruits.

On 30 April 1793, Arthur purchased the position of major in the 33rd Foot and only five months later he rose to the rank of lieutenant colonel giving him the command of a battalion in the field. He led a battalion in the Flanders campaign of 1794–5 and on 3 May 1796 he gained by seniority (purchase not being allowed above the rank of lieutenant colonel) the rank of colonel in the army, although still serving as a lieutenant colonel in the regiment. As such

he then took the regiment to India in 1799, although Arthur (his surname changing in 1798 to Wellesley) now commanded a far larger force and he was rarely with the regiment.

Arthur became a Major General on the 29 April 1802, although the news only reached India in the following September, when he wrote of the 33rd,

'I have commanded them for nearly ten years during which I have scarcely been away from them and I have always found them to be the quietest and best behaved body of men in the army.'

With the death of Lord Cornwallis in October 1805, Arthur Wellesley finally became Colonel of the 33rd Foot, which office he held until 1813, when he was superseded by General Sir

The 33rd at the storming of Seringapatam 1799.

John Sherbrooke. This effectively ended Arthur's relationship with the 33rd Foot, although they did meet again at Waterloo.

Following the death of the Duke of Wellington in 1852, on the anniversary of the Battle of Waterloo in 1853, because of his long association with them, Queen Victoria formally granted the regiment, the title of the 33rd or (Duke of Wellington's) Regiment and they were from then on, known affectionately as 'the Dukes'. The new regimental insignia included a lion taken from the Duke's own coat of arms.

Shako plate 33rd Foot.

13: English Violin circa 1790

A rthur had followed his late father in his love of playing the violin, at which he was apparently quite adept. He was however, soon to end his days of violin playing in dramatic fashion.

Only some 30 miles from his family home at Dangan castle, resided the Pakenhams, another influential Anglo-Irish family. It is unclear when Arthur first encountered Catherine Pakenham, 'Kitty' to everyone, but it is believed that they had often met as children, but only seriously took an interest in each other in 1791, when he was 22 and she was 19 and described as having 'an indefinable beauty'. Her natural gaiety and rosy complexion, with dark curls and very statuesque figure, made her a great favourite with the younger gentry. She also had a serious side and could often be found immersed in a book and was quite accomplished on the harp, both traits that particularly attracted her suitor. Certainly, by 1792 they were openly courting and Arthur was often writing from 'the Castle' the name everyone used when referring to Pakenham Hall. Arthur asked Lord Longford for Kitty's hand, but he refused, despite the open support of Kitty's grandmother

Kitty's brother Tom had succeeded as Lord Longford that year, on the death of their father, but this was not welcome news for Arthur, for Thomas, two years younger than his sister, saw no reason to lose his popular sister to a virtually penniless young officer with few prospects. During the following year, Arthur did everything he could to earn the appreciation and respect of Tom and made his maiden speech in the Irish parliament.

In the spring of 1793, Arthur decided to try his luck and asked for the hand of young Kitty, but the

offer was rejected outright. Her brother would not entertain a middle-ranking army officer without a fortune and little prospect of obtaining one. Kitty would find herself a young man of independent means from the veritable pack of eligible young nobility in the Pakenham circle.

Rejection forced Arthur to reappraise his life. He was a younger son of minor nobility without independent means. He had never committed himself properly to anything apart from Kitty, his military career to date being mediocre and uninspiring. He had simply enjoyed the high life, wasting his time playing at cards, chasing women and playing his violin, but to what end?

It was a moment for taking stock and devising a serious plan of action, to earn his fortune in order to return to claim Kitty's hand, he immediately gave up the gaming tables and apparently burnt his beloved violin, although some claim he gave it to a friend, although no trace of it has ever been found. Soldiering was to be his only serious pursuit from now on.

In a letter to Kitty, Arthur wrote that if circumstances changed, which could alter Tom's mind, his determination to gain her hand would remain, as he stated 'my mind will still remain the same'. To a man of honour such as Arthur, these few words were binding and were akin to an oath.

Pakenham Hall.

14: Automaton Owned by Tipu Sultan

When Richard Wellesley arrived in India, he soon became aware that the greatest threat to British possession of the subcontinent was Tipu Sultan, who controlled Mysore.

Three wars had already been fought by British troops against the Mysorean armies, the first two waged against Tipu's father, Hyder Ali, who had proven a formidable opponent. The first war against Mysore, from 1767–9, almost ended in a terrible defeat for the British and the near loss of Madras, but they were saved by the Nizam of Hyderabad, who changed sides at a critical moment. A second hard-fought war of 1780–4 ended with the death of Hyder Ali from cancer. Tipu Sultan took his father's throne and, allying himself to the French, he invaded Travancore, a state allied to the British, and a third war raged from 1789–92, which ended with Tipu having to cede half of his kingdom.

Tipu Sultan's hatred of the British was legendary and his favourite automaton pictured himself as 'the Tiger of Mysore' devouring a red-coated soldier, representing the East India Company and British interests. The musical box incorporated within the body of the tiger was

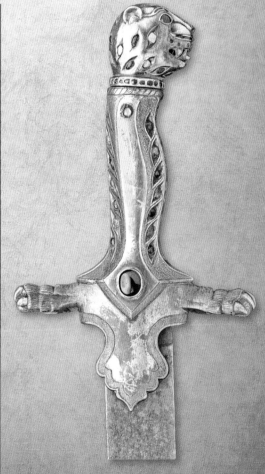

Jewel-encrusted sword owned by Tipu Sultan.

meant to replicate the roar of the tiger and the squeals of the dying soldier. Tipu corresponded with Napoleon Bonaparte and retained French military instructors in his army. It is uncertain that Napoleon could have ever marched an army from Egypt to India, but he certainly wrote to Tipu hinting at such an event and encouraging the sultan to rise against British interests in India again.

Richard Wellesley became aware of this correspondence and was very worried by the threat of French forces joining Tipu. He therefore organised two large British armies and also garnered the military support of the Nizam of Hyderabad and of the Maratha Confederacy, which controlled huge swathes of central India. It was planned that these four armies would invade Tipu Sultan's lands simultaneously, crushing his heavily outnumbered forces.

Arthur was to command the Nizam of Hyderabad's contingent purely on the back of a very strange incident. Colonel Henry Aston of the 12th Foot, having been given the command, got embroiled in an argument with a Major Allen, which ended in a demand for satisfaction and a duel with pistols. The two antagonists arrived at the appointed duelling ground, apparently having drunk way too much alcohol and all attempts at an apology fell on deaf ears. Aston received a ball through his shoulder and he died of the wound a few days later. His death led to Arthur being given the command.

Lord Mornington ordered the invasion of Mysore on 3 February 1799. Tipu's forces fought using delaying tactics, especially at Mallavelly on 26 March, but were slowly forced back to the Sultan's great fortress capital of Seringapatam (modern-day Srirangapatna).

Surrounding the city, the British found that five outposts were maintained by Tipu's troops in thickets (topes), which would need to be taken

Tipu Sultan.

before they could properly attack Seringapatam. Arthur was ordered to clear the Sultanpettah Tope and was given no time to recconoitre before the attack was launched. The area was criss-crossed with deep irrigation channels full of water the confused attack in the dark came under a heavy fire including from rockets and the 33rd was forced to retreat precipitately. It is often quoted as Arthur's only ever military defeat.

General Harris who commanded, wrote in his diary that 'Colonel Wellesley came to my tent in a good deal of agitation, to say he had not carried the tope'. Being well aware of his relationship to the Governor General, he added 'It must be particularly unpleasant to him'. Some junior officers openly wrote that but for this relationship 'he would never have had a chance of getting over this affair'.

Arthur certainly viewed it as a hard lesson, and he wrote to Richard determining 'never to suffer an attack to be made by night upon an enemy who is ... strongly posted and whose

One of Tipu's cannon.

posts have not been reconnoitred by daylight'. The following morning a renewed attack on the tope led by Arthur was completely successful and Tipu's troops were now fully confined within Seringapatam.

The army began a regular siege of the fortress and peace proposals from Tipu Sultan were ignored as the trenches were dug and the batteries of cannon set up. Harris was under orders from Richard to ignore all offers of peace: Tipu's reign must end.

On 3 May a regular breach had been made and on the morning of 4 May 4,000 men under the command of Sir David Baird launched a furious assault, whilst Arthur commanded the reserve which was to remain in the trenches until called for. Within fifteen minutes the impetuous attack brushed aside all of the ingenious defences and huge numbers of the garrison were put to the sword until resistance was overcome and the remaining defenders surrendered.

Tipu Sultan had feared the worst, the omens he had consulted that morning predicting his doom. He had fought tenaciously at the North Gate until seriously wounded and whilst being removed by his guards was shot by a British soldier. That night Baird and Wellesley led a torchlight search for Tipu's body and having found it, his remains were buried alongside his father the following day.

On 6 May General Harris appointed Arthur as Governor of Seringapatam and he turned to restoring order and collecting the immense treasure of Tipu Sultan (valued at nearly £1.2 million – or approximately £50 million today) for the East India Company. Arthur was eventually to receive £4,000 as his share of the Prize Money, making him financially independent for the first time in his life, athough he still owed his brother for purchasing his rank.

Mausoleum of Tipu Sultan.

15: Button of the 19th Light Dragoons

Dhoondiah Waugh (or Dhondia Wagh), the leader of a Maratha raiding party which had been pillaging Tipu's lands, had been captured and although initially employed by Tipu, he was eventually imprisoned at Seringapatam by the Sultan. During the confusion of the British assault on the fortress and the death of Tipu, the prison gates were destroyed allowing Dhoondiah to escape and, having recruited numbers of Tipu's soldiers, to continue his path of pillage and rape across the Deccan valley, declaring himself the 'Lord of the Two Worlds'.

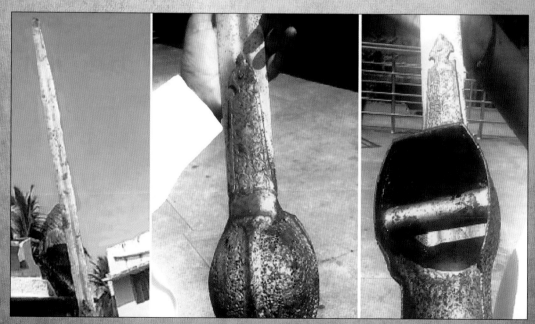

Dhoondiah Waugh's sword.

Soon relieved of the governorship of Seringapatam, Arthur Wellesley took command of all forces remaining in Mysore, after the main army returned to their bases. His three years of rule were marked by a firm but just rule and a determination to eradicate the unruly bands of rebels which blighted the country. A new Sultan of Mysore was put in place, but even his own officials viewed him as little more than a British puppet and it is certainly true that Arthur effectively ruled the state. Arthur wrote to Richard stating that 'If we do not get him, we must expect a general insurrection'. Dhoondiah's raiding parties were continually pushed northward by Wellesley's troops and his band eventually disappeared back into Mahratta territory and Arthur turned his focus against other rebellious groups.

Early in 1800, Dhoondiah's name came to prominence again, with strong rumours of a plot to kidnap the Sultan of Mysore and Arthur himself! Indeed, during a subsequent hunting party, the protective screen did come into contact and skirmish with Dhoondiah's men, giving confirmation of the intelligence. Arthur's men drove the bandits off and he characteristically remarked that 'the gentlemen succeeded against the blackguards'.

Dhoondiah again retreated into the safety of Maratha lands, but this time, rather than halting the pursuit, Richard ordered him to continue his pursuit until Dhoondiah was

Victorian print of Arthur Wellesley and the body of Dhoondiah Waugh.

caught and immediately hanged from the nearest tree. Arthur gained the assent of the Marathan leaders to enter their lands and they supplied their own forces to rid the state of this pest. The pursuit was relentless and Dhoondiah was chased throughout the Maratha lands and eventually back into the Deccan, where he was slowly squeezed between a force commanded by Arthur and a secondary force under his subordinate Colonel Stevenson. On 26 July 1800 Dhoondiah's camp at Dambal Fort was attacked and many of his men and equipment captured and on 10 September Arthur finally saw an opportunity to end the chase, but he would have to act swiftly, before he disappeared again.

Arthur, for the one and only time in his life, acted as a cavalry commander and placed himself at the head of four regiments, the 19th and 25th Light Dragoons and the 1st and 2nd Native Cavalry Regiments. He launched a mass charge on Dhoondiah's troops, sweeping them away with their speed and killing Dhoondiah, ending his reign of terror. This action received loud acclaim from the army, one colleague congratulating him for showing 'what has never yet be shown in this country, that is, what cavalry can do'. This campaign and the method of its successful termination certainly regained much credit for Arthur after his failure at the tope before Seringapatam.

When his troops pillaged the baggage of Dhoondiah, they discovered his little 4-year-old son, Salabat Khan, cowering in fear, and brought him to Arthur. He immediately took him under his personal protection and arranged to finance his future education. Salabat eventually worked for the Sultan of Mysore, but unfortunately died of cholera in 1822.

16: Etching of General Sir David Baird

Richard Wellesley continually looked beyond India to strengthen British control of the region and following Arthur's success against Dhoondiah Waugh, he trusted his military judgement enough to canvas his views on projected attacks. A previous project to send a naval force to Dutch Batavia to summon its surrender now that Holland had been overrun by the French was momentarily resurrected but soon abandoned for even more ambitious plans.

In November 1800 Richard sent two projected plans to his brother to comment on. The first, a secret expedition to take the Isle de France (modern-day Mauritius), with Arthur leading the army contingent. Richard had been persuaded that the invasion would be child's play and he sought Arthur's support by promising to make him Governor and Commander-in-Chief there. Arthur replied enthusiastically, seeing his opportunity to act alone and gain his laurels and he made his way rapidly to Ceylon (Sri Lanka) to meet the expedition.

However, having become excited with the prospect of an independent command, Richard sent a hasty letter to meet him at Ceylon, informing him that the troops being assembled were no longer being sent to Mauritius, but were now to sail as part of a much larger force to the Red Sea where they were to form a part of a major British expedition, intended to defeat the French army in Egypt. This change in destination was not in itself a problem, but such a large expedition was way beyond the command of a colonel and Arthur was disappointed to learn that he would be under the command of General Sir David Baird. Richard was aware of the animosity existing

between the two, but he had been forced to give Baird precedence and was also clear that Arthur could not withdraw from the expedition at such a late stage. Arthur was furious, but Richard was able to deflect his criticism, pointing to a fortuitous note from the British government ordering that the attack on Egypt must be the priority. However, this did not appease Arthur, as he correctly pointed out that the government had not made any recommendation as to who should command the troops, so he could have commanded it.

Arthur decided, without instructions and against all advice, to take his troops to Bombay where they could pick up supplies and bullocks for transport, rather than have them sent after him, so when Baird arrived at Ceylon to take command of the expedition, he found the troops had left for Bombay and he was forced to sail after them.

In the midst of this hostile atmosphere, with criticism of his actions ringing in his ears and Arthur still firing off letters excusing them, he suddenly became quite unwell. A doctor consulted at Bombay diagnosed the 'Malabar itch' – actually a skin infection like scabies, caused by the fungus *Trichophoton*, which erupts as a number of large patches of hard overlapping scales. It is not a form of ringworm, as some historians have claimed. His cure required him to bathe in nitric acid, which was so strong that it burnt the towels he dried himself on.

Arthur was so upset with matters that he seems to have seriously considered quitting both India and the Army forever. Luckily, on his arrival,

General Baird sought to offer his sympathy as an olive branch to the irate colonel and Arthur calmed down to the point where he agreed to sail to Egypt as Baird's second-in-command. This shows clearly that Arthur's reputation as a 'cold fish' is far from the truth, his natural tendency was to be quite volatile, with particularly strong reactions to perceived injustice.

A second bout of the 'Itch' meant that he could not sail, this further forced delay proved particularly fortuitous, as the ship *Susannah* went without him and was reputedly lost on the voyage to Egypt with all hands, although there is some doubt over this claim.

Arthur was not, however, a man to dwell on such occurrences and he would never have had any time for those who make claims of the influence of the hand of God.

Colombo harbour circa 1800.

17: Indian Sword Captured at Assaye, Presented to Lieutenant General John Stuart

Having recovered from the 'Malabar Itch', Arthur returned to Mysore, where events were moving at a rapid pace. A feud between two warring factions within the Maratha Empire culminated in victory for Yashwant Rao Holkar at the Battle of Poona in October 1802, the defeated Daulat Rao Scindia retiring to his own territories, whilst his ally, Baji Rao, sought refuge with the East India Company, offering to accept British authority if they would help him regain his territories. The ambitious Governor General of India, Richard Wellesley, would never turn down such opportunities to significantly increase British influence in India and a treaty was soon agreed at Bassein, whereby the company troops would restore Baji Rao, with the understanding that the Company would direct his foreign policy for

him and that 6,000 Company troops would be permanently garrisoned at Poona.

Richard organised a force under General Lake to enter the Maratha territories from the north, whilst Arthur, who had been promoted to Major General in April 1802, was given command of the troops which would advance from the south. His force consisted of 15,000 Company troops and 9,000 troops supplied by the Nizam of Hyderabad. The Maratha leaders saw British involvement in their affairs as a very dangerous precedent and Scindia formed an alliance with the Rajah of Berar in a coalition against the British. Arthur attempted to conduct negotiations with the Maratha leaders, but when they failed he did not hesitate to immediately declare war. The British were, however, successful in dividing the Maratha leaders, with Holkar

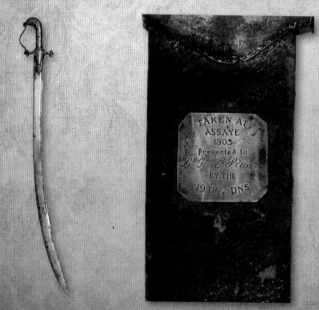

Assaye Fortress.

remaining neutral and the Gaekwad of Baroda placing himself under British protection. Arthur was clear that action must be swiftly taken as he wrote 'a long defensive war would ruin us'.

General Lake would actually face the main Maratha army commanded by a French mercenary, Pierre Perron, but Arthur still faced a significant force, particularly of fast-moving light cavalry who lived off the land. He launched a two-pronged attack, sending his trusted Colonel Stevenson with 10,000 troops to prevent raids into the Nizam's territories whilst he marched northward with a force of just over 13,000 men towards Scindia's nearest stronghold at Ahmednuggur and on arrival Arthur ordered an immediate storming of the walled town, which was successful and the adjacent fort surrendered a few days later following a heavy bombardment.

A British cannon still lying in the streets of Peepulgaon.

Scindia's forces successfully slipped past Stevenson and raided the Nizam's territories, but Stevenson did not react as expected, continuing his march into Maratha territory and capturing the city of Jalna, forcing Scindia to call off his raid. Meanwhile Arthur turned his force to meet Scindia.

Hearing of Wellesley's approach, Scindia called in all of his forces, including infantry and artillery and his formidable force now numbered around 60,000, of which 11,000 were well-equipped regular infantry who had been trained by European officers and some 35,000 were irregular cavalry. Such a sizeable threat caused Wellesley to combine his force with Stevenson's, which met on 21 September. Arthur was informed that the Maratha army was then encamped just 30 miles (48km) to the north, the bulk of the cavalry having already moved on, but the infantry had yet to march.

Believing their intelligence to be perfectly correct, Wellesley, aiming to catch the Maratha infantry before it marched off, made the near-fatal mistake of marching his force in two columns either side of a large range of hills, until they could combine again at Bokardan on 24 September, the other wing again commanded by Stevenson. This decision was nearly catastrophic.

When near to Bokardan, Arthur was surprised to find himself facing the entire Maratha army in a very strong defensive position on a tongue of land lying between the Kailna River and a tributary. Arthur's force consisted of only 4,500 infantry, some 5,000 Indian cavalry and 17 cannon, with no sign of Stevenson's force. The Maratha chiefs believed that the British were in no position to launch an attack given the disparity of numbers, but Arthur was determined to bring them to battle and he launched an immediate attack.

The Maratha army, commanded by a Hanoverian named Colonel Pohlmann, was deployed along the northern bank of the Kaitna River, with his cannon arrayed in front. Arthur's

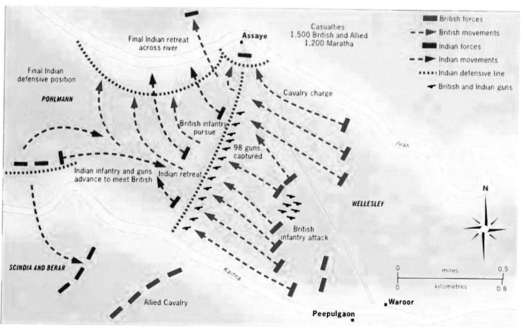

Battle of Assaye 23 September 1803.

troops were to the south of the river and the only known ford was directly in front of the Maratha cannon, but Arthur quickly disregarded this as an obvious death-trap for his forces.

The local guides assured Arthur that there were no other fords in the vicinity, but whilst reconnoitring the area, he noticed that two villages beyond the left of the Maratha forces, Peepulgaon and Waroor, faced each other on either bank of the river and he made the assumption that a ford must exist between them, which his engineers quickly found to be true. Wellesley ordered his army to cross here and by 3pm his whole force were formed up on the left flank of the Maratha army, his six battalions of infantry in two lines and his cavalry forming a third behind them.

Pohlmann soon learned of Wellesley's manoeuvre and his force swiftly redeployed in a new line facing the British and Arthur ordered his line to extend so that his force covered the entire peninsula from the bank of the river to the banks of the tributary, therefore preventing the Maratha troops passing around his flanks.

The 100 or more guns of the Maratha army cannonaded the British troops and soon overpowered the few pieces that Wellesley was able to deploy against them and his casualties were mounting fast under such an intense barrage. Arthur boldly decided that the only way to relieve the situation was to fix bayonets, abandon his own guns and to march directly on the Maratha cannon. The 78th Highlanders on the left of his line reached the Maratha lines first,

Arthur Wellesley at the Battle of Assaye 1803.

halted briefly at fifty paces, fired a devastating volley, gave one loud cheer and charged with the bayonet. The Maratha gunners bravely stood to their guns and were cut down and seeing this, the Maratha infantry behind the guns promptly turned and fled northwards. Four battalions of Madras infantry to their right performed the same manoeuvre, but became disorganised and were attacked by Maratha cavalry. They began to fall back until supported by the 78th which had retained its order.

The attack on the left was succeeding, but Wellesley's right was in serious trouble as the pickets supported by the 74th Foot mistakenly pressed their attack too strongly and suffered severely from a crossfire from the guns mounted in front of Assaye and from the left of the Maratha line. Seeing the British line here retiring, Pohlmann launched his cavalry at them, virtually annihilating the pickets, although the 74th saved themselves by forming a rough square.

Seeing his right in serious trouble Arthur Wellesley ordered the 19th Light Dragoons and the 4th and 5th Madras Native Cavalry to attack, routing the Maratha cavalry and continuing their charge on into the guns and infantry beyond.

At this point the battle looked won, but many of the Maratha gunners had feigned death and they now re-manned their guns, turning them to fire into the rear of Wellesley's infantry. He immediately ordered the 78th Foot and the 7th Madras Native Cavalry to retake the guns. It was soon done and this time it was fully ascertained that everybody lying around the cannon was really dead.

British casualties were 428 killed and 1,154 wounded, over a third of the force engaged, Maratha losses are much harder to ascertain but it is estimated that up to 6,000 were killed or wounded and 98 cannon were captured. Arthur later said that Assaye was 'the bloodiest for numbers that I ever saw.'

Stevenson had heard the cannon and marched towards the battle but was misled by his guide and did not arrive until after the battle was over. Suspecting that his guide had led him astray on purpose, Stevenson promptly had him hanged.

Arthur was recognised for being in the thick of the action at Assaye and had a horse killed underneath him. When in old age, the Duke of Wellington was asked which was his finest battle, he answered without hesitation, 'Assaye'.

18: Gawilghur Fortress

The Battle of Assaye was followed by the bloody Battle of Laswari on 1 November 1803, where a British cavalry force under General Lake destroyed one of the last significant Maratha armies in the field and forced them to pull back into their fortresses. The casualties on both sides were very heavy, however. Indeed Lake later wrote admiringly 'I never was in so severe a business in my life or anything like it ... these [Maratha] fellows fought like devils, or rather like heroes.'

In the south, Arthur Wellesley marched his troops in pursuit of the remnants of the Maratha army which had escaped from Assaye and on 29 November, his entire force came up on their camp near the village of Argaum (or Argaon). He did not hesitate and ordered his troops to advance immediately, but the high vegetation made the Maratha force virtually invisible to the advancing troops until the last minute.

As his advance guard emerged from the dense vegetation onto an open plain, they were struck by the massed fire of fifty Maratha cannon. These soldiers who had braved the cannon fire at Assaye without flinching, now turned and fled and this panicked two further sepoy battalions, who joined the rout. Arthur was very close at hand and saw it happen, but his attempts to rally them by waving his sword in the air failed spectacularly and he was forced to send them to the rear to re-form. He calmly waited for them to form up again and then marched them back into their place in the line, where this time, with his encouragement they stood.

Once the rest of his troops had arrived and formed up in line, he ordered the advance, when the sepoys were attacked by a screaming horde of Maratha cavalry. They stood bravely and drove the horses off with controlled volleys and soon the Maratha cavalry was routed. It had been a close call, however, and Wellesley spoke frankly afterwards, stating that

'If I had not been there to … restore the battle, we should have lost the day.'

There was, however, still the formidable thirteenth-century fortress of Gawilghur (or Gavilgar), which stood on top of a steep hill and was garrisoned by 3,000 troops. The fortress was considered unassailable, having never been taken, but this did not deter Wellesley. A bombardment was begun on 12 December and a practicable breach already formed by the 14th when an assault was ordered for the following day. The main attack quickly succeeded in gaining the walls, only to discover that there was a second ring of walls within. Their attack on the main fortress was, however, aided greatly by two feint attacks made against the impossibly steep southern face of the fortress, but in which Captain Colin Campbell of the 94th Foot somehow led his light company over the walls and succeeded in opening the gates to the fortress, allowing the main attack to enter.

A fortress, which one historian has described as being so strong that 'Boy Scouts armed with rocks could have kept out several times their number of professional soldiers', had fallen very easily. This ended the Maratha War.

British losses totalled only 132 killed and wounded whereas the Maratha troops lost around 1,200 men, a disproportionate loss when the strength of the fortress is taken into account. It would seem, that Arthur Wellesley's reputation was now so high, that it had cowed the Maratha troops into offering little resistance, an effect he was to achieve again in 1813–14. Arthur did admit years later however, that the ease of taking Indian fortresses may have heavily influenced his sieges in Spain and caused him to badly underestimate the difficulties of capturing fortresses when expertly defended by the French.

Indian cannon in Gawilghur Fortress.

19: The Briars Pavilion, St. Helena

On his long voyage home from India in 1805, Arthur's ship stopped at St. Helena to replenish supplies and he hired a small pavilion to enjoy some time ashore. The pavilion was on the estate known as the Briars, which had very recently become the home of William Balcombe, who worked for the East India Company – who owned the island – as superintendent of public sales, his wife Jane (née Cranston) and their two daughters, Jane then aged five and Elizabeth who was just over two years old. Arthur has not left us any thoughts on the Balcombes, but it is clear that he regarded the island as very pleasant and a very healthy place to live, describing it as 'apparently the most

healthy I have ever lived in'. Arthur stayed for a month.

Arthur never visited the island again, but when in 1815 Napoleon was sent there to ensure that he could never attempt another escape,

he was intrigued to hear that Napoleon was temporarily staying at the pavilion of the Briars, whilst the building works at Longwood House were completed. Indeed Napoleon particularly enjoyed spending time in the company of the Balcombe's daughter Elizabeth, who was now 12 years old and known to everyone as 'Betsy', whom he found to be charming. 'Betsy' has gone down in history, although Napoleon only spent eight weeks at the Briars.

Arthur heard that his good friend Admiral Sir Pulteney Malcom was sailing for St. Helena, to command the naval force which secured the island. He wrote him a short note wishing him well and noted the coincidence with his typical sarcastically dry humour.

'Paris 3 April 1816
My dear Malcolm,

I am very much obliged to you for Mr Simpson's book, which I will read when I shall have a moment's leisure. I am glad you have taken command at St. Helena, upon which I congratulate you. You must never be idle if you can avoid it.

You may tell 'Bony' that I find his apartments at the Elysee Bourbon [Palace] very convenient and that I hope he likes mine at Mr Balcombe's. It is a droll sequel enough to the affairs of Europe that we should change places of residence.

I am yours most sincerely, Wellington'

The original Briars was eventually destroyed by termites, but the pavilion was saved and reconstructed. It is now one of three sites on the island linked with Napoleon which are now owned by the French government.

THE BRIARS AND PAVILION.

20: Pencil Drawing of Kitty Pakenham in 1814

Arthur had spent some nine years in India and he was now a man of considerable wealth (he wrote that he had £42,000, worth around £2 million today) and was also a renowned general – even if all his battles had been fought in India. He was, however, quite sick of India and his health was far from good, constantly complaining in his letters of rheumatism, lumbago and ague. He was therefore overjoyed when he was ordered home, without his regiment, in March 1805, indeed in later life he clearly felt that his recall may have saved his life.

Whilst in India, we do know that Arthur was not celibate, with some claiming that he had a penchant for other people's wives, particularly a Mrs Isabella Freese, the wife of the acting commissary of stores at Seringapatam, but moral codes were a little different then. There is no evidence that he ever once wrote home to Kitty during his entire time in India, nor any reference to her in any of his correspondence. To all intents and purposes he acted as he had completely forgotten her very existence.

Kitty had continued to be a glamorous addition at her brother Tom's regular soirees at Pakenham Hall and had indeed attracted the eye of a certain young colonel named Lowry Cole.

Their relationship would seem to have blossomed to the point where the family assumed that they would marry, but Kitty ultimately turned his offer down, as it seems she still held out for Arthur, believing in his promise to return for her. No letters went from her to Arthur either, but one did come from a friend of the family, a Colonel Marcus Beresford, with an enclosure from her friend Olivia Sparrow, which clearly sought to gauge Arthur's feelings, if any still remained for

Arthur as Kitty would have last seen him – painted by Hoppner around 1795.

him in his actions when he finally did arrive back in Britain in 1805.

Kitty was shown this correspondence by her matchmaking friend, and her letter to Olivia openly admits her deep love for Arthur, but stated that she would not write to him, as this might be seen as binding on him and force him to renew her pursuit anew on his return. She very unselfishly wished to release him from any obligations, but if he did freely and genuinely wish to renew their relationship, then she could not be happier.

Arthur reached England in September 1805 and remained in London for a considerable period, long enough for Olivia to write, accusing him of neglecting Kitty, but he wrote back excusing pressure of business and hinted that he

Kitty. It was written in January 1801 and therefore probably did not arrive in India until the middle of that year. This strange letter dishonestly portrayed Kitty's life as almost that of a hermit, with no suitor in view, clearly seeking to infer that she was loyally awaiting Arthur's return. There are only hints as to why this letter was sent making such dishonest claims, or what Arthur's real thoughts were when he received it. Arthur did reply to Olivia, but his reply recalled bitterly his disappointment at his offer having been refused by the family and he did little more than ask Olivia to 'remember me to her in the kindest manner', which was hardly a declaration of his undying affection for Kitty. The correspondence with Olivia continued, albeit that a letter and reply took over a year to arrive, it is clear that Arthur also still held feelings for Kitty, but was still heartbroken by the refusal and he makes no hint at renewing the offer unless sure of success. It may, however, have subconsciously confirmed

St George's Dublin.

only had one event in contemplation, but was it to be marriage?

Both were undoubtedly guilty of building impossible expectations of the other during such a long absence, expunging all faults and overstating their virtues to impossible heights, a sad tragedy was almost certain to be the outcome. Kitty could only see perpetual domestic bliss, whilst Arthur saw marriage as a simple contract, with the wife running the home and looking after the children whilst he was engaged in higher issues of state, and he certainly did not envisage too many evenings of domestic bliss in his already busy schedule.

Arthur later recalled meeting Olivia at Cheltenham, where she demanded that he offered Kitty marriage, but Wellington was a notoriously poor witness regarding his own life in later years and the evidence is that such a meeting never happened. Arthur wrote directly to Tom Pakenham for permission to make a formal permission and quickly received a very positive reply. He was now able to write to Kitty direct and renew his proposal initially made some twelve years before, which of course Kitty accepted immediately. Still they did not meet as in the December Arthur was ordered to embark with an expedition to North Germany, but he was back in England in the February and he was now colonel of the 33rd Foot, Lord Cornwallis having died in India.

A prenuptial agreement was soon drawn up and agreed, to which Kitty would bring £4,000 and Arthur £20,000. Arthur arranged the wedding like any other business transaction, fitting in only a few days in Ireland to get married between his election for Parliament at Rye on 1 April 1806 and his brother Richard's impeachment hearings commencing on the 22nd of that month. Arthur and his brothers arrived at Pakenham Hall on 8 April, with a requirement to take his seat in Parliament on the 16th. No record of their first meeting in twelve years has actually survived and the ungallant quip supposedly made by Arthur to his brother Gerald that 'She's grown ugly, by jove' seems overly harsh and unlike him.

They married on 10 April 1806 in the Longford Drawing Room in Rutland Square, Dublin and officially registered at St George's Church, married by his brother, the Reverend Gerald Wellesley.

Unfortunately the marriage was not to be as happy as either hoped for.

21: Dress Coat Worn by Admiral Nelson at the Battle of Trafalgar

Some time just after his arrival in London in September 1805 (most likely on the 12th), Arthur was to accidentally meet the very epitome of the age and one whose star was already blazing in full glory, Admiral Horatio Nelson. Admiral Nelson, already the victor of the Nile and Copenhagen, had returned from his fruitless pursuit of the French fleet from the Mediterranean to the West Indies and back and they were now holed up in Cadiz. Nelson had returned home for a brief period and was to receive orders to sail again and to try to bring the joint Franco-Spanish fleet to battle. This he so famously succeeded in doing only one month later on 21 October 1805, when his fleet won the crushing victory of Trafalgar, which effectively ended Napoleon's ambitions at sea, but at the cost of the life of Nelson, shot by a musket ball that broke his back.

Arthur Wellesley was not of course anywhere near as famous as Nelson, but the newspapers had been full of his exploits in India for a number of years and his relatively recent victory at Assaye was well known to everybody. Arthur was nine years the junior of Horatio Nelson and bore no obvious scars of war, whilst Nelson was blind in one eye (although he had not lost it) and had lost his right arm. The meeting occurred at

the Colonial Office at No. 14 Downing Street, which was unfortunately demolished in 1876.

We have only Arthur's account of the incident, recalled to the diarist John Wilson Croker in October 1834 and therefore we must be a little suspicious of his version of events, but it does ring true as regards the personalities of the two characters involved.

Arthur recalled

'It was soon after I returned from India. I went to the Colonial Office in Downing Street, and there I was shown into a little waiting-room on the right hand, where I found, also waiting to see the Secretary of State, a gentleman whom, from his likeness to his pictures and the loss of an arm, I immediately recognised as Lord Nelson. He could not know who I was, but he entered at once into conversation with me, if I can call it conversation, for it was almost all on his side, and all about himself, and in really a style so vain and so silly as to surprise and almost disgust me.

I suppose something that I happened to say may have made him guess that I was somebody, and he went out of the room for a moment, I have no doubt to ask the office-keeper who I was, for when he came back he was altogether a different man, both in manner and matter. All that I had thought a charlatan style had vanished, and he talked of the state of this country and of the aspect and probabilities of affairs on the Continent with a good sense, and a knowledge of subjects both at home and abroad that surprised me equally and more agreeably than the first part of our interview had done; in fact, he talked like an officer and a statesman.

The Secretary of State kept us long waiting, and certainly for the last half or three quarters of an hour I don't know that I ever had a conversation that interested me more. Now, if the Secretary of State

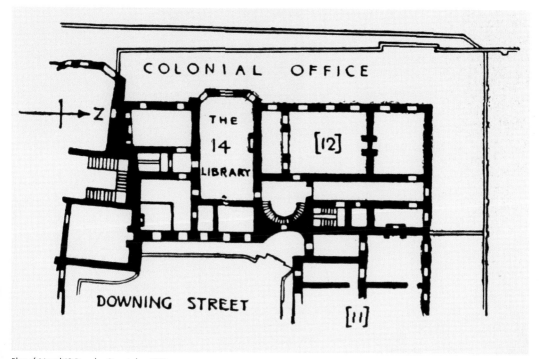

Plan of 14 and 12 Downing Street circa 1857.

had been punctual, and admitted Lord Nelson in the first quarter of an hour, I should have had the same impression of a light and trivial character that other people have had, but luckily I saw enough to be satisfied that he was really a very superior man; but certainly a more sudden and complete metamorphosis I never saw.'

Arthur's characterisation of Nelson seems to be very accurate, as he certainly could be vain and overbearing. Indeed Admiral Lord St Vincent once described him as 'A great captain at sea, but a foolish little fellow on land'.

We have no idea, unfortunately, what Horatio thought of Arthur as he never wrote a word of their meeting. Neither left a record of what was discussed, but there is much speculation that Nelson thought the projected expedition which Arthur was to go on to North Germany, would prove useless (it was) and that he suggested that an attack on Sardinia would make more strategic sense, but there is absolutely no evidence to support these claims. Nelson left London the following day and sailed from Portsmouth harbour on board his flagship HMS *Victory*.

Arthur Wellesley attended Nelson's funeral at St Paul's Cathedral on 9 January 1806.

Wellesley and Nelson meet – a stylised version.

22: Deerfield, the Official Residence of the Secretary to the Lord Lieutenant of Ireland

Arthur had been linked to the administration of Ireland at Dublin Castle ever since Richard secured him the role of an aide-de-camp to the Lord Lieutenant of Ireland in 1788. This confidential role required him to attend government meetings and provided him with an extra 10 shillings per day in pay. He continued to hold this post even when serving with his regiment in Holland, but was forced to relinquish it when he sailed for India in 1797.

Returning from India in 1805 he was able, with Richard's help, to gain the position of Military Secretary to the Lord Lieutenant at Dublin Castle in May 1807, with a very healthy salary of £6,566 per annum and was able to retain his position whilst on active service at Copenhagen in 1807.

The Ireland Arthur returned to had changed a great deal. The family had parted with Dangan Castle and Mornington House and the Irish parliament building was now a bank. Indeed, much of the talk of Dublin was of the loss of prestige and wealth to the city since the Union and the parliament moving to London. The problem of absentee landlords had also markedly increased, with the rich, powerful and influential now all streaming to base themselves in the real seat of power, London.

One of Arthur's chief roles was in the overseeing of patronage and ensuring that it was issued in the most effective way to maintain

the government's majority. Arthur was possibly not the best man to handle the multitudinous requests and pleas for government favour. His brusque, off-hand nature and desire to keep on top of the heavy workload got him through the huge amount of daily business, but he probably won few friends by his curt responses. A Mr Meeke received the following typical reply to his request for a position for him and a friend. 'You are rather high in your demand of an office … but I hope to place your friend, if he be more moderate than you are.'

His family also inundated him with requests for positions for their friends and servants, his mother sending a list no less than four pages long! Most received a very tart refusal. Bribery was an anathema to him, despite the Irish establishment being renowned then for such corruption. However, when it came to it, Arthur fully defended the corrupt patronage system, arguing that the patronage dished out to the lesser nobility, tied them inexorably to

the Establishment and was a major factor in the preservation of constitutional monarchy and even more importantly, law and order. Arthur also looked on the Catholics benevolently, admitting that the time for full emancipation was yet to arrive, but he intimated that the Catholic laws would be administered 'with mildness and good temper'. He refused plans for a celebration of the anniversary of Vinegar Hill, when the Irish rebels had been defeated, and stopped the appointment of ultra-Protestant bishops and he avoided the use of the Insurrection Act to put down disturbances in Sligo and Mayo, preferring more measured responses.

Arthur undertook a major tour of the island to review the defences against a French attack and made a number of recommendations, interestingly he argued for the construction of Martello towers to cease in favour of increasing the naval presence in Bantry Bay, admitting that Ireland 'in a view to military operations, must be considered as an enemy's country'.

Dublin Castle.

Arthur had left for the Danish expedition with the firm idea that he would not return to Dublin, but following the capitulation of the Danish fleet, Arthur was recalled by the Lord Lieutenant and he returned to the castle for another spell lasting eight months. The threat of invasion had receded again following the removal of the Danish fleet and the escape of the Portuguese fleet to Brazil, allowing Arthur to resume his preferred mild governance. He considered mixed-religion schools to avoid sectarianism, he mulled over the problems of absentee landlords and clergy and considered education of the absentees as a possible solution, He produced statistics that proved that Maynooth College needed to produce 25 per cent more priests annually to meet demand, he reformed the Dublin police and prepared to issue an embargo on corn exports if a potato famine ever threatened again. Along with a domestic life which included the birth of his second son, the family residing at the Secretary's official residence, Deerfield in Phoenix Park (now the American Ambassador's residence). Arthur was however, very restless and on the lookout for an opportunity of some more exciting employment, writing to George Canning, the Foreign Secretary, in October 1807, that he was 'ready to set out for any part of the world at a moment's notice'.

Following failed attacks on Buenos Aires in 1807, the government were still discussing the possibility of sending troops to help Venezuelan rebels overthrow the government and Arthur was canvassed for his opinions. The government had already rashly sent forces to Egypt and to aid the King of Sweden and Arthur was not impressed by the litany of failures. He wrote a very clear and precise memorandum highlighting all of the main flaws in the projected expedition to Venezuela, which he had been earmarked to command and made it very clear that he could not support the project. It was quietly shelved.

23: Gerald's Sick Note Allowing Him to be Absent from his Parish dated 1842

Gerald Wellesley was the youngest of the four brothers, born in 1770. Always a little more studious and straight-laced than the other boys, he was an ideal match for his chosen career, the Church. Gerald went to Eton and then studied at Cambridge University, where he became a Doctor of Divinity.

Gerald gained the position of Chaplain of the Royal Household at Hampton Court in 1793, his income rising from £200 per annum to a very handsome £500 per year by 1805. He married Emily Maud Cadogan on 2 June 1802 (a sister of Charlotte Cadogan who married Henry Wellesley the following year), and they seem to have had a more settled marriage than Henry and Charlotte, having four boys and three girls together before Emily died in 1839.

Gerald conducted the marriage of his brother Arthur to Kitty Pakenham in Dublin in 1806, and as Arthur had to return to Parliament hurriedly, Kitty travelled to London later with Gerald. When Kitty had given birth to two sons, Gerald and Henry were both appointed executors and guardians of the children in case of the death of Arthur and Kitty.

Gerald initially took care of Henry's son 'little Gerald' after his wife had eloped. However, due to his own increasing family and undoubtedly,

some issues over looking after Emily's sisters child in such an awkward situation, Gerald eventually asked Kitty to take the youngster and she readily agreed, writing that 'Gerald, if entrusted to me, shall be to me as a child of my own'. Gerald brought the boy to Kitty on 6 March 1811, when he was only two. She was shocked and wrote in her diary 'On examination, I find he has been badly neglected. May it be in my power to make him well, good and happy.'

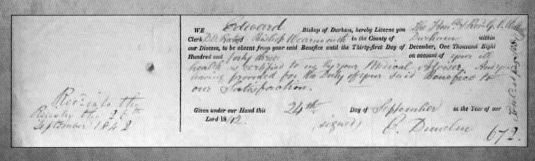

Gerald as a young man.

She also recorded that he cried at night and she took him into her own room for many days until he eventually settled.

In 1805 Gerald became the Rector of St Luke's in Chelsea, a post he held until he eventually resigned in 1832, and during his tenure the church was totally rebuilt into the superb edifice it is today.

In 1827 he was appointed as the 5th Prebendary (honorary canon) at Durham Cathedral and also Rector of Bishopwearmouth in Sunderland, both of which positions he retained until the end of his life. However, by 1842, the Bishop of Durham was granting permission for Gerald

to be absent from his parish (St Michael's, now Sunderland Minster), due to ill health. This was confirmed by a medical certificate and the bishop stated that he had 'provided for the duty of your said benefice to our satisfaction'. In his sick certificate, he is described as 'subject to a chronic affliction of the larynx and top of the trachea, which is very much influenced by the state of the atmosphere, and the air he breathes'.

It would seem that he was only allergic to the air of Bishopwearmouth and the records confirm that he was readily attending meetings in Durham most weeks at this period and was not apparently triggered by the air of the cathedral

Gerald as Prebendary of Durham.

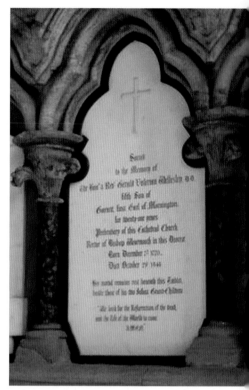

Memorial to Gerald in Durham Cathedral.

close in Durham. This perhaps explains the repeated references in the medical certificate to the 'loaded and impure state of the atmosphere' in Sunderland. In the certificate, the doctor states, 'Were he to reside at Bishopwearmouth rectory it would very materially tend to increase his complaints and shorten his life.' Gerald actually survived until 1848 and he was buried at Durham Cathedral.

He should not be confused with his nephew Gerald Valerian Wellesley (a son of brother Henry) who became Dean of Windsor.

24: Early Painting of Arthur and Kitty's Two Sons Carried by Arthur in the Peninsula

At No. 11 Harley Street, London, Kitty gave birth to their son Arthur Richard on 3 February 1807, but how much Arthur had to do with the event is unclear as he only ever mentioned the birth in one letter, written to his mother-in-law, giving thanks for her care of Kitty 'in the late disturbing & critical moments'. If Kitty had suffered a difficult birth, being a first-time mother at the age of 36, Arthur did not feel the need to be on hand, as the letter was written only three days after the happy event, when Arthur was already at Hatfield House, with a hunting party.

It would seem that Kitty also recovered from the birth quite quickly, they moved to the Chief Secretary's Lodge in Phoenix Park, Dublin in the April and the following month Kitty was pregnant again. Young Arthur developed the measles a few months later, but luckily there were no serious consequences.

When Arthur Wellesley became an Earl in 1812, his son Arthur Richard became his heir

and was titled Lord Douro, a name attached to the Duke of Wellington's first son ever since. Young Arthur was educated at Temple Grove School at Parson's Green, Eton, Christ Church Oxford and Trinity College Cambridge.

A military career was almost inevitable for Arthur Richard, becoming an ensign in the 81st Regiment of Foot in 1823, before transferring to the Horse Guards and eventually into the Rifle Corps. He finally rose to the rank of lieutenant general in 1862. He also dabbled in politics, being returned as the MP for Aldeburgh from 1829–32 and later for Norwich, eventually moving to the House of Lords on the death of his father. His politics always brought him into conflict with his father, General Sir William Napier noting that 'His politics are decidedly adverse to his father's and he is for a thorough reform. He dislikes London society for its heartlessness, and as good as told me Sir John Moore was as great a man as his father.' Arthur Richard married Lady Elizabeth Hay in 1839, but they had no children. Poor Arthur Richard was completely overshadowed by his great father and it is clear that he felt it sharply, once saying to his wife just having succeeded to the dukedom, 'Imagine what it will be when the Duke of Wellington is announced, and only I walk in the room'. Later in life he is described again, noting that the loss of an eye through an infection and his old-fashioned clothes gave him a 'rather grotesque appearance', but he remained active and a renowned wit to the last. When he died on the platform of Brighton Railway Station in August 1884, the title went to his nephew, son of his brother Charles.

Wellington's two sons and their cousin at Stratfield Saye, in their Eton uniforms.

Cartoon from *Vanity Fair* 1878 of Arthur 2nd Duke of Wellington.

Their second son, Charles, was born on 16 January 1808 and was educated at Eton before becoming an army officer, rising to the rank of major general, and an MP from 1842 until his premature death, aged 50 at Apsley House in 1858. Charles had married Augusta Pierrepont on 9 July 1844 and had three sons and three daughters. At the death of the 2nd Duke of Wellington, who had no heir, the title passed to Charles' eldest surviving son, Henry, and when he also died childless in 1900, the title passed to his younger brother Arthur.

As Arthur was away from home during the entirety of their formative years, he had a poor relationship with his two sons, Edward Littleton noting that

'The duke is fond of his sons, but I never saw them riding or walking together in my life and I believe they seldom converse. He seems to like that he and his sons should live independently of each other. But he allows them [to] treat Apsley House as a barrack and to use his table when he dines there.'

25: Walrus Tusk Carved with Image of the Bombardment of Copenhagen 1807

Arthur had returned to the post of Chief Secretary for Ireland at Dublin Castle, which came with a very healthy salary so when he was offered the command of a brigade in an attack on Denmark to seize the Danish fleet, he readily agreed, on the proviso that he retained his position and salary in Ireland.

This large expedition, which eventually included a fleet of 25 ships of the line and 71 lesser warships commanded by the Bible-bashing Admiral Gambier, known as 'Dismal Jimmy' by his sailors, and with some 377 transports carrying the 30,000 troops involved under the command of the overly cautious General Lord Cathcart, set sail in July 1807. Arthur sailed over to Denmark on the little fireship *Prometheus* and met the fleet anchored in a sheltered bay not far from Elsinore Castle, where relatively friendly relations continued with the Danes, who did not yet suspect the destination of the fleet.

Arthur was fully involved in the discussions on how the attack should be made if the ongoing negotiations with the Danish Crown Prince

failed. Copenhagen's sea defences had greatly improved since Nelson's attack on the Danish fleet in 1801, which successfully defeated the Danish 'Reserve' fleet, whilst the main fleet had remained safe and sound in harbour. An attack by sea was soon discounted as impracticable and discussions centred on a landing by the troops and a blockade of Copenhagen. Arthur was keen to land troops on both sides of the city and to force it to surrender by cutting off all access to food or water supplies, in an effort to avoid unnecessary civilian casualties. Others proposed a landing only on the island of Zealand and a heavy bombardment of the city by shells and rockets to quickly force the governor to capitulate and Cathcart eventually decided to go with this option as he was aware that time was not on their side, with the threat of French forces arriving in their rear.

The troops began landing on 16 August and within a few days the city was completely blockaded on the Zealand side. Arthur Wellesley commanded the Reserve or Light Brigade

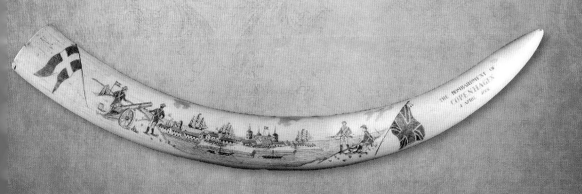

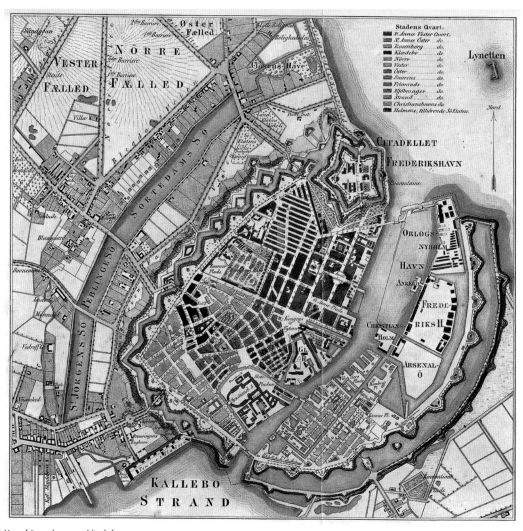

Map of Copenhagen and its defences.

consisting of the 43rd, 52nd, 92nd and 95th Foot and had little to do with the preparations for the planned bombardment.

However, the commander of the Danish Landvaern (militia) troops in Zealand, General Castenschiold, made an attempt to disrupt the siege. General Cathcart sent Wellesley with his Reserve brigade and eight squadrons of hussars and the 6th Line Battalion of the King's German Legion and two batteries of artillery to drive them away. Arthur's troops marched on Kioge in two columns: the principal force under his own command, while a smaller column under Major General Linsingen of the German Legion manoeuvred so as to turn Castenschiold's left flank and threaten their escape route.

Sergeant David Robertson of the 92nd described the Danish position: 'We had not gone far before we perceived the Danes drawn up in line ready to receive us, having their artillery, amounting to six or eight pieces, placed on rising ground, with a windmill in front, and

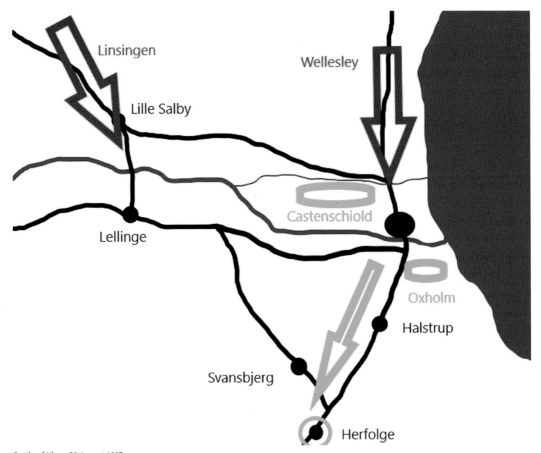

Battle of Kioge 29 August 1807.

the cavalry in the same line, protected by a garden hedge.'

Wellesley formed line, but delayed any attack to give time for Linsingen to manoeuvre around their left flank, but this column was delayed because of broken bridges and he eventually decided to make the attack, the 92nd Foot leading the attack. The Danish militia did not stand long as described by Private William Green of the 95th Rifles: 'the Rifles pushed on in extended order, as is always the case in action. The 79th and 92nd Highlanders made a brilliant charge with the bayonet, and they soon dispersed; our cannon played through the town, and we overtook them; they were shod with wooden shoes, except the officers, so that it was impossible for them to run fast. I believe they were all taken prisoners!'

It was a particular feature of this action, that when the Danish Landvaern turned to flee, they discarded their wooden clogs, so as to run faster. The streets of Kioge were apparently carpeted with wooden clogs and the Danes often refer to the battle, if one can call it that, as the 'Battle of the Clogs'.

Much has been made of this battle, as the first victory of Arthur Wellesley in Europe and hence removing the tarnish (if indeed there really was one) from his reputation as merely being 'a Sepoy General'. Kioge really cannot in any serious terms be viewed as a battle and it was largely dismissed by the troops present as nothing more than a skirmish. Captain Leach of the 95th explained that 'Our loss in this affair was very trifling, as it was impossible that the Danes could offer any effectual resistance to disciplined troops'. British losses were negligible, but Danish losses were 152 officers and men killed, 204 wounded and some 1,500 prisoners taken. It also removed all hope of relief for the garrison of Copenhagen: they were all alone and morale within the city crumbled with the news.

Work had continued to prepare the batteries and by 31 August everything was fully ready and armed with a total of forty-four mortars, eight howitzers and thirty-six cannons, along with a number of heavy rockets. A final demand to the Governor, General Peymann, fell on deaf ears and at half past seven on the evening of 2 September, whilst the populace of Copenhagen were strolling in the parks enjoying the warm summer evening the bombardment began. All of a sudden, the sky rained shells and rockets streaked through the sky, causing instant horror and panic. The rockets, however, made more noise than did devastation, but they certainly frightened the people, General Peymann calling them an 'uncivilised' weapon.

The firing continued for three successive nights, by which time a number of huge fires had taken hold and the wooden houses of the old Medieval quarter were completely destroyed. The third night, the Frue Kirke with the tallest spire in Copenhagen burnt and crashed to the ground and it effectively symbolised the end of Danish resistance, the governor agreeing to surrender on 6 September, just before the British launched an all-out assault. Arthur was one of the three British representatives at the surrender talks signed the following day.

The articles were signed at 2am on 7 September, the British pledging to evacuate the whole of Zealand within six weeks, taking the entire Danish fleet with them. All prisoners on both sides would be returned and Danish persons and private property were to be respected. All

Fragments of a British shell and damaged book.

naval stores were now simply viewed as prizes of war. Colonel George Murray who was also involved in the talks, describes a moment when a Danish admiral attempted to haggle over the naval stores, when Arthur answered brusquely and rather loudly

'Now Admiral, mind, every stick! Every stick!'

Two Danish ships of the line and two frigates deemed unserviceable were destroyed, but within the six weeks, sixteen ships of the line, eleven frigates and twelve lesser vessels, plus twenty-six gunboats were successfully prepared to sail. The general naval stores were loaded on ninety-two merchant vessels allocated for this purpose. The Danish Navy was reduced to two ships of the line which had luckily been in Norway at the time of the attack.

Arthur had always had his doubts on the need to bombard civilians and he was embarrassed by having to put his name to the surrender terms. He therefore claimed that he was needed back in Ireland, so that he did not have to remain whilst the Danish fleet was prepared to sail to Britain.

The government, perhaps equally embarrassed by the action, did not allocate many rewards for it and no battle honour or medal was ever issued to regiments involved. Arthur received no form of honour for his actions, but he gained £1,700 as his portion of the Prize Money. It is perhaps telling that he rarely referred to this episode in later life.

British troops observe the bombardment of Copenhagen.

26: Permission Slip Granted to Carry Firearms, Signed by General Delaborde as Commander of Lisbon

Napoleon had ordered his troops, under the command of General Andoche Junot, to march to Lisbon and to seize the Portuguese Royal Family and their fleet. Despite huge logistical problems, the French army limped into the city on 30 November 1807, only to see the Royal Family and much of the Portuguese nobility sailing off with their fleet to rule from Brazil. This was followed shortly by the news that the Spanish people had risen up against the enforced abdication of the Spanish king and his exile in France. Napoleon had placed his elder brother on the throne in their place and insurrections broke out across Spain, with delegations being sent to London to request arms and money to support their struggle.

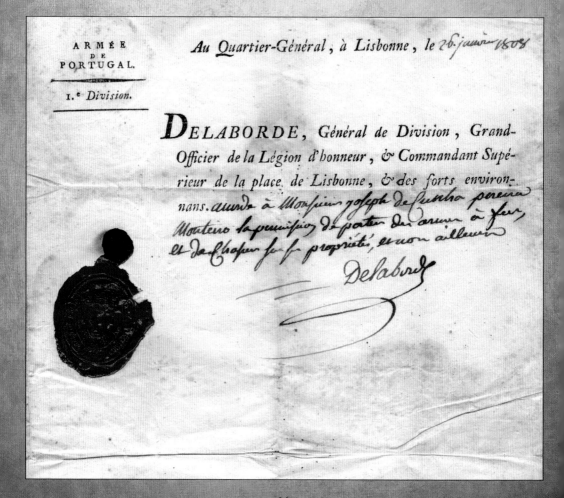

The Grave of Colonel Lake, Roliça.

A force of some 9,000 troops had been assembled for the projected attack on Spanish Venezuela, but now that they were no longer enemies, the government reallocated them to the Iberian peninsula to support both the Spanish uprisings and a Portuguese revolt led by the Bishop of Oporto, which had already liberated Portugal's second city.

Arthur took his new assignment extremely seriously, being the first time that he had faced the all-conquering French armies himself. He studied their tactics and believed that he could beat the French 'because I am not afraid of them, as everybody else seems to be; and secondly, if what I hear of their system of manoeuvre is true, I think it a false one as against steady troops'. Arthur was, however, seen as too junior to be in command of such an army, and General Sir Brent Spencer was allocated to be in overall command, much to Arthur's disdain.

When Arthur reached the coast of Portugal ahead of his troops, he received a letter from Lord Castlereagh informing him that a further 5,000 troops were being added to his force, as the intelligence on Junot's forces in Portugal indicated that he had a much larger army than previously thought. The letter came with a sting in the tail: as the army was now so large, Lieutenant General Sir Hew Dalrymple (presently Governor of Gibraltar) and Lieutenant General Sir Harry Burrard would command instead of Spencer and as both were senior to Arthur, he would only be third in command. However, he and his troops were already on the spot, whilst the reinforcements and the two new commanders were potentially weeks behind, he therefore decided to land and advance on Lisbon, in the hope that he would be able to defeat Junot before they arrived to take over command.

Arthur ordered the troops to begin landing on the beaches of Mondego Bay in Portugal on 1 August 1808 and despite a few mishaps in the heavy Atlantic surf, they were all disembarked within a week, without encountering any opposition and they were joined here by 6,000 Portuguese troops under the command of General Bernardino Freire. Arthur immediately put his troops on the march, south along the coastline, to maintain communications and the ability to receive supplies from the navy.

Arthur had just short of 11,000 troops and he first encountered a French force of only 4,000 troops, commanded by General Henri Delaborde at the village of Roliça, which lies in a basin surrounded by hills. Wellesley sent troops through the hills on both flanks in the hope of surrounding the French, but Delaborde was too aware of the situation and he retired to a very strong position on the hills in his rear. Arthur intended to continue the flank attacks

Wellington's headquarters at Vimiero.

to dislodge the French, but unfortunately Colonel Lake pushed his regiment, the 29th Foot, forward in a suicidal head-on attack. This succeeded only after Wellesley sent forward further troops in support and at a heavy cost to the 29th, including their foolhardy colonel, who was buried on the ridge. Realising that his rear would soon be jeopardised, Delaborde ordered a retreat, leaving the battlefield in British hands, Arthur had won his first battle over the French.

The British troops continued to march south and Wellesley ordered them to take up positions on the southern range of heights overlooking Porto Novo, to allow Sir Harry Burrard and 4,000 reinforcements to land. As Burrard was his senior, Arthur went on board his ship to discuss his plans. Sir Harry had decided to await a further reinforcement that was due to arrive within a few days under the command of

General Sir John Moore (also senior to Arthur), before marching on towards Lisbon. Burrard remained on board for the night and Arthur made his way ashore, unhappy with the outcome of the meeting, but unknown to both men, the French were going to force the issue.

The following morning, General Junot attacked with his force of 14,000 men, not from the south as expected, but from the east, forcing Wellesley to rapidly redeploy his troops on the hills overlooking the village of Vimiero, where he had established his headquarters.

Four separate attacks by large columns of infantry were launched at the British positions and despite French determination, all of the attacks were defeated by the overwhelming firepower of the British infantry deployed in lines only two ranks deep at very close quarters, followed by a bayonet charge, which broke the will of the French infantry and they rapidly fell back.

As the French army streamed back to Lisbon, Arthur prepared to march his troops off in pursuit. However, Sir Harry Burrard had landed during the action and had sensibly let Wellesley complete his battle before taking command, but he now ordered the army to halt and await Moore's reinforcements, much to Arthur's irritation. Within twenty-four hours Sir Hew Dalrymple arrived to supersede them all and he confirmed Burrard's orders. Arthur had held his own commands for too many years by now and was an unwilling junior, he turned away in frustration and apparently suggested to the officers of his force that they may as well go hunting.

However, General Junot now made an unexpected proposal, suggesting an armistice in preparation for a formal convention, the fighting was over.

Miniature of Arthur Wellesley dated 1808.

27: Cartoon Lampooning the Convention of Cintra

Arthur had been determined to follow up the retreating French army, which was demoralised following their defeat at Vimiero, but the arrival of Sir Harry Burrard ended any idea of a pursuit. When Sir Hew Dalrymple arrived the following day, he concurred with this decision, much to Arthur's great irritation and dismay.

Junot was aware of his own difficult predicament, but he sought to use the apparent timidity of his enemy to his own advantage in any negotiations. He sent General Kellerman to request talks on a capitulation and they began to discuss things over dinner at Vimiero. Dalrymple

sent Lieutenant Colonel George Murray to discuss terms, having successfully negotiated the convention at Copenhagen the previous year. The talks were initially difficult as the French wished to include the Russian fleet, then blockaded in the Tagus, within the convention, but Admiral Cotton insisted on the Russian fleet being excluded from the negotiations. Once that was sorted, everything was soon agreed. The French troops were to give up all of their fortified positions in Portugal in perfect condition and to return to France – not as prisoners, but free to serve again immediately. The French troops, numbering nearly 25,000 men, would be

THE CONVENTION of CINTRA, a Portuguese Gambol for the Amusement of JOHN BULL.

Queluz Palace.

transported on British ships to Rochefort and La Rochelle and they could take with them their arms and all military equipment. It was specifically stated in the treaty (although not in the public version) that the French could not take any plunder with them, but unfortunately those appointed to oversee their embarkation turned a blind eye to the mass of treasures plundered from Portugal which they took to France as personal property, causing uproar amongst the Portuguese, who saw it as a betrayal. The convention was named 'of Cintra' because it had been signed by Junot and Kellerman at his headquarters in the Queluz Palace near Lisbon, which is in the district of Cintra and was then countersigned by Dalrymple at his headquarters at the Palace of Seteais in Cintra (or Sintra) which is now a luxury hotel.

When the news of the Convention arrived in Britain, it was not long before the British press were branding the agreement as a disgrace. *The Times* branded it disgraceful and wished 'a curse, a deep curse might wring the heart and wither the hand that were base enough to devise and execute this cruel injury on their country's peace and honour'. Soon the public clamour was so great that minsters felt compelled to hold an inquiry into the convention and Dalrymple, Burrard and Wellesley, who had signed it, were called home to explain their actions. More recently, historians such as Michael Glover have stated that 'Never has a victorious army with every advantage in its hands signed an agreement which gave so much to its defeated enemies with so little to itself.' Murray who had actually negotiated the agreement was strangely not recalled to give evidence, leaving command of the army with General Sir John Moore.

Napoleon's reaction is also very revealing, writing to Junot, 'You have done nothing

Palacio de Seteais, Sintra.

dishonourable; you have returned my troops, my eagles and my cannons, but I certainly hoped you would do better … you have won this convention by your courage, not by your dispositions; and it is with reason that the English complain that their generals signed it.'

At the Inquiry, which was held in the Great Hall at the Royal Hospital, Chelsea from 14 November to 27 December 1808, Dalrymple sought to put all of the blame for the convention on Burrard and particularly Wellesley, while Arthur claimed that having relinquished

Junot and the French army embark at Lisbon.

command he had nothing to do with the negotiations and that he only signed in due form.

It is clear however, from Arthur's correspondence, now that it was too late for military operations to resume, Arthur supported the Convention as the best way of removing the French army from Portugal as he wrote:

'I approve of allowing the French to evacuate the country for I [am] convinced that if we do not, we should be obliged to attack Elvas, Fort Lippe, Almeida and Peniche regularly or blockade them and thus autumn would pass away and it is better to have 10,000 or 12,000 additional Frenchmen on the northern frontier of Spain and the army in Spain, than the Frenchmen in Portugal and the English blockading them in strong places.'

Following the inquiry all three officers were officially exonerated but both Dalrymple and Burrard were quietly sidelined and never actively employed again. Arthur, with the help of his political friends, was absolved of blame, but it is not clear whether he would have been sent straight back to Spain in the New Year had not news arrived of the terrible winter retreat of the army and pyrrhic victory at Corunna, before being forced to embark and the death of his rival, Sir John Moore at Corunna. Tellingly, King George III formally declared his disapprobation of the Convention and Arthur alone was voted the thanks of Parliament on 27 January 1809 for the victory at Vimeiro.

28: Traditional Salt Boats at Aveiro

During Arthur's enforced absence from Portugal for the inquiry into the Convention of Cintra and the debacle following the embarkation of Moore's army at Corunna, a number of changes had occurred in the Peninsula. The British still retained a small army in the vicinity of Lisbon, now commanded by Arthur's old friend from Ireland, General 'Beau' Cradock, but the government was not sure of the wisdom of maintaining their tenuous toe hold in Portugal or indeed of reinforcing this corps. However, Arthur, fresh from his recent absolution from blame, argued strongly within government that he believed that with a force of 20,000 infantry, 4,000 cavalry and a rejuvenated Portuguese army, that he could hold Portugal. He persuaded them to give him the opportunity to prove it, always having the security of knowing that Lisbon could be defended for long enough to allow the army to embark if it all went wrong. Just as Arthur set out for Portugal, news arrived of a French force having invaded northern Portugal under the command of Marshal Soult, capturing Portugal's second city, Porto, on 29 March 1809. With other French forces threatening to enter the country Arthur realised that a decision had to be made swiftly on his arrival.

Contemporary view of the Douro river at Porto and the Seminary (which at the time of the battle was unfinished).

Arthur sailed to Lisbon on HMS *Surveilante* on 14 April 1809 and he endured the almost traditional stormy weather which always seemed to dog him at sea, arriving in the Tagus on the 22nd. Quickly appraising the situation, having formally superseded his friend Cradock, Arthur made an almost instant decision, to march north and deal with Soult whilst he remained isolated, deep within Portugal on his own.

Leaving 12,000 troops under General Mackenzie at Lisbon to secure his rear, he ordered his main force of 18,000 troops, which Cradock had placed at Leiria, 100 kilometres north of Lisbon, to march further north to Coimbra, where he joined them on 2 May. On arrival Arthur re-ordered his force, placing a regiment of the untried Portuguese troops into each of his five British brigades, to give them confidence and giving each brigade a company of riflemen to strengthen their skirmishing line.

Arthur knew from intelligence that Soult had about 23,000 men altogether, but that around 4,000 of these troops under General Franceschi, were established on the line of the Vouga river some 30 kilometres south of Porto as an advance guard. He determined on a surprise attack and arranged to send two brigades of infantry, commanded by General Hill, in a flotilla of the salt boats of Aveiro up the Aveiro lagoon to Ovar, where they could land in their rear. Unfortunately the French were able to retire before the trap could be closed.

Soult, with his forces now fully concentrated at Porto, believed himself to be secure on the northern bank of the Douro, having removed the only bridge (of boats) to the northern bank and

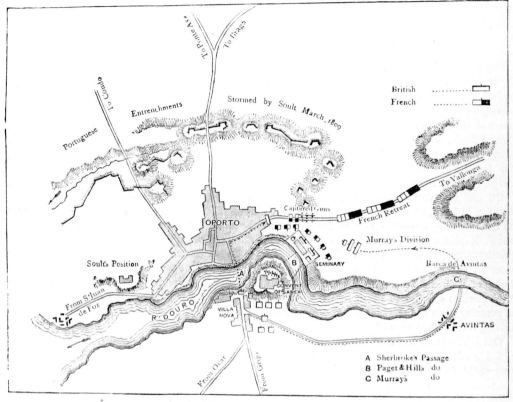

British ....

French ....

Entrenchments

Stormed by Soult March 1809

To Vallonga

Captured Guns

French Retreat

OPORTO

Murray's Division

Barca de Avintas

Soult's Position

SEMINARY

To Pome Av?

To Braga

Portuguese

To Coolbo

R^o DOURO

From S. Juan de Foz

CONVENT OF S. AREA

VILLA NOVA

AVINTAS

C.

From Oxar

From Grijo

A   Sherbroke's Passage

B   Paget & Hills   do

C   Murray's   do

PLAN OF THE PASSAGE OF THE DOURO.

removing all of the boats. However, Portuguese militia acting to the east along the Spanish border had threatened Soult's communications and he began to send his baggage and heavy artillery into Spain in preparation for a full-scale retreat, retaining only 12,000 men at Porto. Arthur's troops arrived on the southern bank of the Douro at Vila Nova de Gaia, but he kept them secreted out of the way whilst he formulated a plan. The Douro is quite broad and flows rapidly between steep banks, making crossing the river hazardous. Arthur sent his cavalry and a brigade of infantry to the east to endeavour to find a ford or a method of crossing, whilst he sought a way forward for the rest of his troops.

A Portuguese barber informed the British officers that a small skiff had been missed by the French and with a few men, they might row to the northern bank of the river and release four of the large wine barges tied up there, which were unguarded. Being around a curve in the river from the town, the French were unaware of the capture of the four barges and remained ignorant of Arthur Wellesley's immediate orders to transport troops over, thirty at a time, as quickly as possible and the troops were ordered to occupy and prepare for defence the unfinished seminary buildings on the heights above. By the time the French realised what was happening, the entire regiment of the 3rd Foot, the Buffs, were occupying the seminary buildings and an attack by three battalions of French infantry was repulsed with heavy loss, Arthur having placed three batteries of artillery on the opposite

Traditional wine barges at Porto.

heights to support the troops in the seminary. A second attack by three more battalions an hour later found the seminary defended by over 3,000 troops and they again were driven off in disorder.

Soult ordered the retreat and the guards on the river front within Porto were removed to support the attacks on the seminary. As soon as they left, the Portuguese inhabitants rapidly emerged to man the numerous boats tied up alongside the quay and soon they were ferrying British troops across in large numbers. Porto was clearly lost and Soult ordered a full retreat along the road towards Spain. The force sent to locate a crossing further up river, had discovered a sunken ferry and had succeeded in refloating it so that this force of nearly 3,000 troops stood on the northern shore. Unfortunately, the commander of this force, Murray, failed to intervene and block their retreat, probably fearing that his force would be overwhelmed. The single squadron of the 14th Light Dragoons did charge however, taking some 300 prisoners although they lost over a third of their own number.

British losses were only 125 men killed and wounded, whilst the French suffered 600 casualties and some 1,800 prisoners including about 1,000 sick. Unable to retreat by the main road, which was still held by the Portuguese, Soult's force was forced to take to mountain roads, abandoning his stores and 58 cannon and up to 2,000 more men during the dreadful retreat into Spain.

Arthur was rightly celebrated for his audacious attack against a superior enemy who still retained a formidable reputation at this time. His surprise attack near Aveiro nearly succeeded in cutting off a French brigade and his determination to push his troops across a wide river in the face of a very strong enemy force, demonstrate clearly that he was not merely a 'defensive general' as many try to portray him. When the strength of his forces were at least equal to those of his opponents he was very capable of launching well-coordinated attacks. The fact that many of his battles were defensive only shows that for most of his battles on the European mainland he was heavily outnumbered.

This success was a valuable morale-boosting victory for the Portuguese troops, although they had not been heavily engaged, but it was significant enough for the Portuguese soldiers that they regularly acclaimed the arrival of 'Douro' with them for the rest of the Peninsular War.

29: Monument to the Battle of Talavera on the Heights of Medellin

The British government had sent Arthur back to the Peninsula to defend Portugal, without having any real ambitions to interfere in Spain again. Indeed, Arthur was positively instructed not to get involved in Spain, if it weakened the defences of Portugal.

Having driven Soult out of Portugal and with Marshal Ney being bogged down in fighting the guerrillas in the north of Spain, Arthur turned his attention to the French I Corps, commanded by Marshal Victor. Leading elements of this corps had briefly clashed with Portuguese troops at Alcantara on the Spanish border on 14 May 1809, causing some concern to General Mackenzie, who feared that this was the start of a drive on Lisbon. However, Victor had been similarly worried that the troops at Alcantara were the vanguard of a much larger Portuguese force entering Spain. On realising that they were not, he halted his movement and returned initially into Estramadura.

Arthur saw an opportunity to strike against Victor who had moved north of the River Tagus whilst the other French armies were scattered and unable to come to his support. This move by the French was designed to enable them to live off the land with greater ease, but it brought them close enough for the Anglo-Portuguese Army to strike in cooperation with the Spanish Army of General Cuesta. Arthur ordered his troops to form up at Abrantes and on 3 July, he led his force

The Casa de Salinas.

of 21,000 men into Spain, reaching Plasencia on the 8th. Here he paused, still vainly trying to agree a concerted attack via correspondence with Cuesta, whose army stood just south of the River Tagus glaring at the French across the wide river.

Finally, the two Allied generals met on 11 July and held a four-hour conference to establish a plan. Both could speak French but Cuesta refused to use the language and everything had to go through interpreters. Victor's corps numbered some 25,000 men and was now in the vicinity of Talavera de la Reina. Opposed to them, Cuesta had an army of some 35,000 which had crossed to the north of the Tagus, but Victor was largely unaware of the Anglo-Portuguese Army also in his vicinity due to effective screening of this force by light troops and Spanish guerrillas.

It was agreed that the two Allied armies would meet at Oropesa on 20 July, when they would march on Talavera together. As this large force approached Talavera, Victor's advanced troops put up some resistance and were soon reporting the alarming news that the approaching army included British troops. Arthur came to an agreement with Cuesta to launch a full-scale attack on 22 July, but when the sun rose, his troops fully prepared for battle, he discovered that the Spanish troops had not formed up. Indeed, it transpired that Cuesta had unilaterally decided that his troops were fatigued and delayed the attack for 48 hours. Victor, now fully aware of the combined army facing him, rapidly retreated towards Madrid, the element of surprise being wasted.

Cuesta insisted on chasing the French on 24 July, but Arthur rightly refused to cooperate, realising that Victor had retired towards significant reinforcements and his troops were starving as the promised supplies from the Spanish had failed to materialise. As Arthur had predicted, Cuesta found himself facing a French army now numbering nearly 50,000 men

and he ordered a return to Talavera in haste, followed closely by the French. Having returned, Cuesta set up his camp in front of the Portina river rather than behind it and only moved back from such a dangerous position after Arthur had virtually begged him. Whilst on reconnaissance this afternoon, Arthur had probably his closest brush with death. Using one of the towers at the Casa de Salinas to view the French advance, he was nearly surprised and he and his staff were forced to run to their tethered horses and flee with bullets whistling past them.

The combined Allied armies lined the Portina stream which runs north from the town of Talavera into the hills, Cuesta's troops protecting the town and extending northward on the line of the Portina for about a mile, Arthur's troops extending the line another two miles to the north and anchoring the left wing on the height of Cerro de Medellin.

Everything was prepared for battle on 28 July, but Marshal Victor launched a surprise attack during the night, pushing forward a division to seize the Medellin, which was clearly the key to the whole position. In the confusion, two of the three French regiments went off course, but the 9th Légere did succeed in temporarily capturing the heights, before they were forced to retreat by a British counter-attack. More concerning to Arthur was the panic caused in the Spanish lines by a few French cavalry skirmishers, four entire battalions firing a full salvo off in the dark at an enemy which was far too distant and then turning tail en masse and fleeing from the field.

The French commenced the attack next day with a further attempt to wrest possession of the Medellin from British hands, but their columns were decimated by British firepower and driven back by a bayonet charge. Another column attack was driven back by the British Guards, who then advanced too far in pursuit. Coming up against a second French force the Guards were badly

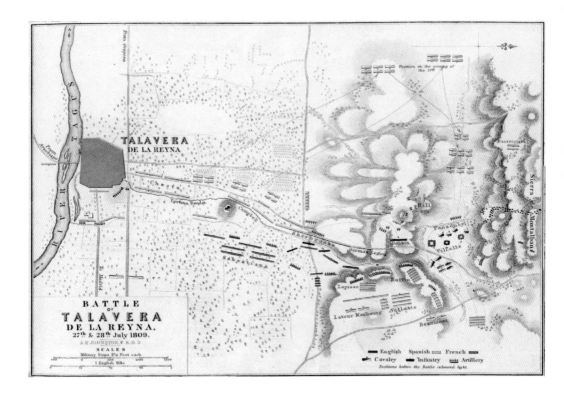

mauled and driven back with loss. Arthur had seen the failure in his centre, quickly reinforced the position and they successfully drove off the French whilst the Guards reformed in their rear. The French attacks had been defeated, although a cavalry affair to the north led to the 23rd Light Dragoons losing a number of men and horses, having unfortunately charged into a sunken ravine.

Losses on both sides were nearly equal at around 7,500 casualties, the British losing five times as many as the Spanish, who were not seriously attacked, but the French leaving the battlefield gave the victory to the Allies. Whilst contemplating a pursuit of the French, a captured message revealing that Marshal Soult was marching into his rear, forced Arthur to order his troops to rapidly march west to Almaraz and to cross the Tagus there into relative safety. Arthur had no option but to leave 1,500 wounded under

Cuesta's protection at Talavera, but within hours, the Spanish army had also crossed the Tagus and the French captured the wounded although they were treated exceptionally well.

Arthur's troops were forced to retire towards Portugal through a land unable to supply much food and many fell sick on this dreadful march. Arthur's troops had won two victories, which were rightly celebrated in Britain, but the consequent retreat did cause some concern. Arthur had, however, learnt a number of valuable lessons. The Portuguese troops had performed well and the Spanish guerrillas had proven very useful in gathering intelligence, but he also learnt that fighting in the Peninsula required an organised commissariat and huge mule trains as the troops could not rely on being able to subsist off the local supplies and that due caution must be exercised when coordinating with his Spanish allies.

30: A Pair of Wellington's Glasses

Following the retreat of the army back into Portugal after the victory at Talavera, Wellington was painfully clear that the army required a thorough reorganisation and drawing on his experiences in India he was just the man to do it.

He had already begun to organise his army into divisions, but as the Portuguese troops were brought up to scratch, he incorporated weak units into brigades with stronger ones and Portuguese and British brigades were intermixed within divisions for mutual support and to integrate them.

The supply of the army had broken down during the late campaign on the false promises of his allies and this had led to huge problems with indiscipline and plundering amongst the troops. He therefore insisted on a sufficient commissariat department responsible for the provision of food for both men and horses.

With the establishment of regular shipments of foodstuffs from Britain, North Africa and even North America, river boats and vast numbers of mules in trains were employed to move the goods up country to localised depots, ready for distribution. Arms, ammunition and uniforms were also constantly transported up to the front. It was a huge operation, which cost a great deal of pain, but once working well, gave his army a freedom of movement within Spain unknown to his enemy.

Regimental and field hospitals were set up to care for the sick and wounded and the health of his men steadily improved as he ensured that they were fed relatively well and that he protected them in battle as a valuable commodity hard to replace. Such obvious care for their welfare caused him to be greatly admired by his soldiers, although his aversion to 'theatricals' meant that he was never loved like a Napoleon.

At the same time Wellington took little interest in what his men wore, as long as their weapons were well looked after and they were always ready for action. He insisted on strict discipline within his army, not a trait often visible in British armies in Georgian times. He insisted that soldiers who committed crimes faced strict punishment and officers were to remember they were gentlemen and to act so at all times. Failure to do so would be harshly dealt with. Youthful boisterousness was not a problem within reason, as long as it did not offend the locals or could be seen to be blasphemous in such a strict Catholic country. His frequent admonishments included such phrases as '... the English public would not bear it ... and I see no reason why the Portuguese public should be worse treated'.

Wellington made it clear that he did not approve of officers absenting themselves from the front to enjoy the fleshpots of Lisbon or to gamble and certainly discouraged the regular taking of long leave in Britain and encouraged the others to follow his example, never returning himself to Britain during the entire six-year campaign.

Such attention to all of these details, whilst still planning future campaigns, answering inordinately long letters from government ministers, generals, admirals and all and sundry, inspecting troops and planning defences and inspecting their progress during construction filled his day and more, but he rigidly stuck to the task late into the night, maintaining his mantra of completing the day's work in the same day.

The workload was immense and the toll on his body was sometimes too much and he occasionally succumbed to illnesses for a day or two, but then he would be back at his desk at full tilt once again. So many long hours reading or writing reports in dim candlelight undoubtedly

damaged his eyesight and he used glasses to read from a relatively young age.

As time went on, the hard work began to pay off, the wheels began to grind efficiently without so much personal involvement and the military machine became a finely-oiled precision instrument, maintaining generally the highest standards of efficiency. Wellington always said that his army of 1814 was the best he ever commanded, but what he did not say, was that was purely down to his insistence on the highest professionalism at all levels at all times. He effectively invented the modern British Army.

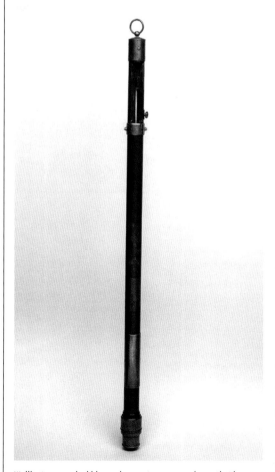

Wellington even had his own barometer on campaign so that he could keep an eye on the weather.

31: The Wellington Monument in Somerset

When news arrived in Britain of the victory at Talavera, King George III and Portland, the Prime Minister, decided that Arthur should be rewarded with a peerage. He would probably have already gained one after Vimiero but for the fuss over the Convention of Cintra.

In Arthur's absence abroad, his brother William was tasked with selecting a relevant and suitable title for him. The College of Heralds required a rapid decision and there was not time to correspond with Arthur for a decision, so William made his thoughts and hoped that Arthur would not be too displeased.

William wrote to Arthur on 22 August, congratulating him on his peerage, jokingly complaining that he had not left any prior instructions on what to do and then explaining the reasoning for his preferred choice. As there was already a Lord Wellesley (his brother Richard), William turned for inspiration to the map of the West Country where the Wellesleys were originally from. His eyes finally rested on the small market town of Wellington which had grown prosperous from being on the great trade route between Exeter and Bristol and became a centre for cloth-making. The government granted £100,000 for the purchase of lands to attach to the title and the manor in the parish of Wellington was apparently available and William oversaw the purchase.

Originally known as Weolingtun, which means 'wealth estate', it was recorded in the Domesday Book as Walintone and the estate was owned by the Bishops of Wells, which could explain how the name quietly changed to its present spelling. There was enough money to purchase a second manor, the land attached to this second manor including the site of the eventual Wellington monument.

William had him officially declared Viscount Wellington of Talavera and of Wellington and Baron Douro of Welleslie in the County of Somerset. When he wrote to Arthur, he announced his title with some trepidation, fearing that Arthur might find it 'unpleasant or trifling'. He needn't have worried as Arthur

was delighted with the choice, writing back 'I think you have chosen most fortunately'. The subsidiary title of Baron Douro has since been traditionally held by the child who is due to succeed to the main title.

Kitty was not so keen on the name apparently, as it referred to nothing really, but as she recorded in her diary 'it is done & I suppose it could not be avoided'. Hardly a resounding seal of approval. Once a few letters arrived addressed to Lady Wellington, she succumbed to the inevitable. Arthur first signed a letter with his traditional 'Wellington' on 16 September 1809, noting casually to his correspondent, 'This is the first time I have signed my new name'.

The monument which dominates the surrounding area, standing proudly atop Wellington Hill high above the town, was initially proposed at a meeting held at the White Hart Inn in Wellington in September 1815. A design competition was won by a Thomas lee in October 1817, with a triangular obelisk shape, standing 53 metres tall and incorporating a circular staircase of eighty steps and there was originally meant to be a statue of Wellington on the top. The unusual triangular obelisk was reputedly inspired by the triangular bayonet used on the Brown Bess musket, carried by Wellington's troops. The foundation stone was laid in 1817, but the project always suffered from financial difficulties and it was abandoned only half built when the money ran out in 1829. When Arthur died in 1852, renewed efforts were made to raise the finances needed to complete the monument and it was finally completed (without a statue on top) in 1854. The original plans incorporated the siting of twenty-four captured French cannon from the Battle of Waterloo around the base and sixteen cannon were shipped from the Royal Arsenal at Woolwich to Exeter Quay, but never went any further, eventually being sunk into the quay at Exeter as bollards. The cannon were iron naval guns and not from the Battle of Waterloo anyway. The single brass gun sent has recently been installed as originally intended.

32: Traditional Portuguese Tiled Mural depicting the Portuguese Victory, Busaco Palace

Following Napoleon's defeat of the Austrian army in 1809, he was able to send large reinforcements into Spain, in order to complete its conquest. The Spanish armies were destroyed in the Battle of Ocana in November 1809 and Seville fell, forcing the ruling Spanish Junta to flee to Cadiz, as one of the last bastions of Spanish freedom. It was obvious that a concerted effort would now be made to drive the British out of the Peninsula and Arthur began to make preparations to defend Portugal to the last.

The remains of Fort Concepion in the 1960s, clearly showing where the walls had been destroyed by British engineers.

Marshal Massena was appointed to the command of the Army of Portugal in early 1810 and Wellington moved almost all of his available troops to watch the northern border of Portugal around Almeida. By the end of April, French troops began to prepare for the siege of the Spanish fortress of Ciudad Rodrigo although it did not commence properly until 5 June. The French initially underestimated the strength of the fortress, but it eventually fell on 9 July, opening the road into northern Portugal. Having been delayed here longer than anticipated, Massena's troops remained in the vicinity for another ten days awaiting further supplies, before they moved forward again. This played perfectly into Wellington's hands, who knew that his best hope for the defence of Portugal against such superior numbers, was based heavily on delaying the French advance until winter forced them to retire or starve.

The French began to move forward slowly and first encountered Wellington's advance guard at Fort Concepcion, which was deemed too small to defend and was abandoned, but rendered unusable as a fortress by a number of mines detonated under the walls by British engineers before they retreated.

Massena advanced his troops to the fortress of Almeida, which guarded the northern route on the Portuguese side. This was a large fortress, in a good state of repair and with a sizeable garrison, which Wellington confidently expected to hold out for eight weeks or more. However, even before the French army began the siege, Arthur nearly suffered a major setback, due to the stupidity of one of his most senior officers.

General Craufurd, commanding the Light Division had been warned not to get trapped to the east of the Coa River when the French approached. Craufurd, however, thinking he

The narrow bridge over the Coa.

knew better, defied Wellington. The result was a surprise attack on 24 July, with overwhelming French numbers pushing forward at speed, with the aim of capturing the narrow bridge in their rear and forcing the entire division to surrender, and it nearly succeeded. It was only by a dogged defence and a rapid retreat over rugged terrain, which luckily precluded the French from utilising their cavalry, that they managed to reach the bridge and cross, only minutes before the French arrived. It was a very narrow escape.

The following day, the French turned to preparations for the siege of Almeida, but it took more than two weeks to get the siege guns there from Ciudad Rodrigo and siege works only began in earnest on 15 August. It was 26 August before the French were ready to begin battering the walls, fully expecting it to take a week or two before a practical breach could be formed. However, a freak accident on the first night changed all of that. It is not exactly clear how it happened, but a spark or a live shell got into the main gunpowder store in the cellars of the old medieval castle. An almighty explosion levelled the castle and blew many of the cannon off the fortress walls, some of the masonry blocks landing over half a mile away and causing casualties in the French lines. Claims that 500 men were killed instantly are now doubted (Portuguese casualty lists count only 110 killed and wounded). However, morale had collapsed and the defences were ruined, and the garrison forced the British governor to submit. The fortress fell on 27 August, only twenty-four hours after the French siege guns had opened fire and 4,000 Portuguese troops marched into captivity. Arthur was very worried when information was received that virtually the whole of the Portuguese garrison had enlisted in the French army, but he soon discovered that they had used it as a chance to desert and most were soon back fighting the French.

The French army was now clear to invade Portugal and as Massena's army of some 60,000 men heavily outnumbered Wellington's army of around 45,000, he had no choice but to retire slowly, destroying the bridges as they went. As the army slowly marched south, the local inhabitants were forced to leave and to take whatever they could with them, as Arthur had ordered a 'scorched earth' policy, to increase the supply problems of the French as they marched deeper into Portugal. Unsurprisingly, although the Portuguese government had agreed to this drastic step, the continued retreat of the Allied army, without any significant resistance to the French at all, began to attract loud criticism.

As the French marched on towards Coimbra, they were now nearly half way to Lisbon and the Portuguese complaints were becoming vociferous, but at Busaco, on a high ridge just 20 kilometres north of the city, Wellington finally turned to offer battle. Every delay Arthur could inflict on the French advance was invaluable, but the political pressure and open criticism of his tactics, both from the Portuguese authorities and the opposition in the British Pparliament also made a stand imperative.

The long, narrow ridge, over 5 miles in length, runs perpendicularly to the then main road to Coimbra and reaches heights of up to 550 metres above sea level, it was a serious obstacle to the French advance. Wellington had arranged his troops sparsely along this long ridge line, but the bulk of his troops were positioned out of sight on the rear face of the ridge, making it impossible for Massena to know where his real strength was. Arthur had also had his engineers construct a trackway along the crest of the ridge to allow rapid movement of his forces to any crisis point.

Massena believed that his greatly superior numbers would soon overwhelm Wellington's forces and led him to launch a number of direct assaults on the ridge with large columns of

The fortified town of Almeida with the ruined castle in the top left.

infantry. Massena's poor view of the Portuguese soldiers also influenced his decision, but he was soon to discover that they had greatly improved.

Each column struggled to climb the steep ascent and arrived at the top of the ridge with the men exhausted, only to be struck by a heavy fire from Wellington's infantry and artillery at close range, decimating their ranks, before a bayonet charge drove them back down the slope. The same scenario played out in all of the French attacks and the final attack was defeated by Pack's Portuguese Brigade unaided.

The French eventually gave up, having suffered over 4,000 losses, whereas allied losses were nearer 1,200, it was a comprehensive defeat. The day marked the re-birth of the Portuguese army and has rightly been celebrated in Portugal ever since with great pride.

The following day however, the French found a way around the western end of the ridge line and Wellington's men were forced to continue their retreat, the French still possessing a great superiority.

The memorial to the Battle of Busaco.

33: Metal-Cased Mysorean Rockets – Part of a Huge Batch Recently Discovered

Soon after gunpowder was developed in the Far East, rockets encased in bamboo were trialled, but they lacked range and stability and were soon superseded by cannon. However, Hyder Ali and his son Tipu Sultan had experimented with rockets using iron tubes to contain the gunpowder meaning that they could develop greater thrust and would travel up to a mile. The metal casing was scientifically designed, with one end sealed and a nozzle on the other end to propel the rocket using the gasses emitted. It was balanced by a stick of up to 15 feet (4.6 metres) in length. The Mysorean design included a long thin sword blade of up to 40 inches (1.016 metres) long which was designed to help stabilise the weapon when fired, but as the propellant became exhausted the rocket became unstable, causing the rocket with sword attached to tumble, the blade acting like a scythe, inflicting nasty injuries on anyone it came in contact with.

Tipu developed a corps of rocketeers 5,000 strong, with 200 rocketeers being assigned to each Mysorean cushion (or brigade). They fired both handheld rockets and also used carts with frames for firing between five and ten rockets in near-simultaneous launches. Both men used the rockets to great effect against British forces and were particularly successful because of their element of surprise at the Battle of Pollilur in 1780, where it is believed a rocket caused the British ammunition store to explode. Tipu went as far as to write a military manual called the *Faithful Mujahidin*, which incorporated the use of rockets in both attack and defence. Arthur Wellesley first came under fire from rockets during his failed attack on the tope at Seringapatam.

After the fall of Seringapatam, 600 launchers, 700 fully-armed rockets and some 9,000 empty iron rocket casings were discovered and a number of examples were sent to the Royal Woolwich Arsenal where a rocket development programme began in 1801. An improved system was designed by William Congreve and brought into operation in the British army from 1807, with two Royal Horse Artillery troops being equipped as Rocket Troops and the Royal Navy developing a number of 'rocket ships' as an advancement on the

A Mysorean rocket man.

Congreve rocket.

They did, however, remain very much a weapon in their infancy, with many of the rockets fired proving to be very inaccurate and even turning back on their own side. Arthur had seen the destructive power of incendiary weapons during the bombardment of Copenhagen in 1807 and he reluctantly trialled the rockets in Portugal in 1809, but was less than impressed with the results, viewing their effect as more psychological than physical, and they were generally used in the Peninsula as signals rather than as a weapon. Perhaps their most famous use during the Napoleonic wars was their use at the bombardment of Fort McHenry where the 'rockets' red glare' soon became a line in *The Star Spangled Banner*.

At Waterloo, Wellington found that he had a rocket troop appointed to his force, but insisted that they put the rockets into store and carry cannon. When informed that the commander of the troops would be devastated if he could not take his rockets into action, Wellington's initial outburst of 'Damn his heart Sir! Let my orders be obeyed', was eventually ameliorated and the troop carried and used both in the battle.

traditional fireships. Very large rockets, weighing up to 32 pounds (14.5 kg) were produced, some even carried cannon balls on the tip.

34: Wellington's Headquarters at Pero Negro

During the autumn of 1809, Wellington regularly rode out to the hills around Lisbon with his engineers, but nothing official was written up about his plans, to maintain secrecy. Being heavily outnumbered, it was only time before the French invaded Portugal again and Arthur was determined to defend Lisbon as long as possible and if necessary to fortify a position to ensure a safe reembarkation.

Drawing on previous proposals by the Portuguese engineer Jose Maria das Neves Costa, Wellington had Lieutenant Colonel Sir Richard Fletcher of the Royal Engineers devise a series of lines of forts right across Portugal streching from the Atlantic coast to the River Tagus. Two major lines were constructed as an outer and inner defence and just west of Lisbon, a third set of defences were to be constructed around Fort St Julian on the banks of the Tagus to ensure a secure point from which to embark, if all else failed.

The works began in secrecy in November 1809, Wellington not even mentioning them to his own government. The defences were multi-faceted: not only were 150 forts constructed in the Lines of Torres Vedras, with 600 heavy

cannon installed, but everything else possible to defend these lines of hills was done by an army of around 7,000 Portuguese labourers being paid 1 shilling per day and later the entire population for 40 miles around were conscripted to complete them. Communication roads were built, rivers were dammed to form lakes, slopes were scarped to make the incline steeper, huge stone walls were constructed across valleys and huge impenetrable abatis were fashioned from sharpened olive trees. Communication masts were erected along the lines and using a semaphore system with balls it was said that a message could travel from one end of the line to the other in under seven minutes. The entire project cost some £100,000 (about £5 million today), all financed without the knowledge of the British government.

As the French advanced into Portugal, the Allied army slowly retreated towards Lisbon, driving the local inhabitants before them and destroying everything in a 'scorched earth' policy. Some 300,000 Portuguese were displaced and they were all moved within the Lines, where they were fed, but despite their best efforts up to 40,000 died that winter.

As the Allied army passed into the Lines on 8 October, the troops were sent to camps just behind the defences of the First Line for rest and recuperation, the forts all being garrisoned by 30,000 Portuguese militia, leaving the main army ready to move to any point threatened by a French attack.

Massena and his forces arrived in front of the Lines on 14 October and on his first reconnaissance his large staff riding with him attracted a cannonball fired from the nearest fort. Massena raised his hat in acknowledgement of the warning and retired. When he challenged his officers as to why he knew nothing of these

The defences of Fort Sao Vicente.

An aerial view of Fort Sao Vicente.

The two main lines of defences – each red star denotes a fort.

defences, they meekly replied 'Wellington had made them'. To which he replied angrily 'The devil! Wellington didn't make the mountains.' Arthur maintained his headquarters at Pero Negro, in the centre of the Lines from where he could ride to any point along the lines with ease. The French never penetrated the First Line and the other Lines never fired a shot in anger.

Massena felt incapable of attacking Wellington in such a prepared position, particularly after his recent defeat at Busaco, so he would wait until he received reinforcements. He held out for a month, but hunger soon turned to starvation and on 14 November he pulled his army back to Santarem, a more defensible position which still had a reasonable stock of provisions.

Wellington declined to attack them in such a strong position but he would wait for winter to do its worst. In fact, on 5 March 1811 Massena finally ordered his very sickly army to retreat into Spain, but finding Coimbra full of Portuguese militia, his troops were forced to take to mountainous tracks having abandoned much of their stores and materiel. Portugal was free of the French once again at the cost of only 4,000 of his troops. Massena had lost over 25,000.

Even though the third French invasion had been comprehensively defeated, Arthur was well aware that they might yet try again and construction on the Lines continued well into 1812, only ending when a French return became impossible. A fourth line of defences, less well known than the others, was also constructed on the eastern banks of the Tagus river, opposite Lisbon to prevent the French firing on the fleet off Lisbon from here, this line was known as the Almada Line.

In recent years Portugal has rediscovered the Lines of Torres Vedras as a tourist attraction and as a commemoration of a proud period in their history.

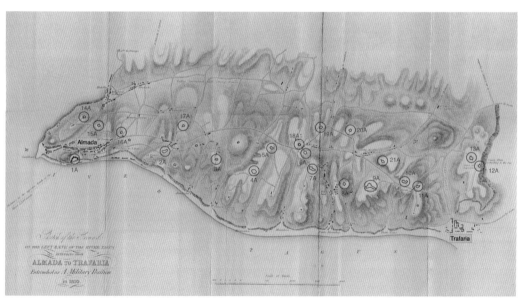

The Fourth Line at Almada.

35: Portuguese Print Commemorating the Victory at Porto 1809

The French invasion of Portugal in 1808 highlighted how poor the Portuguese army was, with useless elderly and often absentee officers and ill-trained soldiers. Portugal had regularly employed foreign officers to organise their army and the Portuguese government therefore had no qualms in offering command of their army to Arthur Wellesley, but unsurprisingly he politely turned down the job, preferring to take the role of supreme allied commander in Portugal. They then chose Major General William Carr Beresford, an excellent, if fortunate choice as he proved to be a very second-rate commander of troops in the field, but a first-rate organiser. Beresford was named as 'Marshal of the Portuguese Army', which in theory gave him a rank higher than Arthur, as the British Army did not then have the rank of field marshal, but he was subordinate to his office as supreme commander.

Beresford arrived in Lisbon in March 1809 and whilst Wellesley drove Soult out of Porto and beat Marshal Victor at Talavera, Beresford settled down to the serious business of 'root and branch' reform of the Portuguese army. Recruitment was not a problem as there was already in place a system of conscription and no lack of volunteers following the devastation of the country and the subsequent high unemployment.

Fugida de Sult. da Cidade do Porto, Wellesley persegue o Exercito Francez: o qual na fugida q. faz, a bandona a sua Artilharia; em.tos Francezes se entregão prizioneiros ao Exercito Portuguez.

One of his first reforms was to recruit a number of British officers into the Portuguese Army by offering them a step up in rank and the subsequent higher salary. Over the six subsequent years of war, some 300 British officers served with the Portuguese forces. In order to avoid national resentment at this large influx of 'foreign officers', he made room for them by forcing elderly and infirm officers to retire and by requiring officers to attend their regiments, a number of the aristocracy voluntarily surrendered their commissions. In the first four months 215 were dismissed and 107 retired. The British officers were then spread through the various regiments in relatively even numbers, ensuring that the British were not congregated together. Virtually half of each rank in a regiment were Portuguese and where a British officer was installed, his junior and senior in line was Portuguese to ensure cooperation between them. The British government produced new uniforms for the Portuguese troops and armed them with Brown Bess muskets and Baker rifles.

In time the Portuguese army grew to about 50,000 men, but the country's economy simply could not maintain such a level of expenditure and Arthur wrote to the British government arguing for them to subsidise the Portuguese army. Over the next six years the Portuguese received nearly £11 million in subsidies (equal to £520 billion today!), but even so Portuguese soldiers were in arrears of pay and were half starved because of poor food supplies. As the war progressed the Portuguese troops accounted for about a third of Wellington's troops in the field and as they gained experience and became more professional, they were seen as equal to the British soldiers they were fighting

British officer's Portuguese shako.

alongside. The light infantry, termed cacadores, were excellent, the line infantry battalions and artillery good, but the Portuguese cavalry was consistently poor.

The Portuguese troops employed at Porto were not particularly good, but by late 1810 when they took part in the Battle of Busaco, they showed themselves to be good, steady troops and it is often seen as the moment when they proved their worth. This is a source of pride to the Portuguese to this day. By 1813 Wellington was calling them 'The fighting cocks of the Army'. In turn, the Portuguese troops loved Arthur and his appearance near a regiment of Portuguese infantry would inevitably lead to loud cheers and cries of 'Douro', their affectionate name for him. The admiration was truly mutual.

Perhaps Arthur's greatest testimonial to the Portuguese troops occurred in Belgium in 1815. When appealing to the British government for more troops, he specifically asked them to subsidise 12,000 to 14,000 Portuguese troops and to arrange to have them transported to Belgium. Unfortunately, the government was worried that it would take too long and more pertinently they could hire more German troops for the money. The point was not lost on Wellington, but he would undoubtedly have preferred to receive his trusted Portuguese troops than German militia of dubious worth. It shows how much he valued them.

A Portuguese line infantryman.

A Portuguese Cacadore.

36: Original Map of the Vicinity of Fuentes de Oñoro (north to the right)

Whilst Beresford watched the southern corridor into Spain, Wellington began a blockade of Almeida, in an effort to starve out the garrison and capture the northern route into Spain. Whilst the siege works were in preparation, the Allied army was spread along the border with Spain, stretching some 25 kilometres to the south of Almeida, to stop any attempt by Massena to relieve the fortress.

Having recently retired from Portugal in disarray, Massena quickly reorganised his troops, and once rested and fed, they were soon ready to advance once again. The French corps marched towards the Portuguese frontier in early May, with the intention of defeating Wellington's army and driving them off, allowing Massena time to re-supply Almeida.

As soon as Arthur received intelligence of the French advance, he ordered his troops to concentrate in the vicinity of the low hill above the village of Fuentes de Oñoro and his right flank stretching southward to Poco Velho. Massena had some 47,000 men of which 5,000 were cavalry, to Wellington's 36,000 with only 2,000 cavalry, therefore Arthur prepared for a defensive battle, placing a brigade of his troops within the stone walls of the village and with his supporting artillery on the low ridge behind.

On 3 May 1811, Massena ordered a direct assault on the village and despite the difficulties of crossing the Dos Casas stream in its front via

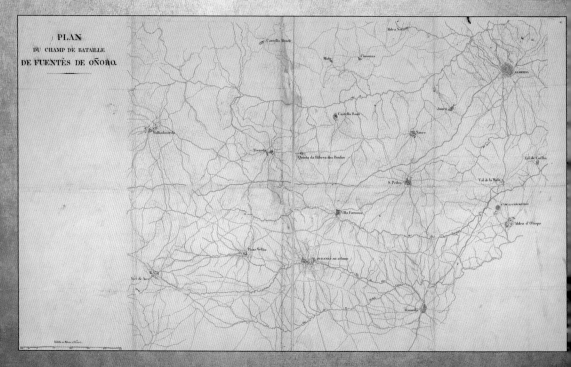

the narrow the stone footbridges and negotiating their way through the village which consisted of a veritable maze of high dry-stone walls with numerous confusing cul de sacs, in the face of determined defenders who resisted with shot and the bayonet, they eventually reached the church which marked the end of the village. However, Wellington sent in reinforcements in the shape of the 71st Highlanders, who drove the French back out at the point of their bayonets. The first day had been one of desperate hand-to-hand fighting, with no attempt at manoeuvre.

The following day was given over to recovering the wounded whilst the pickets of the two armies mingled peacefully at the Dos Casas stream in search of refreshment, no one even considering fighting despite their proximity.

The fighting was renewed on 5 May, but this time Massena tried to manoeuvre Wellington out of his position. He had realised that Wellington's right wing, consisting of one division of infantry at Poco Velho, some 4 kilometres from his main position at Fuentes de Oñoro was relatively isolated and only connected by a thin cavalry screen. Utilising his great superiority in cavalry, Massena sought to drive the Allied cavalry away and then attack the isolated infantry. Arthur could plainly see the threat and he immediately ordered the Light Division, supported by the Allied cavalry, to march to their support and then retire together. The infantry formed squares and marched across the flat plain in this formation, always ready to halt and form up if the French cavalry attacked. Attempts to deploy their

The streambed, footbridge and the village of Fuentes de Oñoro.

The church at Fuentes de Oñoro which was the furthest point the French infantry reached.

artillery at short range to decimate the squares was prevented by the constant threat of a charge by the Allied cavalry. Having reached the 7th Division, the infantry marched back to Fuentes together, the French cavalry swirling about them menacingly, but unable to impede their march.

During this 'pretty field day' as one of the British soldiers observing the march described it, a battery of horse artillery commanded by Captain Norman Ramsay became surrounded by French cavalry and was presumed to have been captured. However, Ramsay had other ideas, and drawing their swords, he ordered his battery to charge through the French cavalrymen and by some miracle they succeeded in escaping.

Having completed a textbook withdrawal with very few casualties, Wellington now formed his army at a right angle on the height above Fuentes. Massena realised that the key to the position was the village and he therefore ordered another attack in order to dislodge the Allied army from its position.

Three battalions of French grenadiers stormed into the village and following bloody work with their bayonets, they slowly cleared the village, inflicting heavy casualties particularly on the 79th Highlanders. A counter-attack by the 88th Foot (Connaught Rangers) swept back through the village, at one time apparently trapping 100 grenadiers in a cul de sac and killing all of them in the ferocious close-quarters fighting. Eventually the French were forced back out of the village and back over the stream, the battle was over, the French having lost some 3,000 casualties to the Allies' 1,800. It had been a difficult battle for Arthur and he wrote soon

Ramsay's Troop escape the French cavalry.

Contemporary print of the Battle of Fuentes de Oñoro.

The narrow bridge in a very steep valley of Barba de Puerco.

after, openly admitting that 'If Boney had been there, we should have been beat'.

Massena's army remained in the vicinity for three more days, but no further fighting occurred and being short of supplies of food and ammunition, he eventually ordered his troops to retire to Ciudad Rodrigo. Massena soon received an order from Napoleon summarily ordering him back to Paris, but this had been sent before he could possibly learn of the outcome of this battle.

Wellington did sustain one loss, which greatly angered him at this time. Just after Massena finally retired, news arrived that the French garrison of Almeida, aware that Massena was now unable to relieve them, blew up the defences during the night of 10 May and during the

confusion in the darkness he successfully got the majority of his 1,400-man garrison safely over the Barba de Puerco bridge into Spain. Arthur was enraged and later wrote: 'They had about 13,000 to watch 1,400. There they were all sleeping in their spurs even; but the French got off. I begin to be of the opinion that there is nothing on earth so stupid as a gallant officer.'

The rest of the year was one of bitter frustration, Wellington's army being too weak to besiege the fortresses of Ciudad Rodrigo or Badajoz and the French too preoccupied within Spain to contemplate another attempt on Portugal. Every man in the Allied army from Arthur down found this period in the campaigns very tedious and extremely frustrating, with little sign of any improvement in the foreseeable future.

37: French Model 1812 Lance

Having seen Massena's force retreat into Spain, Arthur moved his troops back up to the Spanish border. The French forces in Spain were still far superior to his and Wellington could only consider attacking when the French forces were widely dispersed in search of supplies or busy dealing with the remaining Spanish armies and guerillas.

His first targets were necessarily to recapture the fortresses of Almeida and Ciudad Rodrigo covering the northern route into Spain, or Badajoz to open up the southern passage – the French had captured Badajoz from the Spanish on 11 March 1811. However, Elvas on the Portuguese side of the border still remained in the possession of the Allies. Wellington had to maintain a watch over both to ensure the French did not enter Portugal, whilst also awaiting any opportunity to try to capture any of these fortresses. In fact, the French did cross the border capturing Campo Maior on 25 March, Marshal Mortier leaving a small garrison there before returning to Badajoz. Arthur ordered a force of 20,000 men under the command of Marshal Beresford to move towards Badajoz, with a view to besiege it, whilst he commanded the forces on the northern frontier.

Beresford's force surprised the French garrison of Campo Maior, which caused them to retire in haste towards Badajoz. The French troops were at their mercy and General Long was sent with 1,500 cavalry to attack them. Defeating the superior French cavalry, General Long sent his cavalry in hot pursuit of the remnants of the French horsemen in a seven-mile chase which only ended with the guns of Badajoz chasing the British cavalry off.

With Marshal Soult's army having moved south following news of the defeat of the French forces besieging Cadiz at the Battle of Barrosa, Mortier was temporarily isolated at Badajoz and Beresford moved his army forward to invest it, but he lacked a proper siege train of heavy artillery and a number of old cannon had to be borrowed from Elvas fortress. Due to the slow progress, Arthur visited Beresford on 22 April and they agreed a plan of operations, before he left to go north again. Beresford was however cheered by the arrival of support, in the shape of a Spanish army numbering some 15,000 troops under the command of General Blake. Finally the siege began on 4 May.

Hearing that Badajoz was under threat, Soult moved rapidly to break the siege and Beresford

Memorial at Albuera.

Lancers decimate the British infantry at Albuera.

was warned of his approach by Spanish patriots on 12 May. Wellington had left Beresford with discretion to fight or to retire if threatened by an attack and he originally planned to order a retreat, but he was persuaded by the Spanish that their joint force was superior to that of the French, and to offer battle, taking position on some low heights above the village of Albuera.

As Soult's troops arrived, he ordered troops forward to appear to threaten the village of Albuera, causing Beresford to send further support to defend it. The feint having worked, Soult ordered his main force to move by the left on a large flanking movement, which was concealed by some olive woods. Retreating Spanish cavalry soon warned Beresford of the new threat and he ordered the Spanish troops to alter their facing to meet the French attack and all of his cavalry was moved to protect their right flank during the manouevre and the British troops were brought up in support.

The Spanish General Blake did not believe that the flank attack was the real one and only sent four battalions to face in this direction, Beresford soon realised and ordered more Spanish units to move, but the delay caused was fatal and the four Spanish battalions were struck by the French main attack before the reinforcements could arrive to their support.

Despite the localised French superiority, the four Spanish battalions, consisting of probably the best troops in the Spanish army, stood their ground heroically and were only forced to retire slowly, giving time for the other Spanish troops ordered up by Beresford to arrive in support and also the British 2nd Division. The musketry duel was intense with both sides taking heavy casualties but both refusing to give ground and a number of bayonet charges took place, but with only limited success.

At this moment, disaster struck. A heavy downpour of hail and rain suddenly broke over the

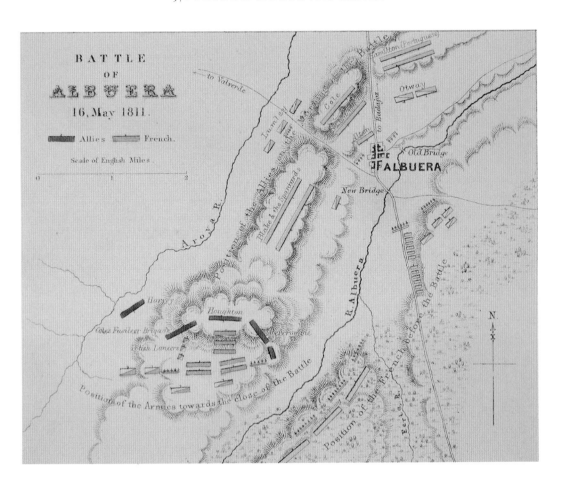

Medal produced to celebrate Beresford's 'victory'.

battlefield, reducing visibility to only a few metres and wetting their ammunition, causing their muskets to become unserviceable. Under cover of this freak weather, the French cavalry commander Latour-Maubourg launched two cavalry regiments at the flank of the British troops. Rolling up the British line the hussars and Polish lancers brought havoc to three of the four regiments of Colborne's brigade, killing large numbers. Only the fourth regiment, the 31st Foot, had time to form square to save themselves, but the cavalry pressed on and also overran the supporting artillery battery. Three battalions had been virtually annihilated and five regimental colours and eight cannon had been captured in less than five minutes, Colborne's three regiments suffering 319 killed, 460 wounded and 479 captured. The rainstorm ending, the French cavalry were driven off and both sides sought to regroup before the final push. At this point the stubborn resistance of the Spanish troops had saved Beresford from complete defeat.

The leading French division had been shattered by the intense firefight and was relieved by a second division. This delay also gave time for the Allies to redeploy and Hoghton's brigade was sent to counter them and this second phase of the battle became even bloodier than the first. The French column supported by a number of cannon sought to break through Hoghton's line, but it held and both sides stood trading volleys of musketry and cannister, which decimated the ranks, Hoghton's brigade losing two-thirds of its

1,500 men killed or wounded, but they still held, the 57th Foot earning the nickname of the 'Die Hards' from this action.

At this point, both armies were exhausted and close to breaking point. Both Soult and Beresford still retained a strong reserve and at this point the French Marshal called off the main attack, although the French feint attack now succeded in gaining the village of Albuera. At this critical moment, General Lowry Cole, advanced without orders towards the left flank of the French attack. In desperation, Soult sent his final infantry reserve to their support and launched four regiments of cavalry against Cole's Portuguese troops, fully expecting them to give way. The Portuguese troops stood firm, however, and drove the French cavalry off.

The brigade of British Fusiliers (two battalions of the 7th and one of the 23rd) traded volleys with the French and both sides again suffered very heavy casualties, but after twenty minutes or so the French finally broke and fled the field and Soult ordered a retreat. By the skin of his teeth Beresford had gained a victory, but at a heavy cost, Beresford losing some 6,000 men and Soult up to 7,000 killed and wounded.

Beresford wrote his report of the battle, but given the shock of such an intense action and with such terrible losses, it was a very depressing read and quite downbeat. Wellington, realising how badly the news of this action would be taken at home, sent it back saying:

'This won't do. It will drive the people in England mad. Write me down a victory.'

The report was rewritten and a victory duly proclaimed, but Arthur privately acknowledged such another battle would ruin his army. Soult paid tribute to the Allies stating that although he had outmanouvred them 'they did not know how to run!' It was also one of the rare occasions

during this war that the Houses of Parliament expressed their gratitude for the steadfastness of the Spanish troops.

It did, however, reinforce Arthur's view that he had few subordinates whom he could give true independent command to.

38: Ivory Miniature of Henry Wellesley

A young Henry Wellesley by John Hoppner.

H enry was the youngest son in the family, but he showed intelligence from an early age. He was educated at Eton, just like his siblings, and then entered the court of the Duke of Brunswick. In 1790, at the age of 17 Henry purchased an ensigncy in the 40th (2nd Somersetshire) Regiment of Foot, but he was clearly ill-suited for a military life, and he was soon being used in more diplomatic roles. In 1791, Henry was appointed as an attaché at the Hague and the following year he became secretary of the legation in Stockholm. He transferred to the 1st Foot Guards and he purchased a lieutenancy in 1793.

The following year, when travelling with his sister Anne on a ship from Lisbon, he was captured by the French and he remained a prisoner of war for over a year. In 1797, he accompanied Lord Malmesbury in his failed attempt to initiate peace negotiations and he then travelled to India to act as private secretary to his brother Richard. He was in India for most of the period 1797–1802 and successfully negotiated two major treaties of alliance with Indian states, whilst performing an invaluable role as go-between for Richard as Governor of India and Arthur who commanded a significant force of troops on the Indian subcontinent. Arthur often wrote to Henry complaining of Richard's actions and he generally successfully negotiated a path which kept both volatile brothers together.

Henry returned to Britain in 1802 and the following year he married Lady Charlotte

---

1. The term for adultery at the time.

Cadogan, who was closely linked to the Dukes of Marlborough. Their marriage seems to have initially been happy and they had three sons and a daughter in relatively quick succession.

Henry was elected to the House of Commons in the election of 1807 for both Athlone and for Eye in England, and he chose to sit for the latter, until he resigned in 1809 due to an unfortunate scandal. Charlotte ran off with Lord Paget and abandoning her children in the process. Henry successfully filed for a divorce in parliament the following year, receiving £24,000 damages for 'Criminal Conversation'.[1] This embarrassing incident also precluded Paget being sent to serve with Arthur at any time during the entire Peninsular War, a significant loss, given his real flare for commanding cavalry. They served together eventually during the Waterloo campaign, when Wellington famously reacted when someone asked how he felt about serving with Uxbridge (Paget's new title), with the words 'I will make damn sure that he will not run off with me!'

That same year, he was sent to Spain as British envoy and became Ambassador in 1811. He corresponded regularly in this role with both Arthur, who then commanded the British forces in Spain and Portugal, and his brother Richard, who was then Foreign Secretary. Henry was knighted in 1812 and he remained as Ambassador to Spain until 1821.

He married again to Lady Georgiana Cecil, daughter of the Marquess of Salisbury in 1816, with whom he had a further daughter and in 1823

Henry Wellesley in 1807.

he became Ambassador to Austria, which office he held for a further ten years. Henry carried out his last diplomatic role as British Ambassador to France in 1835 and again in 1841–6. He then retired for the diplomatic corps, remaining in Paris, where he died in 1847 at the age of 74 from a cold.

Henry had remained close to George Canning throughout his career, and actually acted as his second at Canning's famous duel with Lord Castlereagh, but he eventually lost faith in him, feeling that Canning did not appreciate his service. However, due to the influence of Arthur, who was then in government, he was granted the title of Baron Cowley of Wellesley in Somerset in 1828.

39: Cathedral Tower at Ciudad Rodrigo Still Showing the Marks Made by Cannon Balls

Arthur's troops had remained along the Portuguese border for the remainder of 1811, frustrated that his numbers were too low to challenge Marmont, who had taken over from the disgraced Massena in the field. Attempts had been made to blockade the fortress, but Marmont was too strong and he was always able to send supply columns to the fortress when required. Wellington had however, arranged for a large artillery siege train to be moved to Almeida, perfectly positioned if and when needed.

Winter arrived and the Allied troops looked forward to being ordered to retire into winter quarters, when field operation traditionally

came to an end. However, Wellington was continually monitoring intelligence reports regarding Marmont's troops and towards the end of 1811, he received reports that 12,000 troops had been dispatched far to the south to help in capturing the city of Valencia. Having lost these significant numbers, Marmont still felt secure enough to send his troops into winter quarters and spread his corps over a wide area to feed them more easily, assuming that there was no threat of any fighting before May, when the crops began to grow again. Wellington had very different ideas.

Wellington calculated that Massena had assumed that the fortress of Ciudad Rodrigo, with its garrison of 2,000 men under the experienced General Barrie, would hold out for a minimum of three weeks and probably much longer, giving him adequate time to assemble his troops at Salamanca and march to relieve the fortress with his 32,000 men.

Arthur believed that he could take the fortress in under three weeks and on 6 January 1812, in wintry conditions, he ordered his troops to besiege the fortress. The Allied troops had formed a cordon around the fortress by 8 January and that very night, the Reynaud redoubt on the Grand Teson, a hill lying very close to the walls and which commanded the defences, was captured in a daring raid, allowing work on digging trenches and positions for breaching batteries to commence immediately. Work continued at a pace and by 12 January the guns were being moved into the batteries. The

Aerial view of Ciudad Rodrigo.

following night the outlying fortified convent of Santa Cruz was captured.

On 14 January, the French defenders made a large-scale sortie, with over 500 men rushing out in a bid to destroy the siege works. It initially caused confusion in the Allied lines, but it was eventually driven off with some loss. That night another outlying fortified convent, called San Francisco, was also captured. The way to the walls was now clear for the troops.

The besieging batteries, consisting of thirty-four 24-pounders and four 18-pounders, were all in place and they opened on the walls at 4pm on 14 January and over the next five days, these guns fired some 9,500 cannonballs at the fortress walls, a large number of them flying high and striking the cathedral tower which stood behind

the intended breach and even today the tower clearly shows the marks from dozens of cannon ball strikes. By 18 January, two effective breaches had been formed in the defences and Wellington ordered an assault for the next night.

The 3rd Division, commanded by Major General Thomas Picton, was to storm the greater breach, whilst Craufurd's Light Division would attack the lesser breach. Diversionary attacks were also to be launched in the east and south by the Portuguese, both of which actually succeeded in entering the fortress.

The attacks were made simultaneously in the dark at 7pm, the 3rd Division suffering heavy casualties in the main breach particularly when a mine was exploded under the attackers. However the Light Division did not encounter such serious resistance and they were soon inside the town and they cleared the French attackers from the main breach, by attacking their flank. The fortress had fallen in only two weeks, well before Marmont could interfere. It was a daring attack and it succeeded spectacularly.

Despite this the losses were quite heavy, with 195 Allied soldiers being killed, including Generals Mackinnon and Craufurd, and 916 wounded, the French losing 529 killed and wounded and the remaining 1,500 men being made prisoners. As with all sieges at this time, a successful assault always led to pillaging and there were severe problems with controlling the excesses of the men the first night, but were nothing in comparison with those to come.

The defences were hastily repaired and a Spanish garrison installed, but Marmont never contemplated an attempt to recapture the fortress as his own siege train had been held in store at Ciudad Rodrigo and was captured, meaning that he could not besiege it.

Arthur received a number of rewards for the victory, including being made an Earl and receiving a sizeable pension. The Spanish made him Duque de Ciudad Rodrigo. Arthur now controlled the northern route into Spain and he turned his attentions to capturing the southern route as well.

Print showing the assault on Ciudad Rodrigo.

40: Arthur's Headquarters at Freineda for Extensive Periods in the Winters of 1811 and 1812

During the winters of 1811/12 and 1812/13, Wellington's headquarters was in the small Portuguese village of Freineda. According to Captain Browne, who was in the Adjutant-General's office, it 'was a miserable village … the accommodations of every kind were as wretched as it was possible to conceive'. The village consisted of only about fifty houses and a church, the artillery and engineer departments were located in another village about 5 kilometres away, while the medical and commissary departments, and the Judge Advocate were housed in another village about

5 kilometres in the opposite direction. Wellington naturally occupied the largest house in the town, with a large dining room for entertaining and a separate bedroom. Arthur preferred the meanest shack to going under canvas.

Wellington did not surround himself with a large staff, indeed his headquarters often had the air of a sleepy backwater with nobody there, apart from an odd staff officer darting from one house to another clutching papers. Commissary Schaumann commented on his arrival at Freineda that

'Had it not been known for a fact, no one would have suspected that he [Wellington] was quartered in the town. There was no throng of scented staff officers with plumed hats, orders and stars, no main guard, no crowd of contractors, actors, valets, cooks, mistresses, equipages, horses, dogs, forage and baggage wagons, as there is at French or Russian headquarters! Just a few aides-de-camp, who went about the streets alone and in their overcoats, a few guides, and a small staff guard; that was all! About a dozen bullock carts were to be seen in the large square of Fuente Guinaldo, which were used for bringing up straw to headquarters; but apart from these no equipages or baggage trains were visible.'

Arthur led a spartan life on campaign, normally up at 6am and writing until breakfast at 9am, but was up by 3am at the latest when the troops were on the move and out on his horse by 4am. Breakfast was a short, usually private affair, before he met the heads of each department one after the other, the Adjutant General on troop movements, the Quartermaster General for intelligence reports, the Commissary General on supplies, the Inspector General of Hospitals for sick returns, the Commanding Royal Engineer for reports on the progress of works and sometimes the Deputy Paymaster General or Judge Advocate. This could last until 1pm but sometimes lasted until 4pm and woe betide the officer who kept referring to his notes or did not have the answers to his questions! Arthur would then ride for a few hours in the late afternoon,

A rare view inside Wellington's headquarters at Freineda.

both for exercise and to inspect his troops etc. He would return at 6pm. He would then turn to writing again until dinner, usually about 8pm in Spain, and would read reports and write until 10 or 11pm before he turned in for the night on his folding camp bed.

Wellington's personal staff on campaign is listed in 1813. He had two personal manservants (Bonduc and Smily), three footmen, two grooms, three cooks, three assistant cooks, one Italian, one goat boy, three carmen (driver or carter), two huntsmen, six batmen, three orderly sergeants, twelve Portuguese dragoons, twenty muleteers, two orderly dragoons, three women and three farriers. Colonel Colin Campbell was Commandant of Headquarters to ensure everything went on well, and he along with

the Military Secretary and his aides-de-camp each averaged four servants each. On top of this would be a Portuguese and Spanish liaison officer and an interpreter each with another four servants. His 'very small' personal Staff therefore numbered around 120 people.

He always maintained at least six aides-de-camp, who he paid and fed at his own table and was reimbursed for by London. Arthur's dinners are variously described as good, awful or mediocre, but this is usually explained generally as mediocre food, but the atmosphere varied dramatically on the mood of Wellington himself. When he was in a good mood the meal was often jovial, when in a bad mood everyone ate in silence, but no one was able to leave the table before he himself got up.

Wellington and his Staff.

41: La Torre, Residence of the Duque de Ciudad Rodrigo in Granada

King Ferdinand VII conferred the title of Duque de Ciudad Rodrigo upon Arthur as an honorary title for the victory, 'For his help against the invading army of Napoleon in the War of Independence'. It was and still remains an hereditary title within the peerage of Spain, although since 1984 Spanish nobles no longer receive any privileges from the title. He also received the title of Viscount Talavera from the Spanish crown. The title of Duque came with a grant of 1,000 hectares of land at La Torre and Soto de Roma in the Dehesa Baja de Illora in Granada, which is still owned by the current duke and is regularly used in the summer months by the family. The property had previously belonged to Manuel Godoy but his properties were seized when he fell from power.

Arthur never visited his Spanish property and indeed neither of his sons visited it either because of the threat from local bandits. It was the 4th Duke who first visited the property in 1900, setting off from Madrid with his family by railway and arrived on horseback, the women in a carriage. They were very warmly received by the villagers and ever since it has been a family favourite.

The successors of the Duke of Wellington have traditionally held the title, but this has not always been so, as the Spanish title went to the first heir, male or female, whereas the

main British title only went to a male. In 1943 Anne Wellesley took the Spanish title as the first surviving heir of the 5th Duke, but she renounced the title in favour of her uncle, the 7th Duke of Wellington, in 1949 after it was reviewed in the courts in both countries and they have remained together since. It is believed that the agreement was reached in lieu of a large financial compensation. However, this means that the present 9th Duke of Wellington is the 10th Duque de Ciudad Rodrigo, and he has a daughter who may have a claim for the Spanish title, whilst his son is due to inherit the British title, so a potential split is likely to occur in the future, although the previous case gave British law precedence in the case and this may still stand in future.

There have been some difficulties over the retention of the sizeable estate, as local officials have continually sought to prove that paperwork exists that seems to prove that the lands have on three occasions been returned to the people, but these claims seem tenuous and presently the

The coat of arms of the Duque de Ciudad Rodrigo.

estates remain with the Duke and there does not appear to be any possibility of that situation changing soon.

42: Unexploded Shell Casing from Badajoz

Having captured Ciudad Rodrigo, Arthur now marched the bulk of his army south in an attempt to capture the Spanish fortress which commanded the southern route into Spain, but there would be a significant delay whilst a sizeable siege train could be brought up and he had also had to pick the right moment, when the superior French forces were distracted elsewhere.

In comparison with the second-rate Ciudad Rodrigo, the first-rate fortress of Badajoz, with its much larger garrison of 5,000 men under the command of General Armand Philippon, was not going to be so easy. Two previous attempts to besiege the fortress had failed because of the approach of superior French forces, and this had given the French ample time to strengthen the defences significantly, with new bastions, the

flooding of areas and the digging of mines, ready to explode under any attack.

Wellington's 27,000 available troops moved into position around the fortress on 17 March and the clock immediately started ticking for how long they had to capture it before French relief forces arrived. Work began immediately, building trenches and laying out batteries, but the work was severely hampered by heavy rains, which filled the trenches and made the river swell, breaking the bridges which were essential for the movement of the heavy siege guns and ammunition. On the third day, the French launched a very sizeable sortie by over 1,500 troops, which caused a significant loss to the Allied army, including the wounding of the Commanding Engineer before it was repulsed.

On 25 March a significant outwork, known as Fort Picurina, was attacked at night and captured after losing some 300 men killed and wounded. The capture of the fort allowed much larger siege works and on 31 March the siege guns began the work of breaching the walls. On 2 April, a dam which had formed a lake that hampered the Allied approach to the breaches, was attacked but the explosive charges failed to break it. By 5 April three breaches had been formed and declared practicable by the engineers. News that Marshal Soult was marching to relieve the fortress meant that although Wellington would outnumber him if he abandoned the siege, he could not delay an assault for long.

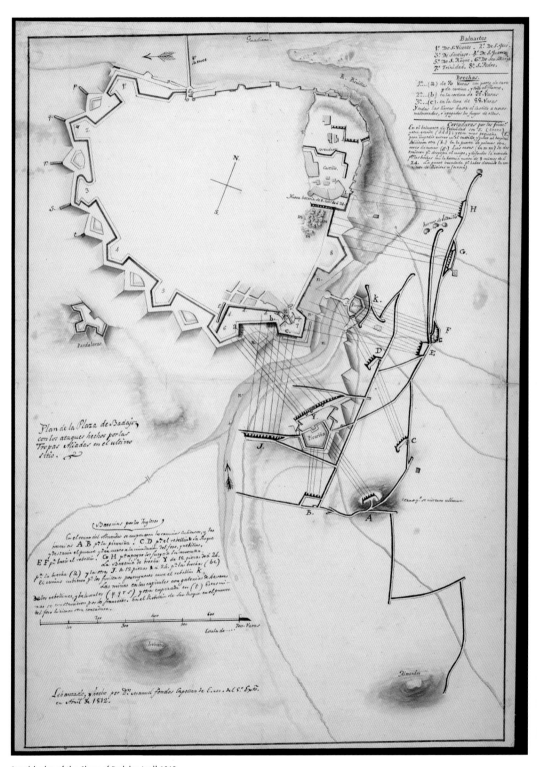

Spanish plan of the Siege of Badajoz April 1812.

Superb diorama showing the storming of Badajoz.

Orders were issued that an assault on the fortress would take place at 10pm the following night, the 6th, allowing the guns a few more hours to improve the breaches. It was perfectly clear to the defenders that the assault was imminent and in these last twenty-four hours, they prepared every possible impediment they could to stop the assailants breaking in. The breaches were mined, cannon placed on the flanks to sweep the slopes, upturned swords and bayonets inserted in the rubble and at the very top huge logs were chained across the breach and swords and bayonets fixed into them (called *cheval de fries*), whilst the defenders had numerous grenades prepared, five loaded muskets each ready to fire and even large stones that they could hurl down on the assailants. They intended to make the breaches a veritable slaughterhouse.

The troops were moved up into position in silence after dark, to avoid giving the alarm, but the French were expecting them. The 4th Division attacked the two main breaches whilst the Light Division would attack the third. At the same time the 3rd and 5th Divisions would make diversionary attacks against the walls well away from the breaches, in an effort to draw off some of the defenders.

As soon as the first troops began to move forward, the French heard them coming and sounded the alarm. In moments the defenders were lining the walls and their cannon were soon spewing death. The attacking troops quickly became disorientated in the dark, causing some to mistake their objectives, and the two attacks on the breaches soon became confused and jumbled. Huge numbers of casualties soon piled up at the base of the breach and those following up the attack had to try to pass this wall of flesh before they could even start to ascend the breaches. The attacks became uncoordinated and the small groups that valiantly launched further attacks rarely got more than half-way up the breach before they were swept away by the fire. The few brave men who reached the top found their way barred by the *cheval de fries* and whilst they cut their hands as they tried desperately to make a way through, a defender would step forward and smash their skulls with the butt of his musket. Not one man got into the town from the breaches and the slaughter just continued to mount over the next two horrendous hours.

Wellington received regular updates and the news was not good. In fact he was very close to calling the whole assault off when incredible

news reached him. The 3rd Division, launching their diversionary attack on the high walls of the old Moorish castle, had actually overpowered the few defenders and captured the castle, but could not break out into the town. The Portuguese troops of the 5th Division had also scaled the walls in their diversionary attack and captured a gate into the town, allowing reinforcements easy access. With two divisions in the fortress, the French realised that all was lost and General Philippon withdrew his troops across the bridge to the outwork of San Cristobal, where he shortly after agreed to surrender.

Arthur's troops had taken the fortress but at a terrible cost. The Allies lost some 4,800 casualties, most of which occurred in those terrible few hours. In comparison the French garrison had only suffered 1,500 casualties,

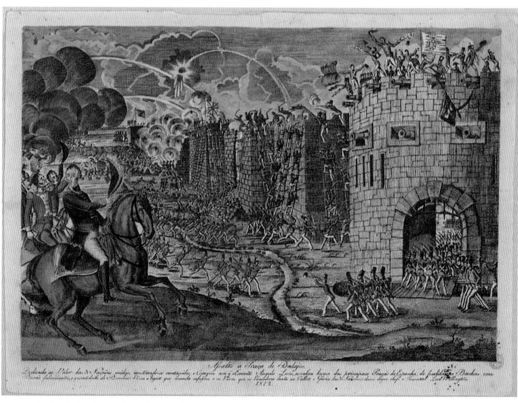

Spanish print showing Wellington at the storming of Badajoz.

but the remaining 3,500 were made prisoners and transported to Britain. Arthur went to the breaches once daylight revealed the true horror and, being struck by the terrible sight and probably bearing much guilt for having caused the death and maiming of so many of his troops, he openly wept at the carnage.

Having captured the town, many of the soldiers who had luckily survived went on an orgy of plunder and in their wild drunken state, they lost all control and self-discipline and many murders and rapes undoubtedly occurred against the poor Spanish population, which rumour claimed had supported the French. Two to three hundred civilians became casualties rather than the thousands sometimes claimed, but there were still too many. Arthur eventually sent fresh troops, untainted by the assault, into the town to restore the situation, and with the erection of a scaffold and a few judicious hangings, order was eventually restored. What occurred cannot be excused however and the Spanish people of Badajoz understandably still bear some real hatred for what happened that night. He now held all of the key fortresses on both major routes into Spain, giving him a great base for the future, but at a terrible cost.

1812 originally picked out in cannonballs – now removed.

43: Water Jug Celebrating the Victory at Salamanca 1812

Having secured the fortresses commanding both major routes into Spain, Arthur had to march his army north again soon after securing Badajoz in order to expel Marshal Marmont's forces which had entered northern Portugal in his absence, even though they could not threaten the fortresses, having no siege artillery.

In May 1812 General Hill succeeded in destroying the bridge at Almaraz, the last intact bridge over the Tagus west of Toledo, severely disrupting the communications between the French forces north and south of the river. Having isolated Marmont, Arthur marched his troops towards Salamanca on 13 June. His troops arrived at the city, to find that the French had converted three of the convents into mutually supporting fortresses garrisoned by 800 men named San Vincente, La Merced and San Cayetano. Wellington's troops found them so strong that they were forced to begin regular sieges against them, using heavy artillery.

This was awkward as they had only brought four 18-pounders with them and a limited supply of ammunition, forcing Arthur to order more ammunition from Almeida.

Marmont was informed of Wellington's move on 14 June and he immediately began concentrating his forces some 30 kilometres north of Salamanca, but he initially only had 40,000 troops whilst Wellington had 48,000 including those involved in the siege. Once

The battlefield of Salamanca with the two key features of the Arapiles.

A jeton made in 1812 celebrating Wellington's victories up to Salamanca.

concentrated, Marmont approached the city and Wellington placed his troops in order to offer battle, whilst turning the siege into a blockade. Marmont eventually retired as reinforcements had not arrived and the siege was resumed.

A premature assault on the forts on the night of 23 June was a costly failure with General Bowes amongst the numerous dead. The ammunition resupply arriving on 26 June, a heavy bombardment caused a number of fires and a practicable breach was formed and the garrisons surrendered on 27 June, just before the Allied troops assaulted them.

Marmont waited until reinforcements arrived in July and now the strength of the two armies was now roughly equal, at about 50,000 men each. This led to a great deal of manoeuvring, and for a number of days the two armies marched alongside each other within cannon shot without coming to blows as each attempted to gain an advantage.

On 22 July, Marmont's troops were marching across a dusty plain a few kilometres south east of Salamanca. He could see a single Allied division on a height and a large dust cloud beyond it, which Marmont wrongly assumed was Wellington's army in retreat. He ordered his troops to march along an L-shaped ridge, which ran around the flank of Wellington's troops, with the intention of cutting his line of communications towards Portugal. Whilst the French troops marched rapidly in order to cut his presumed line of retreat they became strung out along the ridge line.

Marmont had mistaken the situation. Arthur was prepared to retreat if his communications were threatened, but his troops were actually formed in a compact group just behind the ridge where Marmont could see the one solitary division. Arthur watched the French manoeuvre whilst chewing on a chicken leg and having observed how the French were becoming strung out, he reputedly took one last look with is telescope and exclaimed 'By God, that'll do', and turning to his Spanish liaison officer Alava who he always communicated with in French (then the universal language) '*Mon Cher Alava, Marmont est perdu!*' [My dear Alava, Marmont is lost!]

Whilst he launched the 3rd Division and a Portuguese brigade against the head of the column, he simultaneously sent the 4th and 5th Divisions

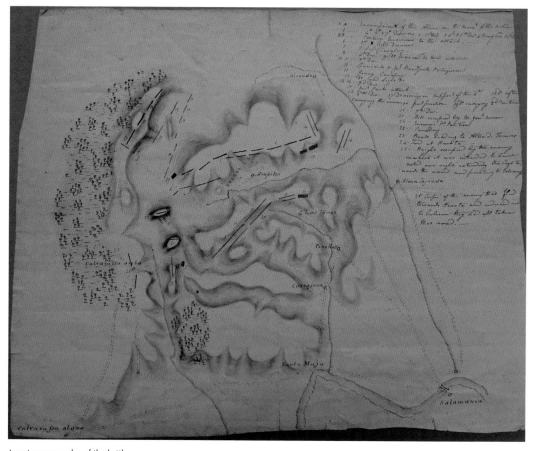

A contemporary plan of the battle.

directly across the valley at the strung-out centre of the French column and sent the 6th and 7th Divisions in reserve: it was a huge hammer blow designed to split the French army in two.

The Allied infantry quickly overwhelmed the French columns with their musketry and as the French left centre buckled, it was devastated by a brilliantly-timed charge by the British heavy cavalry, sweeping away eight French battalions. The French response was disorganised by the wounding of Marmont early in the action by a shell and his second-in-command, Bonet, being wounded minutes later. However, despite temporarily having no leader the attack by the 4th Division on the heights of the Greater

Arapile was repulsed twice with heavy loss by the French infantry.

General Clausel finally took command of the French army and taking advantage of the repulse at the Greater Arapile he launched a major counter-attack, consisting of two divisions and a cavalry brigade, which threatened to upset everything. The 4th Division were driven back and the 6th Division in the second line were engaged but, realising the danger, Wellington sent the 1st and 7th Divisions in to support them and the French attack was finally beaten off.

Clausel now ordered a retreat and told General Ferey to hold off the Allies. While this was effected. Clinton's 6th Division advanced

A Spanish print commemorating the victory.

Eagle of the 22nd Ligne captured at Salamanca.

to take on Ferey's troops and the two divisions fought an intense battle in line at short range, both sides suffering terrible casualties. The French slowly retired fighting until their flank was threatened by the 5th Division, when the French infantry finally broke and fled.

The routed French army poured towards the bridge across the river at Alba de Tormes, which Wellington believed was held by Spanish troops. Unfortunately the Spanish commander had removed the troops without informing Wellington and the French were able to escape, much to Arthur's frustration.

The losses at the battle told the story: the Allies lost just over 5,000 killed and wounded whereas the French lost around 6,000 casualties, but also suffered another 7,000 who were made prisoners of war. Two French Eagles were captured at Salamanca, the 30th Foot capturing the Eagle of the 22nd Ligne and the 44th Foot captured that of the 62nd Ligne.

More than anything, the news of the victory at Salamanca resounded throughout Europe

The monument to the Battle of Salamanca on top of the Arapiles.

and Arthur was feted, Parliament raising him to a Marquess with the news. It also showed that Wellington was much more than simply a 'defensive general', he personally thought it not as good as Assaye, but this was a stunning success in Europe showing his abilities as an 'offensive general', which made everyone take notice.

The French general, Foy, wrote:

'This battle is the most cleverly fought, the largest in scale, the most important in results, of any that the English have won in recent times. It brings up Lord Wellington's reputation almost to the level of that of Marlborough. Up to this day we knew his prudence, his eye for choosing good positions, and the skill with which he used them. But at Salamanca he has shown himself a great and able master of manoeuvring.'

44: Medal Struck to Commemorate the Battle of Salamanca and the Entry into Madrid

Having defeated the French army at Salamanca, Arthur was presented with two options, either to pursue the routed French army relentlessly or to make a political move and free the capital, Madrid. With Soult's army busy besieging Cadiz and many of the other French forces fully engaged in Eastern Spain, the Reserve under the direct command of King Joseph was not strong enough to stand against him. He therefore chose to free Madrid, knowing that it would send a strong message to the people of Spain and encourage them in their struggle.

Arthur advanced with 60,000 men, against which King Joseph could only bring 22,000 men, he was therefore obliged to retire towards the south-east on 10 August, leaving Madrid virtually open. His army was joined by some 15,000 civilians, with over 2,000 vehicles, who had been collaborating with the French and who feared reprisals if they stayed behind.

Wellington's troops arrived at the gates of Madrid on 12 August, the very same day that Marshal Soult finally learnt of the defeat at Salamanca which forced him to reluctantly abandon the siege of Cadiz and he also left Seville two days later. This was an immense relief for the Spanish holed up in Cadiz, but Soult's troops drawing near to Madrid eventually caused problems for Arthur.

Wellington's entry into Madrid was nothing short of triumphal, with the houses all traditionally draped with sheets from the windows and the streets packed with Spaniards who kissed his horse and his boots as he passed in procession. The French had not evacuated the city completely, however, as the Retiro works had been converted into an arms magazine by the French and they intended to defend it. The works were protected by two lines of defence and a star work, manned by 2,000 troops, who were

Cartoon of Wellington's entry into Madrid.

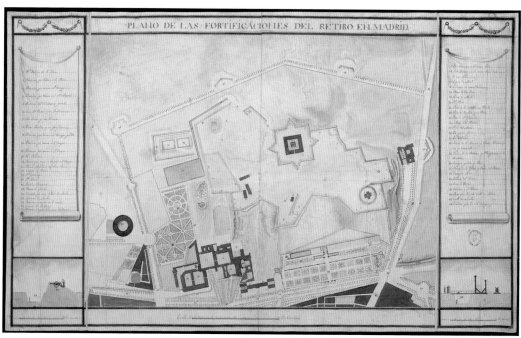

Plan of the Retiro defences.

tasked with holding on until Soult's troops could arrive to relieve them. The biggest fault with the Retiro was the very inadequate supply of water available.

Arthur reconnoitred the works on the day after his arrival in Madrid and an attack in two columns of 300 men each was ordered for that very night, which successfully captured the outer defences with minimal loss. The commandant offered terms on the following morning. Arthur agreed that they could surrender with full honours of war and retain their personal possessions, and they surrendered the fort at 4pm on 14 August. Amongst the huge mass of weaponry, 200 cannon and 20,000 muskets, shot and gunpowder, two Eagles were also captured at the Retiro, those of the 51st Ligne and the 13th Dragoon Regiments.

The strains and pressure of the campaign undoubtedly told on Arthur and whilst in Madrid, he sat for a portrait by Goya, although the painting of a mounted figure had already been started before Wellington arrived in Madrid, most likely an unfinished painting of King Joseph. Of all the paintings of him this shows Arthur as more sallow faced and dark-eyed than any other in existence and probably captures the true man at the time.

In mid-August General Clausel who still retained command of the army since Marmont was wounded, had quickly rallied his defeated troops and advanced towards Valladolid in order to relieve a number of his garrisons which were besieged by the Spanish and Wellington saw a chance to catch him whilst isolated and destroy him. It was a calculated gamble whilst significant French forces were assembling to the south of Madrid, but he decided that the risk was worth taking and he moved north on 31 August where he joined Clinton's covering force bringing his force to 35,000, leaving the remaining 31,000, including most of his most experienced troops, and augmented by 12,000 Spanish troops under the command of Lord Hill to protect the capital.

Goya's haunting painting of Arthur at Madrid in 1812.

45: The Spanish Order of The Golden Fleece

When Arthur's army arrived at Madrid and freed the city, the Spanish people were delighted and Maria Theresa de Bourbon, niece of King Charles IV of Spain, bestowed the Order of the Golden Fleece upon him, accompanied by a very gracious letter. Later in life it was Arthur's favourite Order to wear. He established himself at the Palacio Real and immediately proclaimed the maintenance of law and order throughout the city. A new Constitution was established by the Spanish Cortes, but it was Arthur who signed the proclamation as a Spanish grandee, the Duque de Ciudad Rodrigo. Arthur had no regal ambitions, but for a time, he was effectively King of Spain. He gave and in turn attended numerous balls, concerts and even bullfights, but soon the celebrations would be over and he would have to return to the complicated military situation.

A huge boost to his position in Spain was finally agreed on by the Spanish Cortes on 22 September 1812, which now made Arthur Generalissimo of the entire Spanish army. He in theory now held overall command of all Allied troops on the Iberian Peninsula and finally he could coordinate the entire armed struggle. A number of Spanish officers were horrified by the announcement, however, and some refused to serve under him. General Ballesteros,

An elderly Duke of Wellington wearing the Spanish Order of the Golden Fleece.

commanding the 4th Spanish Army, not only refused to serve under Wellington but sought to instigate an uprising. He was arrested for mutiny and imprisoned at Ceuta, a Spanish enclave in North Africa. The Spanish army still numbered over 150,000 troops, as despite the numberless setbacks they had suffered at the hands of the French, they would not submit. Arthur's control of more distant Spanish commands was probably more theoretical than actual, but some 50,000 of these Spanish troops were ultimately to serve alongside the British and Portuguese in Wellington's Army during the 1813 and 1814 campaigns, increasing his strength greatly.

Palacio Real, Madrid.

46: Button of the Royal Sappers & Miners

As Wellington marched northward from Madrid he believed he had time to defeat Clausel's troops and force the remnants back towards the Pyrenees before the French armies of King Joseph and Marshal Soult could seriously threaten the capital from the south. His force having combined with the small corps under Sir Henry Clinton, which had remained to the north of Madrid covering that flank, he had 35,000 men. The advance northward was slow however and Clausel soon marched away to safety when he learnt of their approach.

As he retired, Clausel left a garrison of some 2,000 troops under the command of General Dubreton in the castle of Burgos, designed to delay the Allies. When Arthur first saw the castle on 19 September, perched high on a hill with very steep slopes making an attack by besieging troops very difficult, he realised that the intelligence reports he had received had badly underestimated its strength. However, he felt

sure that the small number of siege guns available (three 18-pounders and five howitzers) he had available would prove sufficient and declined the generous offer of Admiral Sir Home Popham to deliver a number of naval cannon to significantly increase his siege artillery, as he believed it would all be over well before they could arrive.

The operation began auspiciously, with a night attack on the San Miguel hornwork, which protected a nearby hill commanding the castle defences. It succeeded but with heavy loss, some 421 men killed or wounded. Despite the heavy casualties, it was assumed by many that the taking of the hornwork would soon lead to the fall of the castle itself, but their hopes were to be cruelly dashed.

Formally besieging the three walls running concentrically around the hill was clearly going to be extremely difficult, because the defenders on the ramparts would always tower over the men in the trenches, making the siege work extremely hazardous. Wellington even launched

a first assault as a surprise attack, before the first siege gun had opened fire, but they had only five ladders with which to get into the castle. It was hopelessly inadequate and they were driven off having lost 550 casualties, a severe punishment for failing to besiege the castle formally.

Wellington quickly became frustrated at these failures and he was forced to employ sappers to attempt to dig mines below the walls and blow holes in the defences, but the first attempt failed and this gave warning to the defenders.

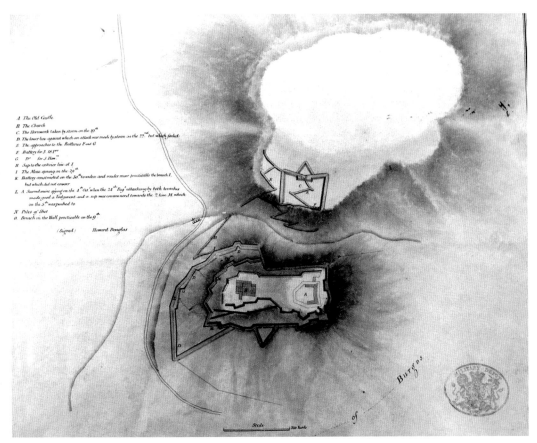

A The Old Castle
B The Church
C The Hornwork taken by storm on the 19th
D The lower line against which an attack was made by storm on the 22nd but which failed
E The approaches to the Batteries F and G
F Battery for 3 18 Prs
G Dr for 3 How.
H Sap to the exterior line at I
I The Mine sprung on the 29th
K Battery constructed on the 30th to widen and render more practicable the breach I, but which did not answer
L A Second mine sprung on the 4th Oct when the 24th Reg.t attacking by both trenches made good a lodgment and a sap was commenced towards the 2 line M which was pushed to
N Piles of Shot
O Breach in the Wall practicable on the 9th

(Signed)   Howard Douglas

Contemporary map showing the siege of Burgos.

A siege battery was constructed near to the castle on the night of 30 September, but the next day, the French brought overwhelming firepower against it and two of the three guns placed in it were damaged and a number of the gun crews were injured or killed. A second attempt the next day caused further losses and finally Arthur bowed to the inevitable and asked Popham for guns, but he had already lost two weeks.

A second mine which blew a 100-foot section of wall down led to an assault which gained a tentative foothold in the outer defences, but strong French resistance defeated all attempts to advance further. The following day, the French made a major sortie out of the castle forcing the Allies to give up their hard won foothold and inflicting large numbers of casualties.

Soon after this, the weather changed drastically and virtually continuous heavy rain made the siege operations almost impossible, with the water filling the trenches and making the troops sick. At the same time, the Allied artillery began to run out of ammunition and the soldiers were paid to collect French cannon balls to be re-used. By now even Arthur was despondent admitting in a letter that 'This is altogether the most difficult job I ever had in hand with such trifling means'. He did not however, admit that the cause for this lack of means rested very much on his own shoulders.

A third huge mine was detonated under the Chapel of San Roman which lay within the defences, two separate assaults were then made but they were not carried out with any real belief and they again failed with heavy loss.

By now superior forces were approaching Burgos commanded by General Souham, forcing Wellington to abandon the siege on 21 October and at the same time a combined army of both King Joseph's and Marshal Soult's troops seriously threatened Hill's troops still protecting Madrid and they were ordered to retire, the aim being to reform as one large army near Salamanca.

Wellington artfully retired, utilising the numerous rivers as defensive lines, destroying the bridges to slow the French pursuit. Meanwhile Lord Hill's force was forced to retreat before a much stronger combined army and King

Joseph re-entered his capital on 2 November, but being anxious to destroy Wellington's army, he continued the pursuit without even leaving a garrison there. Wellington and Hill joined forces at Alba de Tormes on 8 November and they stood defiantly on the Salamanca battlefield once again, offering battle. The Allied army numbered 65,000 men and Marshal Soult, now commanding the combined army had nearly 80,000. Many of the French soldiers saw it as the perfect opportunity to gain revenge on Wellington, but to their astonishment, Soult refused to attack. Arthur was forced to order the retreat to continue.

The failed siege at Burgos following such a number of brilliant successes earlier in the year, was a great shock to both Arthur and his army. He had overstretched his forces in the hope of gaining even further territory, but the French still

The French defenders during the siege of Burgos.

retained a great superiority of numbers and when they combined against him, he could not stand against them in the open field. The blame for the humbling defeat at Burgos has to be largely borne by Arthur, who again underestimated the strength of a fortress defended to the utmost by its French governor and his brave troops. His means for besieging the castle were totally inadequate and clearly proves that he had no inkling that he would need to perform a major siege as he marched into north-eastern Spain and that simply throwing troops at unbroken walls would not succeed. The lucky success of the feint attacks at Badajoz had perhaps caused him to underestimate the difficulties. It is also clear, however, that Arthur was suffering at this time some form of heavy fatigue, if not depression, being so heavily weighed down with work and the stress of command and that he was performing well below par. To be fair, Wellington accepted full responsibility, later stating that 'It was all my own fault'. The hollow, dark-eyed face of Goya's painting at Madrid would seem to accurately portray Arthur's psyche at the time. Doctor McGrigor in charge of the hospitals noted at this period, Arthur's frequent 'bad humour'. It was certainly Arthur's lowest point, but the year was to get much worse yet.

The recently heavily restored walls of Burgos Castle.

47: Duke of Wellington's Necessaire or Travelling Case

Arthur insisted that every officer travel light on campaign and his own personal equipment was suitably Spartan, although he did have the backup of his headquarters wagons. His personal grooming was very important to him, despite the fact that he had lost a number of teeth in early life through decay.

Every officer carried a necessaire on their mule which included combs, toothbrushes, colognes and soaps and scissors. It also included a cut-throat razor – Arthur always shaved himself throughout his life. A travelling mirror was carried separately for this purpose. The necessaire also included a penknife, pliers, corkscrew and cleaning brushes, a drinking goblet and a small saucepan, indeed everything a gentleman might conceivably need.

Wellington also slept on a metal-framed camp bed with a curtain and mattress, all of which could be dismantled and rolled up into a small case. Indeed, the bed was used throughout his life, often sleeping on it in his study, as he preferred it to a more luxurious mattress.

The Duke of Wellington's travelling mirror.

One of Wellington's folding campaign beds.

48: Spanish Pigs Traditionally Reared in the Woods

Having offered battle despite being heavily outnumbered, Wellington was forced to order a continuation of the retreat when Marshal Soult declined to fight, but instead sought to manoeuvre around his flank, threatening his line of retreat. The army began a further withdrawal to the Portuguese border on 15 November and both Arthur and his soldiers would have envisaged a relatively straightforward retreat of only about four days until safe under the guns of Ciudad Rodrigo. It was unfortunately to be four days of hell for the troops.

Colonel James Willoughby Gordon had recently taken over as Quartermaster General and was therefore responsible for the routing of the supply column. He was a man who had a very high opinion of himself and possessed inordinate vanity and ambition, but without much talent for his office. He sent the supplies on a route separated from the line of march for the soldiers by some 20 miles, ensuring that they would not receive any rations during the retreat.

To top that off, the rains were now incessant, turning the muddy tracks into quagmires which would quickly leave the men struggling through it exhausted and shoeless. With nothing to eat in a sparsely-cultivated part of the world, the men were forced to turn to the acorns that were usually devoured by the pigs. Order and regularity quickly dissipated and soon the soldiers became savage in their desperation, pillaging, straggling

and dying by the hundreds if not the thousands. Occasionally the lucky ones stumbled upon a herd of pigs which roamed the woods and an orgy of violence saw the pigs chased and stabbed mercilessly with their bayonets, instantly torn to pieces and devoured ravenously after smoking ineffectively for a few minutes over their smouldering fires. Many describe the cries of the pigs as the worst thing that they ever heard. At another time, Wellington heard heavy firing and, fearing an attack, he rode rapidly to investigate, only to discover that a whole division had fired on a huge herd of pigs that had sought to escape past them, the ranks broke in all directions in pursuit of the pigs, all discipline gone. Most soldiers, however, were not as lucky and many fell by the wayside from extreme exhaustion and malnutrition, the lucky ones being picked up by the pursuing French cavalry, and if not they simply lay down to die.

Three generals decided to take matters into their own hands and chose to ignore their orders received for the direction of march, they eventually led their troops into a serious impasse. When Wellington arrived he instantly realised the gravity of the situation and simply gave them new orders. Turning to the officers he simply stated 'You see gentlemen, I know my own business best' and promptly rode off again.

Things got even worse, when the one-armed and short-sighted deputy commander of the army, General Sir Edward Paget, was actually captured by French dragoons whilst riding between two columns of British infantry during the retreat and would spend the next two years as a French prisoner.

A British wagon laden with stores and camp followers.

After what seemed like an eternity, although in reality only four days, the retreating army arrived safely in the vicinity of Ciudad Rodrigo, when the army was sent to winter quarters to recover and their supplies finally caught up with them.

Arthur was so shocked and angry over the complete breakdown of discipline during the short retreat that he wrote a letter to the commanding officer of each regiment in a sweeping condemnation of the army and the failure of its officers to control the excesses. He railed at how the army had disintegrated

'yet this army has met with no disaster; it has suffered no privations which but trifling attention on the part of the officers could not have prevented ... nor ... any hardship excepting ... the inclemencies of the weather when they were most severe.'

It pulled no punches.

Although intended only for the eyes of the senior officers, it soon found its way into the opposition newspapers back in London and everyone in the army was deeply upset and angered by it. Arthur had a valid point over the complete breakdown of discipline happening so quickly and whilst the French pursuit was so lacklustre, but he had ignored the complete lack of stores and the dreadful weather conditions, which led many soldiers, many of whom had suffered the horrors of the retreat to Corunna, describing these four days as far worse. It was a very bad end to a year that had promised so much with the successes of the first half.

Print showing the capture of Sir Edward Paget.

49: Painting of an Indian Mahout and his Elephant

Whereas the campaign in Flanders had shown Arthur Wellesley how not to do things, India would prove an excellent training ground for him.

Given that armies campaigning in India had to march huge distances across vast swathes of virgin jungle and numberless hills, where supplies were all but impossible to procure, everything they would need had to be carried with them. Because of this, armies had to be supported by huge numbers of camels, elephants, horses, asses, cattle and even human porters to transport the vast array of cannon, ammunition, bridging materials, food, medicines and water necessary for campaigns which could last several months. Arthur estimated that the army of the Nizam alone required a caravan of no less than 150,000 camp followers, who had to be controlled and marshalled into a hollow square, which had to be encircled by a guard of 6,000 cavalry to ensure their protection. Arthur christened the whole unwieldy caravan 'that monstrous equipment'.

Following the success of Seringapatam, Arthur led expeditions to tame a Maratha warlord named Dhoondiah Waugh, who had escaped from Tipu's prison during the final assault and whose followers began to wreak havoc in the Deccan. These expeditions had to move even quicker than Dhoondiah's forces, which were well versed in the local topography, whilst still retaining the ability to supply his troops.

The chaos of an Indian army on the march.

Valley of the Bidassoa 3 Miles above Irun.

London, Published May 1.1828 by John Murray Albemarle Street.

Mule trains passing through the Pyrenees in 1813.

All of this experience in planning and delivery of supplies for his army was to be an invaluable lesson and one which Arthur was to put to very significant use during his many years fighting in Spain and Portugal, where traditionally it was said that large armies starved and small armies were defeated. He was to prove that with a supreme effort of coordinating supplies, utilising both the sea and navigable rivers to deliver goods as far inland as possible and backed up with vast mule trains constantly ferrying supplies to the front line troops it was indeed possible to feed large armies in the Peninsula and thus he eventually gained the upper hand against the far more numerous armies of Napoleon, who attempted unsuccessfully to live off the land. Tens of thousands of mules constantly tracked across the Peninsula, delivering the supplies that Arthur incessantly demanded from government agencies including the coinage necessary to pay for it all. The systems were made as efficient as possible, the commissaries were made fully responsible for supplying his forces and woe betide them if they ever failed!

As much as his skills as a commander of troops on the battlefield led him to unparalleled military success; his voluminous correspondence regarding the needs for supplies of every kind and his indefatigable efforts to clothe and feed his troops by constantly monitoring the work of those responsible, equally led to the admiration of his troops and his ultimate renown as Britain's greatest soldier ever.

50: Drawing of Lady Anne Wellesley

The last of Arthur's siblings was his only sister, Anne, who was born when he was six years old in 1775. Little is known about Anne, who despite her homely beauty, could not stand in the glare of so many prestigious brothers.

In 1790, at the age of 15, she was married to the Honourable Henry Fitzroy, the fourth son of Charles Fitzroy the 1st Baron Southampton, but he unfortunately died at Lisbon of unspecified causes in 1794 at the age of only 28. Henry was a member of the Marylebone Cricket Club and was a keen amateur batsman and bowler, taking 4 wickets in an innings twice in his 44 recorded matches. During their short marriage they had two daughters, Anne and Georgiana.

Anne remarried on 2 August 1799, when she became the wife of Charles Culling Smith (sometimes known as Culling Charles Smith), and was known as Lady Anne Smith for the rest of her life. Charles was the son of Charles Smith, the Governor of Madras and the nephew of Sir Culling Smith, later Baron Eardley. The couple had two further children, a girl and a boy, Emily and Frederick.

Her daughter Georgiana married Henry Somerset, Marquess of Worcester, one of Arthur's aides-de-camp in 1814. They had two daughters, but unfortunately Georgiana died in 1821. She was a favourite niece of Arthur's and he was very upset by the news of her untimely loss, perhaps tellingly stating at the time that 'I did not know death could hurt so much'. The following year Worcester married Georgiana's half-sister, Emily Smith and they went on to have another son and six daughters.

Charles and Anne lived in a grace-and-favour residence at Apartment 8, Hampton Court Palace, and she died there on 16 December 1844.

51: Sabretache of Joseph 'Napoleon' Bonaparte Captured at the Battle of Vitoria

The campaign of 1812 had been one of great highs but ended with the failure to take Burgos and the dreadful retreat back to Portugal. Many soldiers writing home from the army were understandably very despondent, seeing no way of defeating such large French forces. However, news began to arrive in letters and newspapers sent from Britain that Napoleon's invasion of Russia was not going well. This ultimately led to the publication of Napoleon's 29th Bulletin from the army, announcing that the French army was in full retreat and that hundreds of thousands of his troops had frozen to death in the snows of Russia. Intelligence reports soon revealed that a large number of veteran French troops were marching back into France from Spain and the letters home began to indicate a great deal more optimism within the army for the coming campaign of 1813.

Arthur had spent the winter reorganising and reinforcing his troops and in early spring huge numbers of the sick caused by the dreadful retreat also began to return to their regiments, in fact by April the army had rarely been as healthy. With the addition of the Spanish troops now under his command, his army for the new campaign would number over 100,000. For the first time, he would start a campaign with superior numbers to the French and he was determined to take full advantage.

The French, now under the command of Marshal Jourdan, were on the defensive, their front line being entrenched along the River

Tormes from Salamanca northwards, having broken many of the bridges. The French plan was to hold the river line and if forced to retreat, to retire to another position behind the next river and so on. Expecting Wellington to attack in the Salamanca area, these series of costly assaults across the rivers were designed to blunt his attacks and to weaken him, until the French had superiority and could attack.

Arthur played along with the obvious tactics of the French and on 20 May, when the crops had begun growing, providing fodder for his thousands of horses, he advanced with Lord Hill's 35,000 troops towards Salamanca. Intelligence received by the French that Wellington was with the troops moving on Salamanca confirmed to them that this was the main attack. What the French did not realise was that General Sir

The Battle of Vitoria by George Jones.

Thomas Graham had actually been given the larger part of the army and had been ordered to march them over the mountains of northern Spain, an area deemed impassable for cavalry or artillery, and secretly position his force on the right flank of the French defensive line.

Suddenly, Wellington rode north, at one point being transferred across a raging torrent, whilst sitting in a wicker basket hung from a high ropeway. On his arrival with Graham's 65,000 troops, he immediately launched the army across the Esla river on pontoon bridges into northern Spain and soon his troops were passing through Toro and Tordesillas, turning the French defensive line and forcing the French to hurriedly retreat without a fight. As Arthur passed the Portuguese border into Spain, he

rather theatrically raised his cocked hat and loudly declared 'Farewell Portugal! I shall never see you again', such was his confidence.

Hill rapidly marched northward with his troops to join Wellington and his combined army marched along the northern banks of the Douro river, capturing Valladolid and Palencia, turning all of the other French defensive lines on the Carrion, Pisuerga and Arlanzon, and the French troops found themselves in headlong retreat.

Wellington's troops now approached Burgos once again, with a great deal of trepidation after the disastrous siege of last year. When they approached the city, a tremendous explosion at 7am on 13 June both astonished and delighted the Allies. The French had destroyed the defences

British cavalry sweep through the city of Vitoria during the battle.

British troops attack the village of Subijana.

of Burgos and were continuing to retreat. On 17 June the line of the River Ebro was also turned and King Joseph finally ordered his forces to stand on the River Arlanzon in front of Vitoria, to avoid being driven completely out of Spain.

By 19 June, Wellington and his troops began arriving on the hills overlooking the broad floodplain of the River Arlanzon and were delighted to observe that the French were encamped in three defensive lines behind the river line and clearly ready to offer battle. Arthur had 82,000 troops but only 96 cannon, whereas King Joseph had only 60,000 men but over 150 cannon, a major advantage in a strong defensive position.

The river was spanned by a number of bridges, which the French had not broken or barricaded, as they clearly wanted Arthur to order his troops

King Joseph's silver chamber pot.

across the river, where he would see his frontal attacks fail with terrible casualties and the hugely superior French cavalry would then destroy the Allied infantry as they were trapped in a bottleneck, unable to re-cross the bridges quickly.

Arthur, however, had no intention of doing what the French expected him to do. On 21 June

A page from Beethoven's 'Wellington's Victory'.

he launched his attacks. Initially Allied troops pushed along hills forming the south-eastern rim of the floodplain to threaten the French left and force them to draw off some of their reserves from the centre. He then moved his troops across the river and formed up to attack the French lines head on, and, just as Joseph had hoped, the French line centred on Arinez Village and the nearby height. However Joseph was not aware that this was not all of Wellington's forces. General Graham had been sent on a march through the mountains and now appeared to the north, quickly cutting the road to Bilbao, leaving the road towards Pamplona as the only escape route for the French army.

The French first line had been driven back and it fell back in good order on its second position, but the noise of the attack to the north and the obvious threat to their retreat caused French morale to collapse.

The infantry fighting against Graham's attack held on tenaciously in the villages, keeping the road to Pamplona open to allow the troops to flee, but eventually they had to give way themselves. It was not ideal cavalry country, but the British horsemen pursued the disorganised French infantry through and around the city until brought up by the French cavalry who formed a solid rearguard. In the confusion, horse teams were cut from their carriages and hundreds of cannon and numberless carriages full of stores, personal possessions and looted treasures were abandoned in their haste to get away. The pursuit soon halted, particularly as the Allied soldiers became enticed by the possibilities of plunder, but Joseph was nearly captured in his carriage and was forced to flee on horseback, leaving everything behind including his silver chamber pot, which was captured by the 14th Light Dragoons.

Allied and French casualties were roughly equal at just over 5,000 killed and wounded

A teapot representing Victory placing a laurel crown on a bust of Wellington.

each and 150 cannon captured, but Arthur was enraged that only just under 3,000 Frenchmen had been captured, as the opportunity had been there to capture half of the army. However, his army had marched 400 miles in 40 days and the French had virtually been driven out of Spain.

News of this victory resounded throughout Europe and it had far-reaching consequences. For the first time ever a *Te Deum* was sung at St Petersburg to commemorate a foreign victory and Austria felt emboldened to abandon her neutrality and join the coalition against Napoleon, allowing the Allies to overwhelm Napoleon at Leipzig only four months later. As a result of this victory even the German composer Beethoven, now no longer an admirer of Napoleon's, dedicated a piece of music to him, known as 'Wellington's Victory'.

This victory, above all others, put Wellington's name in lights across the world and he was lauded not only by the British public and government, but now by all of the Allied leaders, and he became a household name throughout Europe. King Joseph was removed from the throne of Spain by his brother in an arbitrary act of petulance, the throne no longer being in his gift and Marshal Soult was given the unenviable task of stopping Wellington's troops setting foot on French soil.

52: The Duke of Wellington's Peninsular Despatch Case

The Duke of Wellington was renowned for his capacity for work, but even he found the volume of his correspondence irksome. He was constantly required to report to government on ongoing operations, to request that innumerable deficiencies were urgently remedied, from supplies of weapons and wheat to gold coin, and to justify his future operations.

But Arthur had shown himself to be so adept and efficient at his work and willing to consider matters even beyond his theatre of operations, that it led to an inordinate increase in the volume of his correspondence. The more that he coped with, the more that they sent.

A regular weekly postal packet ship had been organised and the government were able to receive Arthur's well-considered and sage words on virtually every subject within a few weeks. The temptation was too great and soon he was being inundated with correspondence, seeking his views regarding almost every military operation that was either underway or in preparation around the world. However, they wrote on almost

every other conceivable subject and particularly the tangled web that was the current political situation at home and abroad. He was almost certainly his own worst enemy in some respects, because he regularly wrote up reports on various subjects that took his fancy and passed them on to various government departments even when not asked for his opinions.

However, he constantly complained of the excessive workload, but declined to free up any of his time by dictating to his secretaries. Almost all of the unbelievably huge body of writing sent by Wellington was in his own hand, the secretaries purely copying it for other parties or into correspondence ledgers. His handwriting was never good or easy to read, and it is not surprising that it became ever more of a scrawl and some is virtually unreadable, as many a historian can confirm.

On occasions however, the desk jockeys in London occasionally criticised the returns and accounts from the army and it led to a characteristic tirade from an exasperated Arthur. Whilst at Madrid in 1812 Wellington received one such complaint, at a time when he was perhaps not at his best and drew an acerbic reply from him, which Winston Churchill himself would have been proud of.

A cast of Wellington's hands circa 1840.

'Gentlemen,

Whilst marching from Portugal to a position which commands the approach to Madrid and the French forces, my officers have been diligently complying with your requests which have been sent by H.M. ship from London to Lisbon and thence by dispatch to our headquarters.

We have enumerated our saddles, bridles, tents and tent poles, and all manner of sundry items for which His Majesty's Government holds me accountable. I have dispatched reports on the character, wit, and spleen of every officer. Each item and every farthing has been accounted for, with two regrettable exceptions for which I beg your indulgence.

Unfortunately, the sum of one shilling and ninepence remains unaccounted for in one infantry battalion's petty cash and there has been a hideous confusion as to the number of jars of raspberry jam issued to one cavalry regiment during a sandstorm in western Spain. This reprehensible carelessness may be related to the pressure of circumstance, since we are war with France, a fact which may come as a bit of a surprise to you gentlemen in Whitehall.

This brings me to my present purpose, which is to request elucidation of my instructions from His Majesty's Government so that I may better understand why I am dragging an army over these barren plains. I construe that perforce it must be one of two alternative duties, as given below. I shall pursue either one with the best of my ability, but I cannot do both:

1. To train an army of uniformed British clerks in Spain for the benefit of the accountants and copy-boys in London or perchance.
2. To see to it that the forces of Napoleon are driven out of Spain.

Your most obedient servant, Wellington'

The reply, if there ever was one, has not been found!

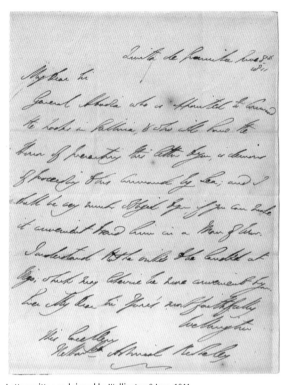

Letter written and signed by Wellington 8 June 1811.

Arthur even went so far as to have his saddles specially adapted, removing the pistol holsters and replacing them with pockets in which he could hold his writing implements. He also began using pads of goat skin, on which Wellington hastily scribbled in pencil, which if rubbed can be cleared so as to reuse them. Four of these survive from the Battle of Waterloo and are preserved at Apsley House.

The text (right) reads 'I see that the fire has communicated from the haystack to the roof of the chateau. You must however still keep your men in those parts to which the fire does not reach. Take care that no men are lost by the falling in the roof, or floors. After they will have fallen in, occupy the ruined walls inside of the garden; particularly if it should be possible for the enemy to pass through the embers in the inside of the house.'

53: Marshal Jourdan's Baton

One of the treasures captured after the Battle of Vitoria was Marshal Jourdan's baton which had been presented to him personally by the Emperor Napoleon. When first handed to Arthur by the colonel of the 87th Foot (The Prince of Wales' Irish), it was missing the two solid gold end pieces. On further investigation, the colonel discovered that Bugler Paddy Shannon had been given the baton by his friend Corporal Fox of the 18th Hussars, who had clearly removed the gold pieces prior to handing it over.

Arthur sent a despatch home and wrote a letter to the Prince Regent enclosing the baton: part of it read

22 June 1813

'... I send this dispatch by my aide-de-camp Captain Fremantle, whom I beg leave to recommend to your Lordship's protection. He will have the honour of laying at the feet of His Royal Highness the colours of the 4th battalion 100th regiment, and Marshal Jourdan's baton of a Marshal of France taken by the 87th Regiment.'

The gold end pieces were eventually recovered and were sent to be refitted to the baton. The Prince Regent sent a reply two weeks later, enclosing a marshal's baton for Arthur as a reward. The rank of field marshal had never existed within the British Army and had to be specially inaugurated so as to present Arthur with the baton. The Prince Regent's reply read as follows:

'Carlton House, 3rd July 1813

To Field Marshal THE MARQUIS OF WELLINGTON, &C. &C., K.G.

Your glorious conduct is beyond all human praise, and far above my reward. I know no language the world affords worthy to express it. I feel I have nothing left to say but most devoutly to offer up my prayers of gratitude to Providence that it has in its omnipotent bounty, blessed my country and myself with such a General. You have sent me among the trophies of your unrivalled fame, the Staff of a French Marshal, and I send you in return that of England. The British Army will hail it with rapturous enthusiasm, while the whole Universe will acknowledge those valorous exploits which have so imperiously called for it. That uninterrupted health and still increasing laurels may continue to crown you through a glorious and long career of life, are the never ceasing and most ardent wishes of,

My Dear Lord, Your very sincere and faithful friend,

GEORGE, P.R.'

Arthur was eventually granted a field marshal's baton from seven other countries as well as his three British ones (from the three sovereigns he served) issued during his lifetime. The batons as shown below are on display at Apsley House in London. They are in order, 1. Spain; 2. Hanover; 3. Russia; 4. Britain; 5. Britain; 6. Britain; 7. Portugal; 8. Netherlands; 9. Prussia; and 10. Austria. The original Russian baton was actually stolen in the 1960s.

The Duke's hat as Field Marshal in 1846.

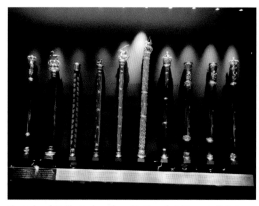

The Duke of Wellington's entire collection of eight marshal's batons.

54: The Spanish Royal Collection at Apsley House

Following the Battle of Vitoria, King Joseph's carriage was found amongst the hundreds of abandoned wagons and rifled for valuables. It was found to contain numerous treasures and a large travelling chest known as an 'Imperial'. When opened, along with state papers and personal letters, they discovered around 200 paintings, which had been removed from their frames and rolled up.

After a cursory look, as the story goes, Arthur and his Staff apparently concluded that they were not particularly valuable. However, rather than simply returning the case to Madrid, he had it shipped to London to his brother William, to ascertain better what was there. William asked William Seguier, who later became the first ever keeper of the National Gallery who realised how important they were and listed 165 of the most valuable. The collection included works by Velazquez, Titian, Correggio and Van Dyck

The list was sent to Arthur, who realised that it was an important collection and almost certainly belonged to the Spanish royal family. He sent the list to the court of King Ferdinand VII, who had been released from French captivity, offering to arrange for the return of the entire collection.

However, the king magnanimously declined them, making the entire collection a gift to Arthur for his stunning victory as they were 'well deserved'. The collection, which was further added to by Wellington in his later years, is too large to be fully on display and some remain in the private quarters of the present duke, and others are occasionally rotated from the stores to let people see them.

It is known that some of the smaller paintings found were still in their frames and at least one, *The Arnolfini Wedding* by Jan Van Eyck, had obviously been looted by one of the soldiers and appeared in London in 1816. It was eventually bought for the National Gallery. When Apsley House was given to the nation in 1947, so was the art collection.

Some of the paintings were damaged and in such bad condition that their authenticity has sometimes been called into doubt. Three paintings termed 'in the style of Titian' and believed to be later copies were restored in 2015 and during the process, they were shown to be genuine Titians.

As a convoy of 100 wagons filled with art treasures had proceeded on to France the day before the battle, it is tempting to wonder what other treasures from the Spanish Royal Collection were taken into France. It is rumoured to this day that many fine paintings in collections throughout Europe came from the Spanish Royal Collection and that Joseph, who was an art connoisseur did extremely well from the sale of these artworks.

A few Dutch paintings in the collection.

55: Dramatic Painting of Wellington and his Staff in the Pyrenees

Having suffered a spectacular defeat at Vitoria, the remnants of the French army retreated over the Pyrenees into France, abandoning almost all of their cannon and huge amounts of equipment. Arthur believed that he would have some months without any threat from France in which to mop up the two remaining French garrisons left in the fortresses of Pamplona and San Sebastian. Pamplona was blockaded by Spanish troops in an effort to starve the garrison into submission, while Wellington turned his focus on San Sebastian, whose capture would give him an excellent supply base close to the French border, for ease of transportation to the front.

However, Napoleon was alarmed at the situation in Spain and he ordered Marshal Soult to take over the remnants of the four armies of Spain as one force. Soult took to the task with gusto and had his army reinforced and resupplied in a remarkably short period of time and was soon planning a counter-attack whilst Wellington was distracted at San Sebastian.

Arthur's 62,000 troops were strung along the Pyrenees guarding the various passes, but this meant that communications between these different units was very difficult. This made concentrating his forces in the event of an attack very awkward and almost impossible if pressed by a determined enemy.

Soult launched his surprise offensive on 25 July 1813, simultaneously launching two large-scale attacks on the major passes of Maya and Roncesvalles, which were designed to break through the Allied defences and converge near Pamplona, the aim being to relieve the blockade of the city and then to turn northwards and break the siege of San Sebastian.

The 4,000 Allied defenders fought valiantly, but were soon nearly overcome by over 20,000 French assailants under the command of d'Erlon at the Pass of Maya, but the timely arrival of another Allied brigade of 2,000 troops, which attacked their flank, prevented the French breakthrough. Despite a successful defence here, General Rowland Hill ordered a steady retreat for the next day, being worried that his flanks might be turned.

The numbers involved in the second simultaneous attack at Roncesvalles were much larger, the Allies having 11,000 troops available to try to hold back no less than 36,000 French troops under the command of General Clausel. General Cole was under orders to defend the pass 'to the utmost' and initially he held his ground with determination, but when thick rolling fog descended on the pass late that afternoon, he ordered a retreat towards Pamplona, being fearful of being outflanked in the poor conditions.

Arthur was now aware of the seriousness of the attack at Maya, but he remained ignorant of the attack at Roncesvalles for a considerable period as General Cole had omitted to send him much news of the attack. Wellington therefore initially concentrated on defending the attack on the Maya pass. By late on the 26th, the French troops attacking through the Roncesvalles pass had driven the Allied troops to within 10 miles of Pamplona, but here they took up a strong defensive position on hills overlooking the village of Sorauren.

The French attack at the Col de Maya on 25 July 1813.

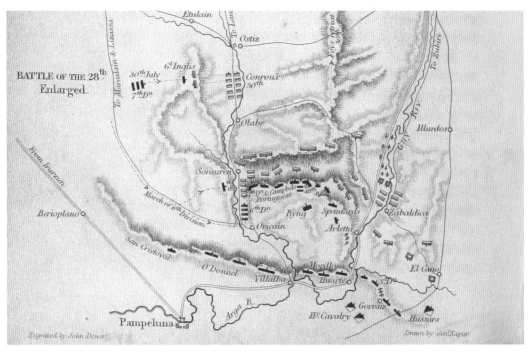

Map of the First Battle of Sorauren on 28 July 1813.

Wellington joined the 17,000 troops at Sorauren on 27 July, fully expecting a serious attack by the French that day. As Arthur arrived at the village only accompanied by Fitzroy Somerset, he dismounted at the bridge to write urgent orders to reroute the reinforcements he had already ordered to concentrate here, to avoid them being defeated piecemeal on the march. Suddenly, shouts from the Spanish villagers notified them to the proximity of French soldiers. Arthur completed writing the order, and handing it to Somerset, he rode off at speed, leaving Wellington alone. As French light cavalry rode cautiously into the village, Arthur mounted and rode at the gallop to join his forces lining the heights above. As he arrived, the Portuguese troops recognised him and shouted 'Douro, Douro' loudly, making Marshal Soult on a nearby hill to wonder what all the noise was. This may have partly caused Soult to decline to attack until all of his forces were up and he therefore delayed until the following day, losing a golden opportunity. Launching his attack with 36,000 men on the morning of the 28 July, Soult found Wellington in position with around 24,000 and all attempts by the French to break through were thwarted with heavy loss.

Wellington drew in further troops, but d'Erlon found it impossible to link up with Soult and therefore he began to move towards d'Erlon. Wellington now felt strong enough to launch an attack on 30 July. The French began to

Wellington and Somerset at Sorauren bridge.

retreat and were held up for hours by a Spanish division which defended a bridge, but the French fought desperately and finally broke through and escaped. However, the French were starving, with no supplies and a mass of Allied troops closing in on their rear and trying to outflank them to cut off their retreat. Panic soon turned their retreat into a rout and the broken French army streamed back into France having suffered some 10,000 killed and wounded and nearly 3,000 prisoners, whilst the Allies lost some 7,000 casualties.

French plans for Spain were now effectively dead and Wellington could contemplate advancing into France, but held off from doing so until Pamplona and San Sebastian were in Allied hands. Napoleon deposed Joseph as King of Spain, releasing Ferdinand VII from his confinement, having extracted promises from him to overthrow the new constitution, which Ferdinand immediately renounced once free again on Spanish soil.

Contemporary print of the battlefield of Sorauren.

56: Cartoon depicting Wellington as a Huntsman and Napoleon as the Fox

Like most gentleman of the age, Arthur had a lifelong passion for hunting. The thrill of the chase, hard riding with difficult jumps and being there for the kill had been signs of masculinity for centuries before and the average Georgian gentleman was no different. Even in Spain during the war, Arthur enjoyed nothing better than riding with the hounds, a pack of which had been specially shipped over from Britain. Arthur was not a refined rider, but he was able to stay in the saddle for many hours over difficult terrain. Riding across country after the hounds with the thrill of the chase was clearly an excellent release from the constant pressures of work. He would ride out most days whenever he could as a form of exercise.

His love of hunting continued throughout his life and when he acquired his country estate at Stratfield Saye in 1818, its potential for hunting and shooting was clearly a very important factor in his decision. He liked both hunting and shooting very much, but whereas he was seen as a good hunter, the same could not be said for his shooting.

Just like his great adversary Napoleon, Wellington was apparently a very poor shot, but who ever said it was a good idea to give a general

Death of the CORSICAN-FOX — Scene the last of the Wellington Hunt.

a musket? Ironically, he was a notoriously 'wild shot' and dangerous to be around, as many were able to testify.

On a hunting trip at Maresfield Park in 1819, Lady Frances Shelley recorded how he managed to shoot very few pheasants, having emptied two and a half powder horns, with very little to show for it. He did, however, wound a retriever early in the day, and later peppered the gaiters of a gamekeeper and finally sprinkled shot into the bare arms of an unfortunate old woman who was washing clothes at the open window of her cottage. Lady Frances went to calm the screaming woman, stating that 'this ought to be the proudest moment of your life. You have had the distinction of being shot by the great Duke of Wellington!' The poor woman now didn't know whether to be proud or furious, but her face broke out in a broad smile when a very contrite Arthur placed a gold coin into her hand. The Duke continued to shoot and Lady Shelley's

daughter eventually became so frightened that she burst into tears, when she suggested that she should stand close behind the Duke, to be protected by him!

In January 1823 at another shooting party at Wherstead Park in Suffolk, Arthur managed to accidentally fire at Lord Granville Leveson-Gower, his host, hitting him in the cheek and nose with somewhere between eight and eleven pellets (reports differ). Leveson-Gower let out a cry of 'I am shot' and Wellington dropped his gun and ran to him, whilst another of the party rode for a doctor who extracted the shot and reported the patient not to be in danger. Apparently Arthur had already shot two of the dogs that day! Ironically, Arthur actually blamed Leveson-Gower for being in the wrong place.

At his later duel with Winchelsea, he is stated as having fired but deliberately missed. Given his general poor aim, this later claim is a little dubious.

The Duke out hunting, his way blocked by a farmer.

57: Silver Fork Plundered from San Sebastian on 31 August 1813

Having to try and carry out a number of operations at the same time across such a very great expanse proved difficult and Arthur later admitted that it had been a mistake. He gave command of the siege operations to his trusted subordinate Sir Thomas Graham, but Wellington still kept a close eye on this operation as it was essential to take this fortress before he could contemplate an advance into France.

The walled town of San Sebastian, which lay on a spit of sand between the sea and the River Urumea and commanded by a rocky promontory, would not be easy to capture. Its natural defences, added to the 3,200 French troops placed in the garrison under the very determined General Rey with 72 cannon lining the walls making it a formidable task. It was not called the 'Gibraltar of the north' for nothing.

However, the British engineers selected two particular sections of wall which might be breached, but the attacking troops were restricted from approaching them except at low water, giving them only a few hours a day in which to storm the defences.

Initially Wellington considered it feasible to starve the defenders into submission, by utilising the British navy to prevent supplies being sent in by boat. However, this proved impossible, with numerous small boats carrying supplies into the town every night. A formal siege was therefore the only alternative.

Operations began successfully with work beginning on capturing the large convent of San Bartolomeo. Having raised two batteries within 200 metres, the convent was battered for four days and then a storming party was sent in, capturing the buildings with only light loss. Trenches were now dug across the sandy isthmus to enable siege batteries to be prepared to fire on the southern wall, although the erecting of batteries at the convent led to the digging up of many ancient graves in the process. Whilst digging the trenches, a storm drain was discovered and

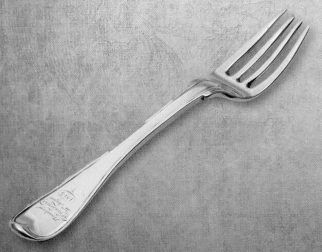

The siege of San Sebastian, drawn by a British officer who was present.

it was planned to place a mine hard up against the town walls whilst breaching batteries on the sand hills to the east were ordered to breach the walls at two specific locations.

When the two breaches in the east wall were declared practicable by the engineers, the mine was exploded at dawn on 25 July and a large-scale assault on all three breaches was set in motion. Unfortunately, the mine was detonated when it was still dark, and the assault was made without any possibility of a supporting barrage because of the lack of light. In all three cases, the infantry assaulted the breaches bravely, but were restricted in their attacks to a thin strip of land by the receding waters and they took terrible casualties at the breach before the assault was abandoned, having lost nearly 1,000 Allied soldiers killed, wounded or captured. News of Soult's attacks in the Pyrenees and a lack of siege ammunition caused the siege work to be postponed and the siege guns were removed to safety on board ships at Passajes.

Having defeated Soult and received new siege guns and an adequate supply of ammunition on 19 August, the siege recommenced with sixty-three guns on 26 August. The French were now down to approximately 2,700 men fit for active service.

Naval boats captured the island of Santa Clara the following day and a gun battery was established here which proved awkward for the French, as it enfiladed much of their defences. The main breach was soon over 150 metres long and two adjoining towers had been demolished, the town was to be stormed at low tide on 31 August at 11am in full daylight. However, the French defenders had also been busy, building new walls and defences behind the breaches, making it almost impossible for the Allied troops to get in.

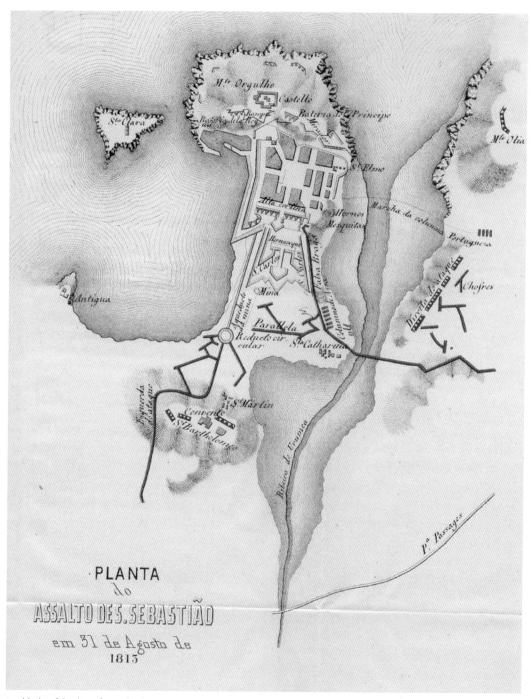

Spanish plan of the siege of San Sebastian.

A contemporary sketch of San Sebastian from the east showing the two breaches.

The assault was presaged by another mine designed to bring down another section of curtain wall and the Allied troops bravely attempted the breaches, but they lost heavily from the incessant French fire. The troops reached the breaches but could not progress further owing to the French retrenchments and after two hours of slaughter, the attack looked doomed to fail once again.

The storming of San Sebastian.

Seeing the terrible situation, General Graham and his commander of the siege artillery considered their options and they chose a desperate measure. The British siege guns were brought into play once again, firing just over the heads of the attackers and they initially caused some panic among the Allied troops. However, it soon became clear that their renewed fire had quickly shattered the French internal defences, providing an opportunity for the storming parties to penetrate beyond the breaches. With this defence line breached, the French rapidly retreated into the safety of the fortress on Mount Orgull, abandoning the town to the Allies, although some 700 Frenchmen were captured. The town began to burn and much of it was destroyed. This was blamed on the Allied troops who had been maddened by the assault and saw the pillage of the town as their right, but witnesses seem to indicate that some of the fires were alight before the French retired. It was a tragedy for the town and it is still commemorated every 31 August with a candlelit ceremony.

Rey and his surviving garrison tried to hold out in the castle, whilst hoping for relief from Soult, but the Allies constantly bombarded the castle and the French garrison suffered heavily as there were no bomb-proof shelters. Eventually with all hope at an end, peace terms were requested on 5 September and the French troops surrendered with the honours of war. The Allies lost nearly 4,000 men taking San Sebastian, the French suffered only 900 casualties but another 2,500 men were sent to Britain as prisoners of war.

Pamplona was starved into submission on 31 October 1813 when another 2,500 French troops became prisoners of war. Wellington could now look to invade France.

58: Contemporary View of the Mouth of the Bidassoa near Fontarrabie

Because of Napoleon's urgent need for more troops in Central Europe to fight the combined armies of Austria, Russia and Prussia, Soult was forced to defend the border with a greatly inferior force, having only 62,000 men facing Wellington's near 90,000 British, Portuguese and Spanish troops. Soult viewed the coastal plain as his strongest sector and only placed 10,000 troops here, positioning the bulk of his force in the mountains to the east, as far as the fortress of St Jean Pied de Port. Neither side could utilise their cavalry in these mountains, so this would be very much an infantry engagement. Arthur stood ready at the end of September, with his army poised to enter France, but Soult had not been idle either, his troops building numerous redoubts on the formidable heights of the French Pyrenees, it would not be an easy task.

Before launching his attack, Wellington issued notices to his troops that the French were to be treated as friendly, being the subjects of King Louis XVIII on his eventual return and insisting that everything taken to provide the troops with supplies had to be paid for. Many of the Spanish troops with his army had seen their families suffer terribly under the French and they burned for vengeance. On their very first opportunity some of these committed wanton acts of depravity and murder on innocent French families in revenge and no threats of punishment could soften their hatred. In a bid to win over the French, who were often plundered by their own starving troops, Arthur ordered many Spanish

units back across the Pyrenees, preferring to reduce his army significantly than risk a French insurgency breaking out in his rear. The policy worked brilliantly and soon the frightened French peasants had reopened their markets and were happily supplying his army, receiving fair payment in return.

The invasion of France was meticulously planned, everything was made ready for the next extreme low tide on 7 October, when Spanish fishermen assured him that there was a ford across the wide mouth of the Bidassoa River.

That morning, Soult was watching the division of Sir Henry Clinton as it marched towards the Maya pass on the left of his extensive line.

Soon, however, he was receiving reports that Wellington's forces had successfully forded the Bidassoa and had quickly swept away the French defenders and captured the heights on the French bank. Realising that he had been duped, Soult rode at breakneck speed to the coast but arrived too late to effect the outcome.

Further attacks captured a number of key heights and by the following morning, the French had abandoned the entire complex of redoubts they had worked so hard to construct and retreated towards the great fortress of Bayonne. The Allies had breached the French defences for a loss of less than 1,600 casualties, a stunning success.

Wellington's troops cross the Bidassoa.

59: La Rhune Mountain

Having gained a foothold within France and consolidated his position, Wellington was ready to move forward again within a month. The French line of defences was still dominated by a series of strong redoubts built on the La Rhune Mountain and its adjoining heights. However, although strongly defended, each height was isolated from each other and so they could not easily support each other.

Arthur realised that Soult would struggle to adequately man his 20-kilometre front, and by showing a disposition to attack at numerous locations along its entire length, ensured that the defences were only lightly manned. Everything was ready for a full-scale assault on the French defences by three powerful columns, but the attack was delayed because of heavy rains and snow on the mountains. Eventually the weather improved and the attack was arranged for dawn on 10 November 1813.

The centre column was by far the strongest and it was led forward by the Light Division at dawn, the light infantry rushing up the sides of the Rhune mountain and storming the redoubts built along its summit. Meanwhile, a feint attack near the coast prevented Soult from moving troops from this sector. The 52nd Foot assaulted a very strong star redoubt on a nearby plateau, charging forward ignoring their exhaustion

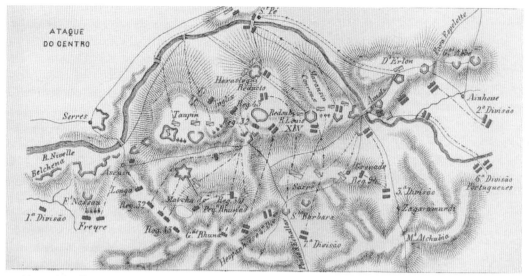

Spanish map of the Allied attack on the French redoubts.

from the steep ascent. The element of surprise and their determination saw them through, the French fleeing as they feared being trapped and forced to surrender. With La Rhune firmly in Allied hands, the centre of Soult's defensive line was breached and his two wings were isolated. As Wellington's main assault was launched along the entire line, the French troops abandoned the redoubts and streamed away over the Nivelles river towards Bayonne. Wellington's army was now completely clear of the Pyrenees and once over the Nivelle, they were onto the vast plains of south western France where his cavalry could operate effectively.

Wellington's troops amazingly only lost about 2,700 casualties attacking such strong defences. The French are estimated to have lost 4,500 casualties and prisoners and also 59 cannon.

60: The Church at Arcangues

Wellington's troops had pushed Soult's troops back towards Bayonne, but the French still held a series of heights about 3 kilometres south of the great fortress. The two wings of Soult's forces were separated by the River Nive and any attack by Arthur's troops would suffer the same problem, but Soult's front was now much more compact, allowing him to defend in force and he also had the advantage of being able to pass troops rapidly from one flank to the other by marching via the bridges over the Nive within the fortress.

On 9 December, Arthur ordered General Lord Hill to take five divisions over the river to the east bank over pontoon bridges, while General Hope with four other divisions drove up the west bank towards Bayonne. Soult saw his opportunity for a counter-attack and he launched eight divisions against Hope on the west bank on 10 December. Hope's troops were badly strung out, with the Guards Brigade being some 15 kilometres behind the front and unable to quickly support the front line.

Soult's attack discovered the Light Division holding a ridge at Arcangues, centred on the church and nearby chateau. Having beaten off one strong attack, the French simply sent skirmishers forward to probe the British, but were unable to progress against the strong defences hastily put together around the church. A second French column attacked the Portuguese troops at the village of Barroilhet, but were held up here and could not progress further. By 2pm the Guards Brigade had arrived to relieve the line and the French opportunity had been lost. That evening Soult's forces were further depleted when two German battalions marched over to the Allied lines and were promptly sent to Germany to participate in the war for German independence. The day had ended in a stalemate, both sides losing around 1,600 casualties.

On the night of 12 December, the Allied pontoon bridge was broken by the strong current, dangerously isolating the two wings of the army from each other, except via a stone bridge some 15 kilometres away. Seizing this opportunity, Soult

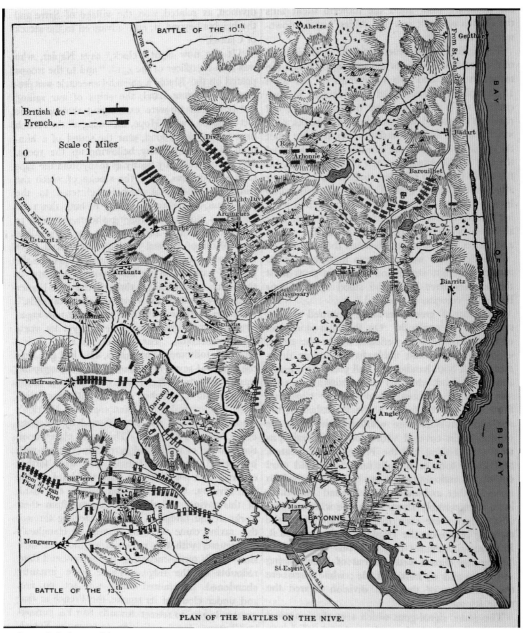

PLAN OF THE BATTLES ON THE NIVE.

North towards the bottom of the map.

transferred six divisions across the river to the east bank during the night. He then launched an attack at dawn on Hill's troops which were now outnumbered by three to one, with little prospect of receiving rapid reinforcements. However, Hill exhorted his troops to fight as hard as they could and they succeeded in holding their line against vastly superior forces for a number of hours until reinforcements finally arrived, when Soult withdrew. French losses had been near 3,000 in comparison with Hill's 1,750, a truly remarkable result against such a superior force.

The interior of Arcangues Church.

When Arthur arrived he congratulated Hill on his stout defence and generously stated 'Hill, the day's your own'.

The winter rains now came on with a vengeance and all operations were forced to halt until the end of February 1814, the roads being washed away and the fields so boggy that horses sank to their bellies in the mud. 1813 had begun on the frontiers of Portugal and ended before the walls of Bayonne, it had truly been a spectacular year of success for Arthur.

61: Photograph of the Bridge of Orthez circa 1855

On 14 February 1814 Wellington had put his army on the move again to break out of the small area he held south of Bayonne, which was to prove a tough fortress to take. He left a sizeable force to blockade Bayonne and with the rest of his army, he steadily drove Soult's forces eastward as they sought to defend each of the river lines.

Soult had been required to send 11,000 more of his troops to help Napoleon in his efforts to defeat the armies of Prussia, Russia and Austria, leaving him with only 36,000 troops in the field. His situation was helped, however, by Wellington's decision to send most of his Spanish troops back over the Pyrenees because of their vengeful attacks on French civilians, leaving him with a field army of around 44,000 men.

Wellington's troops soon breached the French defences on the river Bidouze and Soult's troops fell back to defend the line of the Gave d'Oloron. On 24 February, Wellington launched a feint attack on Soult's right flank, whilst General Hill's troops laid a pontoon bridge near Sauveterre and soon had 20,000 men on the east bank, again breaching French defences. Soult therefore ordered a retreat on Orthez where his troops would defend the Gave de Pau.

Soult's troops held the village of Orthez strongly and the remainder of his forces were

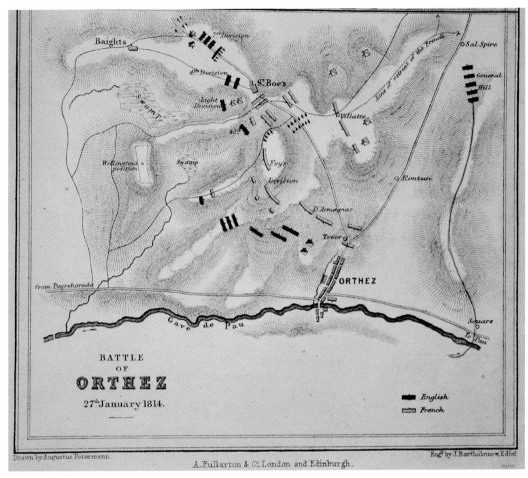

The Battle of Orthez.

lined along a long ridge that stretches above the town with all of his cannon placed here with commanding views of the surrounding countryside.

Wellington sent a force under Beresford to cross a bridge on Soult's right, with the aim of outflanking the strong French defensive line, whilst General Hill's troops threatened a direct attack on Orthez village. Early in the morning of 27 February the leading elements of Beresford's troops attacked the right flank of the French line at St Boes, but the fighting here was very stubborn on both sides and possession of the village seesawed until Cole's troops had finally

had enough and fell back, leaving the entire village to the French.

Wellington had simultaneously launched two divisions under General Picton against the French centre, to prevent Soult reinforcing his right, but the attack was limited to a few spurs of dry land above the marshy fields, restricting their ability to manoeuvre and making them a large target for the French artillery. Eventually the battle in the centre eased into an extensive skirmish, whilst Picton awaited news that Beresford's attack was succeeding. However, Arthur could see that Beresford's flank attack was faltering and he immediately ordered Picton

Memorial at St Boes where General Foy was wounded.

to change from a holding action into an all-out assault on the French centre. He sent every man he could muster and replaced Cole's division with fresh troops which renewed the fight for control of St Boes. The fighting was intense and at close range with both sides stubbornly holding their ground, until General Foy was wounded by a shrapnel shell and French resistance began to falter. Fresh troops sent forward under the command of General Henry Clinton finally broke through with a bayonet charge and the French centre broke.

The French troops in Orthez now saw their line of retreat in danger and pulled back, allowing the Allies to cross the river at the fords and by the bridge once the French had

No. 71 Rue de Saint-Gilles, formerly the hotel La Belle-Hôtesse, where Wellington stayed after the Battle of Orthez.

left. The French infantry were now fleeing as a mob, with a single bridge over the River Luy de Bearn some three miles in their rear. Some have claimed that Wellington's cavalry could have captured thousands here, but the ground was a mass of stone walls and ditches, making it difficult country for cavalry and they escaped.

Arthur was always close to the action and many of his soldiers often saw his survival as little short of miraculous. He was never wounded in any of his battles, but it was at Orthez that he came closest to suffering a severe wound. During the heavy fighting his Spanish liaison officer, Miguel Alava was struck on the bottom and Arthur apparently could not help laughing loudly. Within a minute an iron cannister shot struck his sword hilt, driving it an inch or so into his hip and causing severe bruising. The wound was minor and Alava gleefully regarded it as penance for laughing at his injury. It was painful but did not inconvenience him much, except that he could not gallop for some time without suffering. It did remind his senior officers, however, of how much they relied on him and how easily his life could be ended.

Allied losses at Orthez numbered just over 2,000, whilst the French suffered 2,500 casualties and an additional 1,400 prisoners. Soult's troops retired eastwards towards Toulouse and Wellington's troops followed, but Arthur did not fail to take advantage of the situation, to send Beresford with two divisions to take the great port of Bordeaux, which Soult had left undefended. The city welcomed the troops as their liberators and promptly declared for King Louis XVIII.

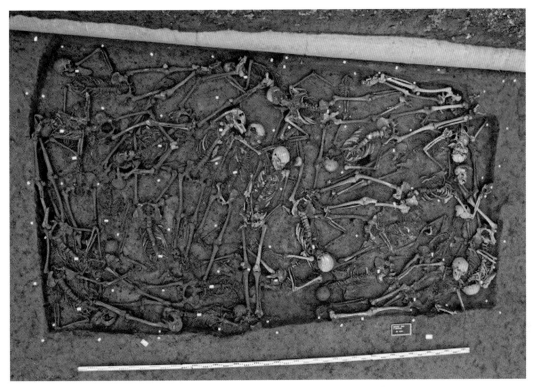

Mass grave recently found at Orthez.

62: Arthur Wellesley, Duke of Wellington, with all his Regalia

Perhaps Arthur Wellesley has become synonymous with one phrase more than any other, that his army was 'composed of the scum of the earth – the mere scum of the earth'. This phrase has been used to castigate Wellington roundly as a member of the governing 'elite', showing clearly his cold disregard for the soldiers who served under him, viewing them as nothing more than scum or 'canaille'.

In fact, he used the phrase occasionally throughout his life when he wished to severely criticise certain groups or individuals. He first described a group of Indian writers in 1800 as the 'Scum of the Earth', whilst the Duke of York's mistress and her cronies, who were found guilty of selling Army commissions to the highest bidder, were not immune, stating 'that these transactions, which have deservedly created so much indignation, have been carried on by the scum of the earth'.

However, the first recorded use of the phrase regarding his own troops, was written as an angry reaction in utter frustration.

In a letter to Earl Bathurst, from Huarte in Spain, dated 2 July 1813, Wellington wrote (my underlining):

'I enclose the copy of a letter from the Governor of Vitoria, which shows how our men are going on in that neighbourhood. These men are detachments from the different regiments of the army who were sent to Vitoria the day after the battle, each under officers, in order to collect the wounded and their arms and accoutrements. It is quite impossible for me or any other man to command a British army under the existing system. We have in the service the scum of the earth as common soldiers; and of late years we have been doing everything in our power, both by law and by publications, to relax the discipline by which alone such men can be kept in order. The officers of the lower ranks will not perform the duty required from them for the purpose of keeping their soldiers in order; and it is next to impossible to punish any officer for neglects of this description. As to the non-commissioned officers, as I have repeatedly stated, they are as bad as the men, and too near them, in point of pay and situation, by the regulations of late years, for us to expect them to do anything to keep the men in order. It is really a disgrace to have anything to say to such men as some of our soldiers are.'

His frustration is clear, but what sparked the outburst? Having won a stunning victory at the Battle of Vitoria, the French army fled the field in total disarray and so he sent his light cavalry in hot pursuit. Unfortunately, just beyond the city, the British troops discovered a huge park of abandoned vehicles which had been filled with the treasures of Spain. The temptation was simply too great and many of the men broke ranks to open the carriages and began looting, diverting them from the pursuit of the French, who were allowed to get away virtually scot free. The 18th Hussars were the worst culprits, according to Wellington, and at a parade, the men were ordered to hand over all the treasure they had taken. Over £2,600 in cash (£100,000 today) was handed in plus a huge amount of jewellery and other items from this regiment alone! Arthur let the regiment know that he was so displeased with them, both officers and men, that if he heard one further complaint about them, that he would dismount them, march them to the nearest port and send them back to Britain. The reason for his outburst is therefore clear, with all

Soldiers drinking in camp.

ranks of his army, showing themselves to be little more than common thieves.

However, within only a few months, when the army had resumed their professionalism and were fighting hard in the Pyrenees, he could write on 21 November 1813 of his army, that it was 'The most complete machine for its numbers now existing in Europe.' Indeed, later in life Arthur confirmed to Lady Salisbury, that by the end of the Peninsular War he had put the army into such good shape that 'I could have done anything with that army it was in such perfect order.'

The only other record of him using the phrase again was on 4 November 1831, when he declared in a conversation with Philip, Earl Stanhope that his soldiers

'... I may say it in this room – are the very scum of the earth ... people talk of their enlisting from their fine military feeling – all stuff – no such thing. Some of our men enlist from having bastard children – some for minor offences – many more for drink.'

Here, Wellington complains of the raw materials with which the majority of the army was composed, but as he himself said further: '... but you can hardly conceive such a set brought together, and it really is wonderful that we should have made them the fine fellows they are.'

This of course, alters the entire meaning of his statement, which admits that the soldiers that they made out of these 'scum' were no less than superb. It was in fact high praise of the common British soldier from him. Arthur believed totally in duty, and he expected nothing less from his men and these rare rants were born out of frustration when they failed to live up to his high standards, it was not an unfeeling assessment of the common soldier, as it is so often portrayed.

His honest admiration for the common soldier was ably demonstrated during an interview he had in Brussels just before the Waterloo campaign opened. Asked if he could beat Napoleon, Arthur looked at a British soldier in the park and said 'It all depends on that article there!' he said 'Give me enough of it and I am sure'. This offhand comment was actually very high praise indeed.

63: Cartoon of Wellington Driving King Louis Back to his Throne

Wellington's troops had followed Soult to Toulouse, where the French troops were positioned behind the River Garonne and occupied strong defences around the city.

On his arrival, Arthur sought ways of getting his army across the river to attack, but it would not be easy. The Languedoc canal ran across the north and eastern faces of the city to effectively form a large moat with every bridge defended by a redoubt. To the east was also a long range of heights called the Calvinet which was crowned by several very strong redoubts. The southern face therefore appeared to be the most favourable, but this was discovered to be marshy land and unsuitable for large-scale troop movements. The city was also defended on the western bank by the fortified suburb of St Cyprien.

On 4 April 1814 Allied engineers threw a pontoon bridge across the Garonne a few miles north of the city and nearly 20,000 troops crossed before the bridge was swept away by a storm surge. The troops on the eastern bank were very vulnerable for three days until the bridge was restored. However, Soult was ignorant of the fact or simply lethargic, as he failed to take advantage of the situation.

On Easter Day, 10 April, Wellington launched his attack, sending General Hill with a force of nearly 13,000 men to make a feint of attacking

Need's must. when Wellington Drive's or Louis Return!

British troops attack the Canal.

St Cyprien, whilst the remaining 36,000 of his army would attack on the east bank. General Picton was ordered to make a movement as if to seriously attack the bridges over the canal to the north of the city, but unfortunately he turned it into a real attack and his men were repulsed with serious loss.

Meanwhile, Wellington had sent General Beresford with two British divisions to march south between the River Ers to their left and at the foot of the heavily defended Calvinet heights to their right, calculating that the French would not risk descending the heights to attack them. Once in position, they would turn to attack the Calvinet heights from the southern end, whilst the Spanish troops simultaneously attacked the northern end. It was intended that both attacks having taken the two ends of the ridge, would

then roll up the rest of the defences and the French would retreat into the city.

Unfortunately, the Spanish commander mistook the heavy firing caused by Picton's ill-judged attack for the main attack on Calvinet ridge and they attacked early and alone. The Spaniards fought stubbornly and bravely, but they were repulsed twice with very heavy losses.

Finally, Beresford's troops arrived in their position and the two divisions advanced one behind the other, determined to capture the ridge. In bitter fighting the British infantry captured two redoubts, only to see them regained by the French in a strong counter-attack, before being finaly secured by fresh troops. Forming up on the southern end of the ridge, they now proceeded to push northward as planned, rolling up the French defences. Realising that the heights had

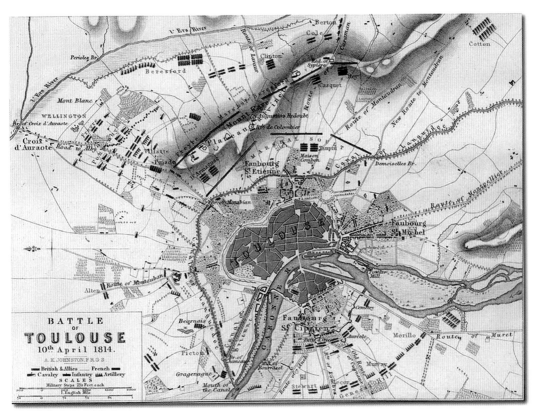

Plan of the Battle of Toulouse.

The Battle of Toulouse.

Obelisk commemorating the Battle of Toulouse.

been lost, Soult ordered his troops to retire over the canal bridges into the city. They held the city the following day, then marched out to the south that night, surrendering the city to Wellington's troops, who immediately marched in pursuit. The French lost over 3,000 men, whereas the Allies lost over 4,500, nearly all suffered by the troops assaulting the Calvinet heights frontally.

On the morning of 12 April the city surrendered to the Allies and later that day Arthur received news that Napoleon had abdicated and the war was over. He sent the news on to Soult who received it the following day. Soult doubted the news until he finally received a dispatch from the French government confirming it was true and an armistice was signed on 17 April.

Arthur probably believed that he had seen his last battle.

64: Bayonne Citadel

As Soult's forces were forced eastwards, Wellington took the opportunity to surround Bayonne, with the intention of blockading it and starving the garrison into submission.

The French defenders assumed that the 500-metre wide mouth of the River Adour, with its sand bar, preventing only the shallowest boats from entering, would prevent any Allied crossing to the west of the city and they therefore concentrated on defending the approaches from the east. However, Wellington had different ideas.

Once Soult had been driven far enough away to prevent him supporting Bayonne, Wellington tasked General Hope with 30,000 men with

French memorial in Bayonne.

blockading the French garrison of 13,000 troops, which Soult had left in the city. Admiral Penrose arranged for a number of small vessels and supplies to be collected at the port of St Jean de Luz, but bad weather delayed any attempt on a crossing.

Finally, the weather calmed enough to allow an attempt on 22 February and although the first vessels were dashed to pieces by the waves with the loss of a number of lives, a safe entrance was eventually discovered and twenty-six boats successfully entered and were moored in line across the river using huge cables anchored by the weight of heavy cannon barrels. Planks were then set across them and within hours British troops were passing to the north bank, to the amazement of the French. Once 600 men had passed across, the bridge temporarily broke and the situation became precarious as the French sent a column of infantry towards them.

However, the stubborn defence of the sandhills and the shock use of Congreve rockets, which frightened the French soldiers, caused them to retreat to the city. The bridge was repaired and soon 8,000 men were across and the blockade was completed.

An air of lethargy seemed to settle on both sides, the governor General Thouvenot meekly remaining within his defences whilst Hope's troops carried on a relaxed blockade with no intention of formally besieging the fortress. This passive blockade continued for six weeks, until 12 April when General Thouvenot received unofficial news of Napoleon's abdication. Despite the fact that peace would shortly be declared and the British troops remained quiet, Thouvenot decided to strike in an act of defiance.

At 3 o'clock in the morning of 14 April, he launched three columns of troops, totalling some 6,000 men on the unsuspecting Allies. The

BAYONNE - CIMETIÈRE DES ANGLAIS - THE GOLDSTREAM GUARDS CEMETERY - A. B.

Coldstream Guards Cemetery Bayonne circa 1900.

Allied pickets were taken completely by surprise and overrun and General Hay was killed. In the confusion of the half light, the alarm was sounded and Allied troops began to form up, but Sir John Hope, commanding the Allies, rode into a group of French cavalry and was wounded and captured, adding further to the confusion.

General Hinuber rallied the Allied troops and launched a determined counter-attack, and quickly recaptured the village of St Etienne, whilst another column was stopped by the British Guards Brigade who repulsed them and then counter-attacked.

By 8 o'clock the two Allied counter-attacks were beginning to threaten the French line of retreat and they were ordered to retire. The sortie had cost the Allies nearly 850 casualties, whilst the French lost marginally more. Formal news of peace arrived soon after, but Thouvenot refused to hand the fortress over until 27 April when he had received formal orders from Marshal Soult to that effect. It was a sad waste of nearly 2,000 lives.

65: Hotel du Charost, Paris

With King Louis XVIII restored to his throne in Paris, the British government had no qualms regarding the appointment of the general who probably did most to achieve his reinstatement, being sent as the first British Ambassador to Paris for a quarter of a century.

Arthur was appointed Ambassador whilst on his visit to Madrid and he immediately wrote to Kitty, enquiring whether she felt equal to joining him in Paris and assuming the role of Ambassadress. For once, Kitty's reply was firm and unequivocal, thanking him for allowing her to decide for herself and confirming that 'I have no hesitation in deciding to go, no other wish than to go'.

Having arrived in London in late June he was on his way to Paris by early August. He travelled via the Netherlands and found time to inspect the border fortresses and suggest improvements, but also identified a very good position to defend Brussels if needed, just south of a village named Waterloo.

Arthur took up his post as British Ambassador to the Court of the Tuileries on 22 August 1814. Planning ahead, he had already secured a home for himself, which would become the permanent British Embassy in Paris. The Hotel de Charost at No. 31 Rue de Faubourg St Honore, had belonged to Napoleon's sister Pauline since 1800, but she was now desperate to sell so that she could join Napoleon in Elba.

Wellington bought the mansion on 26 August, signing for the property and contents for the sum of 870,000 francs (about £40,000 or £2.5 million today), to be paid in instalments and he was in residence there before the end of the week.

Within the week Arthur had been received at court and his first diplomatic success was to

The Peace Illuminations, London 1814.

The Red Room with a portrait of the Duke of Wellington.

persuade Louis to end the slave trade in France. Wellington had warmed to this task, viewing the trade as 'horrible' and he made himself such a master of the topic that the abolitionists in London acknowledged that the new ambassador needed no guidance from them. The French public were not particularly aware of the slave trade and some even thought that Britain was simply looking for a new method of throttling the prosperity of their overseas colonies. Arthur thought deeply on this and arranged for Wilberforce to ensure that criticism of the French government did not appear in the British press at this critical moment and encouraged Madame de Staël to champion the anti-slavery cause in France. Louis was persuaded by these

The formal dining room.

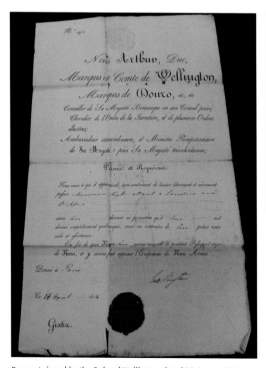

Passport signed by the Duke of Wellington dated 26 August 1814.

subtle methods and promised to end the trade within five years, the first government in mainland Europe to agree to it.

Arthur also met many of his former adversaries, Marshals Ney, Soult and the half-blind Massena. When the latter met Wellington, he declared 'My lord, you owe me a dinner – for you made me positively starve!' Arthur laughed and quickly replied 'You should give it to me, Marshal, for you prevented me from sleeping'.

Kitty did not join Arthur in Paris until the October, by which time he was already the lion of Paris and she found it virtually impossible to do justice as his consort. She was upset by his obvious fascination with the singer Madame Grassini, but also deeply missed her children and only cheered when they joined them in Paris for the Christmas holidays.

Arthur also found the time to point the Prince of Orange towards fostering a good relation with his new Belgian subjects, rather than keeping to his English and French circles. The prince reacted with candour that he had avoided the 'idiots the Belgians', but would now court them as per his sage advice.

But all was not well in Paris as Louis' government slowly sank into the mire and in September whilst at a review of the troops, bullets whistled past the Duc d'Angoulême and Arthur and by November the British government were becoming very alarmed for the safety of their ambassador, many in the city now referring to him as 'Mr Villainton'. Finally in December a solution was found. Lord Castlereagh was called home from the Congress of Vienna on government duties and Arthur was appointed in his stead. In January, Arthur travelled to the Congress at Vienna, but Kitty and his Staff would remain in Paris, holding the fort.

The British Embassy is still located in the same building and is recognised as one of the most prime locations in all of Paris.

66: Portrait of Giuseppina Grassini

When Arthur arrived in Paris, he was lauded as a hero and saviour of France, everywhere he went the orchestra invariably struck up 'See the Conquering Hero Comes' and ladies swooned. Others gave more admiring glances and Wellington was soon to be seen with a woman on his arm at every occasion and more often than not the same woman. Indeed, such brazen behaviour was openly condemned by many amongst polite society and earned a great deal of sympathy for Kitty who remained in England.

There were rumours of affairs whilst commanding the army in Spain, but there is little hard fact either way, beyond a note from a Spanish noble lady named the Duquesa de San Carlos, who signed herself in one letter to Arthur as his '*apasionada Amiga*' [Passionate friend], which hardly proves the case.

However, in Paris, there seems little doubt that the adulation and pretty women of Paris sorely tempted a pent-up sexual appetite following five years of campaigning and finally led Arthur astray. One who certainly caught Arthur's eye was the famous contralto Giuseppina Grassini who had formerly been a lover of Napoleon and was known as '*La chanteuse de l'Empereur*' [the singer of the Emperor]. Now turning forty, she still possessed a radiant beauty that certainly attracted Arthur and she was often to be seen on his arm at all of the great functions he was invited to.

The Countess de Boigne recorded that

'I recall that on one occasion he decided to make Grassini, then in possession of his favours, the queen of the evening. He placed her on a raised sofa in the ballroom and never left her side. He had her served first before anyone else, arranged everyone so that she could dance, gave her his hand to take her into supper first, sat her next to him, and finally paid her the kind of attention normally granted only to princesses.'

Arthur's interests in her appear to have continued in 1816, when he commanded the Army of Occupation and at times despite the presence of Kitty.

Arthur also showed much attention to the 27-year-old Mademoiselle Georges, real name Marguerite Weimer, who was the star of the Théatre Français. She had also been a former lover of Napoleon's and later famously compared the two great men, stating that 'The duke was by far the most vigorous/stronger'. However, her claims cannot be substantiated and if she did say so, she had only recently stopped entertaining Tsar Alexander I, as she had given him an illegitimate daughter, Maria Parijskaia, in March 1814.

67: Seals and Signatories of The Congress of Vienna

The Congress of Vienna had begun meeting in September 1814 and every kingdom, principality and city state in Europe sent a deputation, as well as all those representing states that had simply vanished in Napoleon's wholesale changes, seeking redress. They did not all meet, the real power being in the hands of Russia, Britain, Austria, Prussia and, after some wrangling, France, the others simply seeking to influence the big players on their behalf. It was therefore as much a continuous round of balls and entertainments of every kind as a hard-nosed redistribution of territory.

Arthur was sent to replace Castlereagh, who sent him an update on proceedings, which in brief simply stated 'no progress'. Castlereagh and Wellington had both come to realise that they needed France and Austria to join them against the ambitions of Prussia and Russia. Wellington therefore began to influence events even before

Austrian print of the Congress of Vienna.

Two chairs used at the Congress of Vienna.

he had left Paris, by convincing Louis to order Talleyrand to cooperate fully.

Arthur arrived in Vienna on 3 February 1815 and was relieved to discover that most of the major sticking points, including Poland, had been solved, leaving only the thorny issue of Saxony to deal with. Having received a thorough briefing from Castlereagh, Arthur launched himself into the fray, being determined to 'go straight forward without stratagems or subterfuges'. He was a breath of fresh air in a sea of chicanery and double dealing.

But then all was sudden change as messengers arrived to both Prince Metternich of Austria and Arthur announcing the news that Napoleon had left Elba and soon after it was clear that he had landed in France on 1 March. Having hoped in vain that the French army would stop Napoleon's progress, the Congress unanimously agreed on 13 March to declare Napoleon an outlaw and Arthur was one of the signatories. In this declaration, the word *vindicate* had been used. The opposition in Parliament claimed that the word meant that Wellington had signed up to the assassination of Napoleon, but as Arthur pointed out that *vindicate* actually meant justice and he remained unrepentant. By the end of the month, huge armies had begun to mobilise across Europe and subsidies promised by Britain to enable the war-racked countries to pay their soldiers. Arthur had retained his position of commander-in-chief of the Allied forces in the Netherlands and he left Vienna for Brussels at the end of March.

Although Arthur's time at the Congress was over, his influence was seen to have succeeded when the final act of the Congress, signed on 9 June, declared the slave trade to be unworthy of Christian states.

Europe after the Congress of Vienna 1815.

68: Cloak Worn by Wellington during the Waterloo Campaign

Arthur arrived in Brussels on 4 April 1815 and immediately set to organising his army ready for the joint advance planned with the Prussians, Russians, Austrians and Spanish in a coordinated strike designed to completely overpower Napoleon's forces. It was not an easy task, however, as it took him nearly a month before King William of Orange granted him the position of commander-in-chief of the Netherlands troops, giving him control of all his force. Many of the British troops were young and inexperienced, many of his Peninsular regiments having been sent to fight the Americans (a role he had declined) and many other veterans having retired from the army after peace had been declared, their time served. Even his Staff did not please him, some being new to him and others not well thought of. He therefore wrote to Horse Guards requesting that the trusted officers of his Peninsular staff were sent to him. Beyond everything else he needed a huge increase in numbers and the German states were persuaded to supply them for cash subsidies, Arthur's own preference for Portuguese soldiers to be shipped to Belgium being deemed far too expensive by the government. Arthur also smoothed things over for Marshal Blücher's Prussian army, which could not afford to feed itself, King William finally accepting responsibility for feeding them when on his soil.

Slowly everything was made ready for the advance, but the Austrians and Russians were delayed on their long marches and Prince Schwarzenberg commander-in-chief of all the European forces put the date back for the start of operations to the end of June.

Arthur was fully aware of Napoleon's fearsome reputation on the battlefield and he met Blücher to arrange how they would advance into France, but also discussed how they would react if Napoleon attacked them. Wellington was well

Wellington and his troops march to Quatre Bras.

Battle of Quatre Bras.

aware that Napoleon was capable of launching a surprise attack with the aim of destroying Blücher's and his own armies before the other Allies had arrived and capturing Brussels, giving him control of Belgium once again. However, Arthur could not be certain by which route Napoleon would come and he was forced to keep his troops spread out over a large area, watching a number of major roads.

When the attack did come at dawn on 15 June, initially against the Prussian forces holding the bridges over the Sambre river around Charleroi, the French troops were successful in gaining the crossing points intact and Napoleon's army was soon streaming north in search of the Allied armies. Wellington was only made aware of this attack around 5pm that afternoon and even then, he feared that it might be a feint, with the real attack coming elsewhere. By midnight, Arthur was certain that it was the main attack and he ordered his troops to march to their forward assembly point at Nivelles at first light. He and a number of his officers did attend the Duchess of Richmond's Ball that evening, but this event has since reached fabled status, almost all of the officers present actually leaving abruptly to return to their regiments.

Napoleon hoped to hold one enemy army back whilst destroying the other and on 16 June he nearly succeeded in his design. Blücher had stood at Ligny and offered battle with three-quarters of his army, which even so, outnumbered the force Napoleon could bring against him. Meanwhile Marshal Ney attacked Wellington's Netherlands' troops at Quatre Bras, believing that Wellington's army would be concentrating much further to the rear.

Wellington had, however, ordered his troops to march on Quatre Bras and as units arrived they were thrown straight into the confused battle until finally he outnumbered the French

and was able to end by reoccupying the positions they had held at the start of the day. This was Napoleon's day. Wellington's army had been held in check as planned whilst Blücher's army had been defeated at Ligny.

Learning the following morning that Blücher had been defeated and had retired to Wavre, Wellington decided to order his army to retreat to a position he had already reconnoitred a year before just south of Waterloo. He then wrote to Blücher to confirm that he would offer battle in his chosen position if he would send one of his corps to join him on 18 June, which he promised to do.

Napoleon began 17 June in a very favourable position, having defeated one army and stopped the other from joining it: in fact at that moment, the campaign could be said to be his to lose. Napoleon mistakenly believed that Blücher's army was destroyed and was streaming back down the roads to Germany. He therefore sent Marshal Grouchy with some 34,000 men to pursue them and ensure that they were completely out of the campaign. After much delay, he eventually learnt that Wellington's army was still concentrated at Quatre Bras, offering him an opportunity of smashing it with overwhelming numbers and he ordered his troops to march rapidly towards the crossroads.

The delay in moving that morning gave Wellington all the opportunity he needed to regain the advantage. Having moved his troops off from Quatre Bras early that morning, Napoleon's troops eventually arrived early in the afternoon, only to find a cavalry screen, which fell back as they advanced.

Napoleon was furious, having missed the perfect opportunity to destroy Wellington's army and all attempts to catch up with his retreating army were foiled by atrocious weather, making the fields a quagmire. Arriving that evening

Wellington's troops retreat to Waterloo.

at the inn of La Belle Alliance, Napoleon was both surprised and delighted to discover that Wellington's army had formed on the next ridge offering battle. Napoleon was sure that the following day he could destroy Wellington's army: his plan was still working.

Arthur had determined to give battle with his army of numerous nations and experience on this ridge just in front of Mont St Jean. He was not confident of success against the veteran French army, but he knew something Napoleon didn't, Blücher was marching to join him.

69: Saw and Bloodied Glove from the Amputation of Lord Uxbridge's Leg

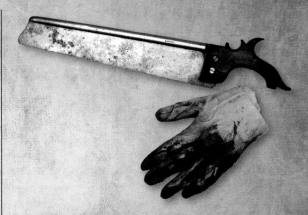

Henry William Paget, the first son of the 1st Earl of Uxbridge, had undoubtedly met Arthur during the inglorious Flanders campaign of 1794, when he commanded the 80th Regiment of Foot which he had just raised in the temporary rank of lieutenant colonel commandant, even though he did not hold a commission in the army. This awkward situation was solved when he bought a lieutenancy in the 7th Foot on 14 April 1795 and had been promoted to lieutenant colonel by 19 May and was colonel of a regiment by 3 May the following year!

Despite this inordinately rapid promotion, Paget had gained his spurs on the battlefield and in 1808 he proceeded to Spain as a lieutenant general commanding the cavalry in Sir John Moore's army. His hussars saw great success at the Battles of Sahagun and Benavente, where Paget showed his abilities as a rare talent in command of cavalry and he was possibly the best cavalry officer the British army then possessed. He was personally brave and cut a dashing figure in his hussar uniform and was a very able cavalry tactician, who understood that a cavalry charge was more complex than simply going out on a hunter, something few British cavalry officers seemed to comprehend.

As such, Paget was an ideal candidate to command the cavalry in Portugal for Arthur, but circumstances made such a situation impossible. Having returned from the Corunna campaign, Paget ran off with Charlotte, the wife of Henry Wellesley. Charlotte's brother even fought a duel with Paget in May 1809, although it was settled without either being wounded, honour being satisfied. Henry took Paget to court for 'Criminal Conversation' the following year and he was awarded £24,000 (around £1.2 million today) in damages. No sooner had the divorce proceeding concluded, than Henry Paget married Charlotte in 1810. They had six children together, the first Emily, being born in March 1810 proving that their relationship had been consummated by June 1809.

Following this scandal, Henry went out to Spain as British envoy and it was impossible to put Paget on Arthur's staff, so he was destined to see out the war in Spain in England. However, when the campaign of 1815 began, Henry Paget, now the Earl of Uxbridge, was sent out to command the cavalry under Arthur. There is no evidence that Arthur made any representation to have the appointment cancelled, although the fact that the Prince Regent had insisted on his appointment instead of Viscount Combermere, who had commanded the cavalry to Arthur's great satisfaction in the Peninsula, may account for that.

He however reputedly made short work of someone who mentioned the threat of renewed

Paget circa 1809.

The Marquess of Anglesey.

scandal. When asked why, they replied 'Your Grace cannot have forgotten the affair with Lady Charlotte?' to which Arthur replied 'Oh no! I have not forgotten that'. They continued

'That is not the only case, I am afraid. At any rate Lord Uxbridge has the reputation of running away with everybody he can.' To which Arthur replied without any hint of emotion:

'I'll take good care he don't run away with me: I don't care about anybody else.'

Claims that Arthur and Uxbridge later conversed during the battle when the latter was wounded in the knee, with 'By God, Sir, I've lost my leg' do not bear investigation, as the fact he would need to have his leg amputated was not determined upon by the surgeons until many hours afterwards.

Although their relationship was probably never warm, Arthur did not bear grudges and during his term of office as Prime Minister, he readily employed the Marquess of Anglesey (Uxbridge had superseded his father in 1815 shortly after the battle) as Lord Lieutenant of Ireland and he was always welcome at the Duke's annual dinner on 18 June at Apsley House.

70: Russian Miniature Commemorating the Victors of the Wars against Napoleon, the Russian Kutuzov, Wellington and Blücher

Arthur rose early and checked the positions of his troops and ensured that the three farm complexes in front of his main line were manned and well prepared for defence. For Arthur this was a defensive battle, having a smaller army of dubious character to Napoleon's, simply holding on to his position until his Prussian allies arrived to dramatically alter the odds in his favour. However, he had never faced Napoleon in battle before and was well aware of his reputation for manoeuvre, and therefore placed a large force well to the right of the battlefield, to prevent any threat of an outflanking movement. He had anticipated that the Prussians would march at dawn and would be with him by late morning at the latest, it was to be a lot longer before they actually did arrive. He placed his artillery on the crest of the ridge and sent out skirmishers, but kept the rest of his troops behind the ridge where they were invisible to the French artillery and hid his reserves.

For Napoleon, the sun rose on a day of great hope. Blücher's army had already been destroyed and if he could defeat Wellington comprehensively, he would have knocked two armies out of the war and recaptured Belgium. The odds of coming to an agreement with the Austrian Emperor, his father in law, would have risen dramatically and Russia alone could be brought to heel: the impossible was nearly in his grasp.

Napoleon's troops breakfasted and it was nearly midday before all of his troops were in position to begin the battle, but Wellington still stood on his ridge. Having launched a major

Wellington's Waterloo telescope.

Wellington was often in the thick of the action.

assault on Hougoumont in a bid to re-enact the French victory on the very same battlefield in 1794 and to force Wellington to deploy his reserves, he softened up the Allied forces with an intense artillery barrage all along his line, although his gunners could not see their targets.

Napoleon launched his main attack with d'Erlon's entire corps of nearly 20,000 men against Wellington's left wing which was outnumbered two to one. Despite suffering heavy losses from Allied artillery as the huge columns of troops marched across the battlefield, they successfully reached the ridge and began to drive back the Allied infantry as they looked to march to Mont St Jean village, thereby cutting Wellington's army in two. At this critical moment, Uxbridge, commanding the Allied cavalry, ordered in two brigades of British heavy cavalry, who smashed through the French columns, causing horrendous casualties and capturing two eagles. The columns broke and ran and over 3,000 prisoners were captured, but the cavalry rode on towards the French guns and were caught by French lancers in their turn and no more than half returned to their own lines.

In the afternoon Napoleon launched huge attacks by French cavalry on the Allied centre. The Allied infantry formed squares and the French cavalry exhausted themselves whilst failing to destroy any of the squares. Wellington was everywhere, always at the point of greatest pressure, encouraging the troops by his presence and sparingly calling up his reserves as needed. Many soldiers comment on his charmed life that day, when so many around him were struck, but Arthur was seemingly oblivious to the danger, so focussed was he on the task in hand.

It was around 4:30pm when Napoleon's troops were attacked by Blücher's Prussians at

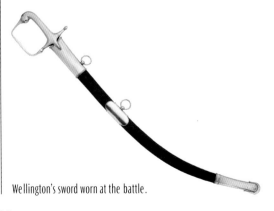

Wellington's sword worn at the battle.

Wellington and Blücher meet after the battle.

Wellington's defences, just as they had done at Ligny two days previously. This time however, Wellington had hurriedly collected his last reserves and when Napoleon's Guard was sent forward piecemeal in three uncoordinated attacks, they were beaten. As the words '*La Garde Recule*' rang out, the morale of his army collapsed and they began to retreat. Wellington, spotting the opportunity, raised his hat as a signal for the army to pour forward and complete the victory. Some around him cautioned him against such a movement, to which Arthur reputedly replied 'Oh, damn it! In for a penny, in for a pound.' During this confused advance others again feared that Wellington was endangering his life too much, but he is said to have replied 'Never mind, let them fire away. The battle's won; my life is of no consequence now.'

Wellington and Blücher met (probably at Maison du Roi not La Belle Alliance) and congratulated each other on a stunning victory. The Prussians took over the pursuit and Wellington rode back to his headquarters in Waterloo village for something to eat and to get some rest. He lay down without even washing. During the night, his surgeon, Dr Hume woke him to recite a long list of casualties, many good friends of Arthur. In total, some 25,000 of all nations had been killed and 65,000 wounded over the four-day campaign. Hume felt tears on his hand and looking up he could see them coursing down Arthur's grimy cheeks: Wiping them away, Arthur said:

the village of Plancenoit in the right rear of the Army and Napoleon was forced to deploy much of his reserve to prevent them breaking through into his rear. He was now fighting two battles simultaneously and was outnumbered, exactly what he had spent the last four days trying to avoid. He now had a choice of retiring from the field to fight another day or attempting to gain a victory from the jaws of defeat by deploying his last reserves, his Old Guard.

Napoleon chose to send his Old Guard forward, believing that one final push would break

'Well, thank God, I don't know what it is to lose a battle; but certainly nothing can be more painful than to gain one with the loss of so many of one's friends.'

He hoped it was his last battle, he got his wish.

There was little further fighting before the Allies captured Paris and Napoleon was exiled once again, this time to St. Helena, where he died of stomach cancer six years later.

Few battles can really claim to change the course of history as dramatically as Waterloo did and Wellington's renown, already great, became stellar after this victory.

71: The Grave of General Miguel de Alava at Vitoria

In January 1810, General Miguel de Alava y Esquival was appointed by the Spanish Cortes to attend Wellington's headquarters in Portugal as a military attache and their mutual respect rapidly turned into a firm friendship which continued throughout the rest of their lives.

Born into nobility in Vitoria in 1770, Alava was only just younger than Arthur and aged 13 he became a cadet in the 11th Seville Regiment, rising to the rank of second lieutenant in 1787. He then served with the Spanish Navy from 1790, becoming a frigate lieutenant in 1794 and was then in South America until 1800 when he was captured by the British but soon released. He was later present onboard Admiral Gravina's *Principe*

de Asturias at the Battle of Trafalgar. His uncle was captain of the *Santa Anna* and was severely wounded in the battle and his ship captured. Miguel rose to the rank of frigate captain and he initially accepted the constitution of Joseph Bonaparte as King of Spain, having escorted him into Madrid and retired from the navy.

Following the Spanish uprising and the defeat of Dupont's French army at Bailen in 1808, he switched allegiance and transferred to the army, to take part in the war of liberation against France, seeing combat at the battles of Calatayud, Tudela and Medellin. Having joined Wellington's headquarters he was present at the sieges of Ciudad Rodrigo and Badajoz, as well as the battles of Talavera, Busaco, Salamanca,

General Alava at the Battle of Vitoria.

Vitoria and Orthez. Alava was made a general in 1812.

His wound in the backside at Orthez has been previously mentioned, but he had reason not to find his wounds as hilarious as Arthur did on that occasion.

In a letter written by Staff Surgeon John Hulme in April 1813 he refers to a wound which Alava had sustained the previous year and his recovery:

'Alava had a very odd wound in the root of his [penis] which threatened no very pleasant consequences. In short I had some apprehensions that as he married by proxy and had never slept with his wife, he might possibly be obliged to consumate by proxy also … I recommended him to try the hot baths at Guimaraes and I am happy to say that he has reaped every advantage that could be hoped for, being in all respects *ad munerum veneris aptus* [Being in all respects capable of functioning for sexual pleasure] & having practised at Oporto with great success.'

When King Ferdinand was restored to the throne, Alava was thrown into prison, but by the influence of Arthur he was soon released and gained the favour of the king, who appointed him Ambassador to the Hague in 1815 as a favour to Wellington, meaning that he was alongside Arthur again for the Waterloo campaign. He became Ambassador in Paris until retiring on health grounds to Spain in 1819.

Miguel became a politician in 1820 and fought to maintain the authority of the Cortes against the rebels in 1823. Alava was deputised to negotiate with the French invading army commanded by the Duc d'Angouleme but he failed and was condemned to death. Alava was forced to flee to Britain via Gibraltar.

Arriving in Britain virtually penniless, he sought out the Duke of Wellington. Arthur welcomed him with open arms, provided him with a house on the Stratfield Saye estate and set up a bank account for him at Coutts Bank stating 'This is my friend, and as long as I have any money with your house, let him have it to any amount he thinks proper to draw for.'

Miguel returned to Spain on the death of King Ferdinand in 1833 and he was appointed Ambassador to London in 1834. He was then proposed as Prime Minister of Spain in 1835 but declined but became Minister of the Navy and refused to sign the new constitution of 1837. He remained in London until a month before his death, he returned to Spain and when he died, he was buried in his home town of Vitoria.

General Miguel de Alava.

72: The Gravestone of Copenhagen at Stratfield Saye

A number of myths surround the horse Copenhagen which Arthur so famously rode throughout the day of the Battle of Waterloo. He was not brought back as a prize from the campaign in Denmark in 1807, indeed Wellington did not own the horse until late 1812.

In fact, Copenhagen was sired in 1808 by Meteor who was a runner-up in the Derby, on Lady Catherine, a half-breed sired by the 1792 Derby winner John Bull. On his birth in England at the stables of General Thomas Grosvenor, he was named after the recent victory at Copenhagen, where the general had served. General Grosvenor may have taken Lady Catherine with him to Copenhagen but that is far from certain and there is no evidence that she foaled there. Because of Copenhagen's ultimate fame, Lady Catherine is the only half-breed listed in the famous *General Stud Book*.

Copenhagen stood fifteen hands high and had a compact, muscular frame. He was later described as being 'a dark chestnut with two white heels, a hollow-backed, powerful horse'. He also apparently had a unique habit of eating whilst lying down.

He was raced until he was four years old, winning two races, but was retired in May 1812, probably indicating that he was not good enough as a racehorse. He was then sold shortly after to Sir Charles Vane, who was ordered out to rejoin Wellington's headquarters as Adjutant General in 1813. Copenhagen was sent out with a number of other horses in advance of sailing himself. However, Vane's appointment was altered to join the Allied headquarters in Germany and he sent instruction for his horses already in Spain to be

sold rather than face the difficulties and expense of transporting them to Germany.

Copenhagen was then bought by either Colonel Wood or Colonel Gordon (sources differ) for Wellington, the price varying anywhere from £200 to £400 depending on the sources. Arthur rode him in Spain and Southern France along with the rest of his stud.

It was at Waterloo that Copenhagen rose to fame, as the horse that the Duke of Wellington rode throughout the Battle of Waterloo and possibly on the two days prior to the battle. Arthur invariably maintained a stable of eight chargers on campaign so it says a lot that he was the only horse he used that day. On the day of Waterloo, Wellington was in the saddle continuously for some seventeen hours. Wellington, despite all

cut from
"Copenhagen"
on March 13. 1830 by
Samuel Wise, usher
of the hall to the Duke
of Wellington and
presented by his
daughter to Rev.
J.S. Malarin

A lock of hair cut from Copenhagen in 1830.

of the dangers of that day, survived unscathed, and just as miraculously so did Copenhagen. However, that night, on his return to the inn at Waterloo, when Wellington dismounted he gave Copenhagen an appreciative pat on the rump, which he took great exception to, kicking out wildly and just missing the Duke! Arthur later complimented his faithful horse, saying that:

'There may have been many faster horses, no doubt many handsomer, but for bottom and endurance I never saw his fellow.'

He remained as his primary horse throughout the occupation of France until 1818.

Arthur continued to use him for a number of years for ceremonial occasions, even riding him to No.10 Downing Street in 1828 when he became Prime Minister, but finally when too old, he was retired to Stratfield Saye where he lived out a long retirement before finally dying on 12 February 1836 aged 28 years. The horse was buried with military honours the following morning, Arthur was there to witness it and apparently 'flew into a most violent passion' when he noticed that one of his hooves had been cut off.

There are a couple of stories regarding the hoof, one saying a farmer bought it for 3 shillings and then returned it, but the most likely is that a servant removed it but thought better about returning it when he heard of the Duke's fury. It was eventually handed over and the 2nd Duke had it made into an ink stand.

No headstone was erected and when the United Services Museum requested to exhume the skeleton to put it on show next to Napoleon's Marengo, the Duke claimed that he had no idea where he was buried. The oak that now marks his grave was not planted until 1843 and was

A print of Copenhagen.

actually planted by the housekeeper to mark her twenty years' service. The 2nd Duke wrote an epitaph after Arthur had died and had a lead plaque and some coins buried at the gravesite and the headstone put up with the same epitaph

It is a good thing that Copenhagen was not exhumed to go on display alongside Marengo as recent research appears to prove that Marengo is a fake.

Here Lies
COPENHAGEN
The Charger ridden by
THE DUKE OF WELLINGTON
The entire day at the
BATTLE OF WATERLOO.
Born 1808. Died 1836.
God's humbler instrument though meaner clay
Should share the glory of that glorious day

73: Pieces of the Prussian Service given to the Duke of Wellington

Following the stunning victory of Waterloo, both Wellington and Blücher were feted everywhere, but when the elderly German returned to Prussia exhausted after a few months, he retired into obscurity and died in 1819, so therefore most of the rewards went to Arthur.

He was granted the hereditary title of nobility in both Holland and Belgium (after their separation in 1831) as Prince of Waterloo, which only continues down the male line. Wellington was also granted 10.5 kilometres of land and a yearly grant of 20,000 guilders (the Dutch guilder being recognised as worth 0.45 of a Euro for historical contracts) which equals E9,090. The rights to the estates are owned to this day by the Duke of Wellington, despite occasional attempts by modern members of the Belgian government to rescind it. It is estimated that these lands produce over £100,000 per annum from rents.

Arthur was given command of the multinational Army of Occupation that was initially meant to garrison part of France, to give time for King Louis and his ministers to re-establish the monarchy, to stabilise the country and to ensure that the huge indemnity to the Allies was actually paid. The Treaty of Paris was signed on 20 November 1815 and it soon emerged that it was much harsher on France than that previously agreed in 1814. France was reduced to the borders it had in 1790 and the Allies now demanded reparations totalling 700 million francs (then about £32.2 million or £1.5 billion today),

The crest of the Prince of Waterloo.

payable within five years. Until settled in full, an Army of Occupation numbering 150,000 Allied soldiers would garrison twenty-six of the northern and eastern border fortresses and were to be fed entirely at French expense. The Army consisted of 30,000 men each from Austria, Britain, Russia and Prussia and the other consisting of 10,000 from Bavaria, and 5,000 each from Denmark, Saxony, Hanover and Württemberg.

The French government seriously struggled to pay the indemnity and their Prime Minister, Richelieu, sought the help of Wellington to ease the burden. In 1817 it was agreed to reduce the force occupying France to 120,000 and in 1818 Arthur helped arrange a large loan from Barings Bank to pay off the reparations and it was agreed that the Army of Occupation would leave by mid-November 1818.

Following the end of the Army of Occupation, Arthur was also presented with a number of huge sets of dinner ware from the various states, which are still on display in Apsley House. The Egyptian Service (depicting Ancient Egyptian sites) was originally ordered by Napoleon Bonaparte for Josephine as a mark of her divorce

and unsurprisingly she rejected it in 1812. In 1818 King Louis XVIII presented the service to Wellington on behalf of France. The Prussian Service (depicting Wellington's military career) was made in Berlin in 1818–19 and was presented to Arthur by King Frederick William III. The Saxon Service made at the Meissen factory in 1819 (depicting battles of the Napoleonic Wars) was presented by King Frederick Augustus IV. Finally, the Austrian Service (depicting busts of Ancient Greeks) was produced at Vienna and presented by Emperor Francis II.

One other tribute to Arthur and his victories greatly amused him. This was the huge statue of Achilles erected at Hyde Park Corner by 'the ladies of England' costing £10,000 (£600,000 today) and made reputedly from 36 tons of metal from guns captured at the battles of Salamanca, Vitoria, Toulouse and Waterloo. The giant figure of Achilles was portrayed as a very muscular, nude young man, holding a sword and shield and was the first nude statue erected in London on public display. The figure was not originally supplied with a fig leaf, but his genitalia being on show greatly shocked the gentlefolk of London and a fig leaf was hastily fashioned, but the artist left his rear fully exposed, all to the Duke's great amusement.

Wellington riding past the statue of Achilles.

74: A French Cavalry
Officer's An IX Pistol

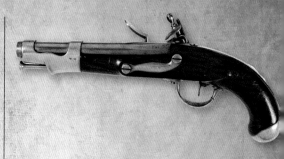

Whilst Wellington remained in Paris, he was always in some form of danger from vengeful Bonapartists. In 1816 an attempt to cause a major fire in a property where he was attending a ball was luckily detected before it took serious hold. However, the nearest he came to being assassinated was on 11 February 1818, when a retired officer named Marie André Cantillon, fired his pistol at the Duke as he arrived home in his coach late at night. He had been aided by a Monsieur Marinet, and they were both tried in 1819 but eventually acquitted, because the pistol ball was not found and the jurors therefore accepted that he may have fired a blank cartridge. The detail regarding the case is best explained in a letter written by Lieutenant Colonel Lord FitzRoy Somerset to Wellesley-Pole dated Thursday, 12 February 1818

'My Dear Mr. Pole,

You have so often expressed apprehensions for the Duke's safety, that you will be more shocked, than surprised to learn, that he was shot at, the night before last, just as his carriage was entering the Porte Cochere of his house. Fortunately, the shot missed entirely; but however one may exult at his escape on this occasion, the fact that it is intended to take away his life is so clear, that one cannot but dread that another attempt may be more effectual.

It appears by the evidence of the coachman and footman, that as the carriage passed by the Hotel d'Abrantes, which you may recollect is at the entrance of the Rue des Champs Elysees, they observed a man standing opposite to it, who, on the approach of the carriage moved on and kept pace with it till he reached the nearest sentry box at the Duke's door, when he stopped and as the carriage was in the act of turning into the gateway the villain fired his pistol. Upon hearing the shot, the horses rather quickened their pace, which the coachman had checked to go more easily over the gutter, and the Duke arrived without accident at the house, totally unaware that he had been fired at, till the footman opened the door and said 'J'espere, Monseigneur, que votre Excellence n'est pas blesse'. [I hope, my Lord, that your excellency is not injured]. He had conceived that one of the sentries' muskets had gone off by accident. Upon ascertaining how the fact stood, the Duke ordered the assassin to be pursued, but as no steps had been taken till he gave the directions to that effect, the scoundrel of course made good his retreat. If however, the sentries had been as indeed they ought to have been outside the Porte Cochere, instead of being in it, or if the footman (a Frenchman) had had his wits about him, and upon seeing the man fire, had immediately jumped down and run after him, or had even cried out he must have been taken; for two of the Duke's English servants were at the moment coming down the street, and heard the report of the pistol, and whilst they were debating upon what was the cause of the shot at such an hour (it was after midnight) they met the man running: and as one of them had said that the shot might have been fired at the Duke's carriage they had a great mind to stop him, but hearing no alarm they thought it most prudent to let him go by without molestation.

Shortly after, some of the guard detached from the Duke's came up to them and asked them if they had seen anybody, to which they replied in the affirmative, and immediately joined with the soldiers in the pursuit. One of the servants ran so fast, that he thinks he saw the same man go into a house in the Rue de la Madeleine, and stay at the door till he came up, when it was slammed in his face. This house was afterwards examined some hours after, I believe, and it appears that the only lodger is a laquais-de-place now in the service of an Englishman. The soldiers and servants continued their researches but ineffectually. The whole of yesterday was occupied by the police in the examination of everybody who could throw any light upon the affair …

Measures are taken to guard the Duke's house and to watch the streets immediately leading to it, and he will have an aide-de-camp always in the house, and he will have a person armed though not in uniform with his carriage. He has promised also never to go about alone and will not make use of his own carriage which is so well known.

Should I hear anything further before the messenger is dispatched I will communicate to you.

Yours most affectionately, FitzRoy Somerset.

P.S.—Since writing the above, ... I have heard nothing further, except that an officer of the Lancers de la Garde was close to the carriage at the time, whose first impulse was to rush upon the villain, but upon second thoughts he judged it best not to attempt to seize him lest he should fail and being seen to run should be suspected of being the assassin. He therefore contented himself with enquiring if the Duke was hurt.'

Having been acquitted Cantillon soon sank into oblivion, but Napoleon brought him to the heights of fame once again by naming him in his will, which became public after his death in 1821. In it he wrote:

We bequeath 10,000 francs to the subaltern officer, Cantillon, who has undergone a trial upon the charge of having endeavoured to assassinate Lord Wellington, of which he was pronounced innocent. Cantillon had as much right to assassinate that oligarchist, as the latter had to send me to perish on the rock of St. Helena. Wellington, who proposed this outrage, attempted to justify himself by pleading the interest of Great Britain. Cantillon, if he really had assassinated that lord, would have excused himself, and have been justified by the same motives—the interest of France—to get rid of a general who had, moreover, violated the capitulation of Paris, and by that had rendered himself responsible for the blood of the martyrs, Ney, la Bedoyere, &c, and for the crime of having pillaged the museums, contrary to the text of the treaties.

Napoleon was severely criticised for this mean-spirited declaration in his will which appears to justify assassination. There is, however, some doubt as to whether the bequest was ever actually paid in full, some claiming that he received a payment in 1823 whilst it is widely believed that Napoleon III paid it in part or in full when he took the throne.

Arthur's view of the whole episode was that it showed Napoleon was 'small minded' and it further proved that he wasn't a gentleman.

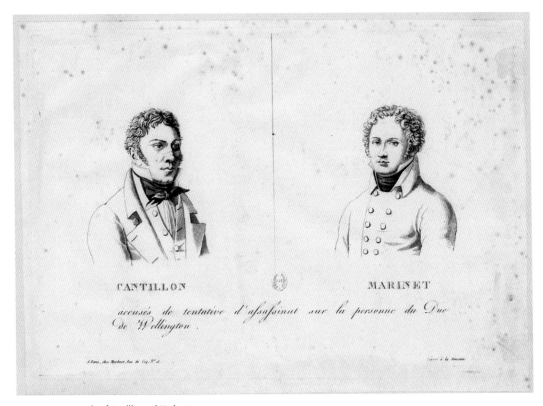

Contemporary portraits of Cantillon and Marinet.

75: Statue of Napoleon as
Mars the Peacemaker by Canova

Arthur Wellesley and Napoleon Bonaparte were both born in 1769, but in truth their upbringing and their careers and life experiences made them into very different characters, very often the complete opposite of the other. Arthur's first and guiding principle was 'service' to his monarch and his country, Napoleon's was 'ambition' and using all means to achieve it.

Napoleon had directed the artist Canova to come to Paris in 1802 to model a bust of him which he could then work up into a full sculpture. It was completed in 1806 and transported to the Musée Napoleon (as the Louvre Museum was temporarily renamed) but when Napoleon saw it there in 1811, he did not like it, saying it was too athletic, and banning it from being put on public display. In 1814 it was under a canvas cover in the museum and when the artworks were returned to their original owners (something Canova supported) the statue was sold to the British government for 66,000 francs (about £175,000 today) and the Prince Regent presented it to Arthur later that year, it is not known what the Duke thought of it. It was put into the stairwell of Apsley House in 1817 when Arthur bought it from his brother Richard. A bronze replica of the statue stands in the Palazzo Brera in Milan.

Wellington was not a great admirer of Napoleon, but he did admit his morale effect on his troops on the battlefield. His much repeated phrase was that: 'I used to say of him [Napoleon] that his presence on the field made the difference of forty thousand men'. However, in later life he felt that he needed to qualify this statement, as he felt that it was being misrepresented.

'It is very true that I have said that I considered Napoleon's presence in the field equal to forty thousand men in the balance. This is a very loose way of talking; but the idea is a very different one from that of his presence at a battle being equal to a reinforcement of forty thousand men.'

More than anything, Arthur was scathing of Napoleon's raw ambition and his lack of morals as to how he achieved his aims writing scathingly that:

'Buonaparte's whole life, civil, political, and military, was a fraud. There was not a transaction, great or small, in which lying and fraud were not introduced … Of flagrant lies, the most important in the military branch of his life that I can now recollect are – first, the

expedition from Egypt into Syria, which totally failed, and yet on his return to Egypt was represented to the army there as a victory … The next was the battle of Eylau. This he represented as a great victory. It is true that the Allied army retired after the battle. So did Buonaparte…. I should think that Spain would afford you instances of fraud in his political schemes and negotiations…. Buonaparte's foreign policy was force and menace, aided by fraud and corruption. If the fraud was discovered, force and menace succeeded; and in most cases the unfortunate victim did not dare to avow that he perceived the fraud.'

On a professional level, the two only ever faced each other at Waterloo. During this campaign Wellington had shown a great deal of respect for Napoleon, admitting that with such a dangerous opponent, he feared making a mistake more than doing nothing. He clearly was surprised by Napoleon's early attack from a direction which Arthur had not expected, but he was less complimentary of Napoleon's performance later in the campaign. Having fully expected Napoleon to manoeuvre his troops with speed and precision and expecting a flanking movement, Wellington was undoubtedly surprised, and disappointed, that Napoleon simply chose a battle of attrition with little finesse, which Arthur could deal with relatively easily, his army simply needing 'bottom' as he put it, to stand and hold their ground until Blücher arrived as planned. His final words on Napoleon, reputedly said at the end of the battle, do reflect his obvious professional disappointment at his lack of finesse, 'so he is a mere bludgeoner after all'.

As to what Napoleon thought of Wellington, there is again limited evidence. It is clear that Napoleon had ridiculed his senior officers who had cautioned the emperor from attacking Wellington in a prepared position, recommending him to manoeuvre him out of his position. Having been beaten at Waterloo Napoleon rarely spoke on the subject, but when he did he spoke disparagingly of Wellington, stating that:

'[I]t is very certain that I gave [Wellington] a terrible quarter of an hour [at Waterloo]. This usually constitutes a claim on noble minds; his was incapable of feeling it. My fall, and the lot that might have been reserved for me, afforded him the opportunity of reaping higher glory than he has gained by all his victories. But he did not understand this. Well, at any rate, he ought to be heartily grateful to old Blücher; had it not been for him, I know not where his Grace might have been today; but I know that I, at least, should not have been at St. Helena. Wellington's troops were admirable, but his plans were despicable; or should I rather say, that he formed none at all. He had placed himself in a situation in which it was impossible he could form any; and by a curious chance, this very circumstance saved him. If he could have commenced a retreat, he must infallibly have been lost. He certainly remained master of the field of battle; but was his success the result of his skill? He has reaped the fruit of a brilliant victory; but did his genius prepare it for him? His glory is wholly negative. His faults were enormous. He, the European Generalissimo, to whose hands so many interests were entrusted, and having before him an enemy so prompt and daring as myself, left his forces dispersed and slumbered in a capital until he was surprised. And yet such is the power of fatality!'

Napoleon failed to see that by berating his enemy, he therefore lowered his own standing, claiming that Wellington had only won because of luck. Such a lowly regard for his enemy may well have been a factor in his defeat, but he was oblivious to that and remained bitter towards his vanquisher throughout his life. Virtually all of Europe was shocked and saddened by Napoleon's grant of money to Cantillon who was charged with the attempted assassination of Wellington.

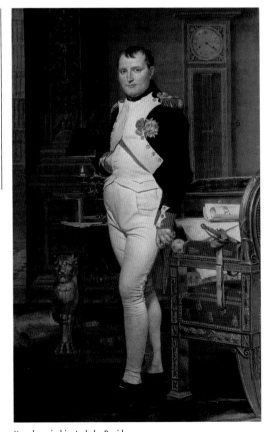

Napoleon in his study by David.

76: Apsley House, London

Arthur required a London base, whilst carrying out his duties in Parliament as well as his purchase of Stratfield Saye and as his brother Richard was in financial difficulties following his separation from his wife, he offered to purchase his London house to ease his burdens. Previously the site of a public house called the Hercules Pillars, a red-brick house designed by Robert Adam was completed on the site in 1778 for Lord Apsley, then the Lord Chancellor and has retained his name ever since. The site of the house, very close to Hyde Park and the toll gate for London, meant that it stood on the very edge of the city and hence earned for itself the address of No. 1 London, which is still a valid postal address, although officially it is now No. 149 Piccadilly. Richard had bought the house in 1807 for £16,000 (£750,000 today) and sold it to his brother for a handsome £42,000 (£2.5 million). Arthur was usually a hard-nosed negotiator and it seems likely that he happily paid over the odds to help his brother, in repayment for Richard's generosity during his early years in the army.

Arthur employed Benjamin Wyatt, just as he was to do later at Stratfield Saye to make renovations. In 1819 he added a three-storey extension on the north east side of the house, providing additional bedrooms and a state dining room. Later in 1828 Wellington undertook a much more ambitious refurbishment, which included a new staircase, the Waterloo Gallery and the entire red-brick façade was clad in yellow Bath stone. The bill for this second phase

Apsley House in 1807.

was originally estimated to be £23,000 (£1.6 million today) but ended costing over £61,000 (£4.3 million). Arthur was Prime Minister when this second phase was undertaken and he resided for eighteen months at No. 10 Downing Street, but as soon as the work was completed, he returned there. When presented with the final bill, he is reported to have raged about having been 'cheated' and that it would ruin his family, even threatening to sell the house, but he was eventually calmed down by his friend Mrs Arbuthnot.

Across the road from the property a great arch was designed as part of the renovations of Hyde Park, Green Park and St James's Park which were begun in 1825. This arch (originally known as the Green Park Arch) and Marble Arch, which was originally built standing in front of Buckingham Palace (where the statue of Queen Victoria now stands) were both designed as grand triumphal entrances to the palace and the architect

The original Wellington Arch.

The modern Wellington Monument.

The Wellington Statue now at Aldershot.

Decimus Burton was chosen to undertake the work. Burton originally envisaged a smaller triumphal arch modelled on the Arch of Titus in Rome, with highly decorative panels adorning it and topped with a four-horse chariot. The design was rejected and a larger, plainer arch was built in its place and topped a number of years later by a 40-tonne bronze equestrian statue of the Duke of Wellington on Copenhagen. The figure alone stands over 8.5 metres high and is said to be the largest equestrian bronze ever made. Indeed the statue was much too large for the arch and looked terribly ungainly. Efforts led by the Prime Minister Sir Robert Peel to have the statue placed elsewhere failed and it was placed on the arch in 1846. Arthur's thoughts on the oversized statue directly across from his house are unfortunately not recorded, although I think that he would have found it vulgar.

By 1882, traffic congestion at Hyde Park Corner had become so bad that it was decided to move the arch and a campaign to remove the Duke's statue at the same time was also successful, a chariot and four horses similar to the original concept replacing it on its new site. It has, however, retained its name as Wellington Arch. The arch is hollow and can be climbed to gain a good view of London and it housed the smallest police station in London until it closed in 1992. A smaller equestrian statue of Wellington, protected at each corner by soldiers in uniforms as worn at Waterloo, now stands opposite Apsley House.

After the giant statue had been removed, it was originally placed in Green Park whilst a decision was made on where it was finally to go. It was eventually decided to put it at Aldershot, the home of the British Army, and was transported there in August 1884, having been cut into pieces. It was reassembled on site, rededicated in 1885 and has recently undergone major restoration.

77: Ivory Coach Pass of
William Wellesley-Pole

William, the second son of Garret Wesley, is the forgotten brother, and is often viewed as a non-entity, an embarrassment and the black sheep of the family, but this is to do him a great disservice, as he was just as instrumental in forging the Wellesley dynasty.

Educated like all of the boys at Eton, William initially entered the Royal Navy as a midshipman in 1777 and served for some six years, actually seeing action aboard HMS *Lion* at the Battle of Grenada in 1779, where a British fleet commanded by Admiral John Byron (the grandfather of Lord Byron) was defeated by a superior French fleet which was attempting to relieve Grenada.

Following the death of his father, the family was in financial difficulties, but luck would have it that William was offered the estate of his childless Godfather, William Pole, if he took the family name and so in 1781 he became William Wesley-Pole. Wesley-Pole married Katherine Forbes, daughter of Admiral Forbes in 1784 and they had one son and three daughters together. Later, like the rest of the family, he altered his name to Wellesley-Pole.

William now turned to politics and initially sat in the Irish House of Commons for the family seat of Trim, but transferred to the British House of Commons in 1790 when he gained the seat of East Looe until 1795 and then following the Act of Union, for Queen's County (now County Laois) from 1801 until 1821. This gave him access to well-paid government positions and he was Secretary of the Admiralty for two years from 1807, then Chief Secretary for Ireland until 1812 and most significantly he was to become Master of the Mint in 1814, a post he held until 1823. That year he became *Custos Rotulorum* (effectively a precursor of Lord Lieutenant) for life for Queen's County and the Master of the

William as a 14-year-old by Benjamin West.

The 'Bull Head' coin of George III issued in 1817 by William.

The Pistrucci Medal.

Hounds to King George IV. In 1809 William had become a member of both the British and Irish Privy Councils and in 1821 he was elevated to the peerage as Baron Maryborough in Queen's County. He became Postmaster General in 1834 although his appointment only lasted one year and in 1838 he received the honorary post of Captain of Deal Castle.

His greatest achievements were undoubtedly when he served as Master of the Mint. When he took up the post, he was horrified to discover that the Mint held no proofs of previous coinage, so with the aid of Sir Joseph Banks, who donated his remarkable collection of coins, he set up the Royal Mint Museum and William ensured that a full set of every new coin and medal produced by the Mint was preserved in the collection. At the same time, William was tasked with the design, manufacture and distribution of a completely new set of coinage, including the recovery of all the old coins throughout the entire country, a massive undertaking. The manufacturing operation was completed in total secrecy and the coinage distributed throughout the British Isles without alerting the general public, until

the entire process was ready to go country wide on 'Great Re-coinage Day'. Once launched, the public was given only two weeks to exchange their coinage before theirs became worthless and then the huge numbers of redundant coins had to be returned to the Mint for re-smelting. Indeed Sir Joseph Banks declared William's plan as 'excellently arranged …I have seen a multitude of public men, but no one whose conduct has been as energetic and so perfectly successful'. By 17 January 1817 no less than 57 million coins had been produced and were ready for distribution. The public were informed of

William by Thomas Lawrence.

the new coinage on the same day and told that the exchange would begin on 3 February. The Cabinet deferred the date until 13 February but all of the new coinage had been issued by 1 March when the old coinage ceased to be legal tender. The entire operation was a complete success and went through without a single hitch, indeed the lack of drama associated with the whole event is probably why the operations is now largely forgotten as is William.

William was also in charge of the issue of the first British campaign medal issued to all ranks, when a one-ounce silver medal was issued in 1816 to everyone who had served at his brother's great victory at Waterloo.

He also brought the Italian sculptor, Benedetto Pistrucci, to the Mint and the government commissioned the artist to produce a medal which would be presented to the crowned heads of Europe who had participated in the overthrow of Napoleon. The design was not completed until 1844 and the medals were not struck until 1849, when the only actual major participant in the wars still alive was Arthur Duke of Wellington.

When his brother Richard died without an heir in 1842, William was to inherit the title of 3rd Earl of Mornington, but he did not enjoy it for long, dying himself on 22 February 1845.

William lived with his family at No. 3 Saville Row and Arthur stayed here with them on his return from the Peninsula in 1814. The house was later bought by the Beatles and it became the headquarters of Apple Records, the Beatles once famously performed live on its roof.

William is sometimes confused with his son and heir, William Pole-Tylney-Long-Wellesley, often referred to as 'Wicked William', who married the richest heiress in England and became renowned as a profligate, womanising (hence his other nickname 'Long Pole' Wellesley) gambler, who dissipated the entire fortune.

78: Stratfield Saye from the Garden

The vast sums of money granted by Parliament for Arthur to procure a ducal home to rival the Duke of Marlborough's Blenheim Palace were not a major priority for him. He tasked Benjamin Wyatt, who had been his clerk in Ireland and India but came from a family of architects, with finding him a house, but it proved more difficult than had been imagined and no property had been identified by the end of 1814. Arthur's demands were relatively straightforward: it had to be within reach of London and possess extensive grounds ideal for hunting with no turnpike roads to get in the way. Wyatt struggled to find an imposing edifice and Arthur suggested knocking down an old pile and building one from scratch.

Wyatt eventually identified Stratfield Saye in Hampshire, the property of Lord Rivers, as 'the estate possesses great beauty & dignity; & is capable of being made a princely place' and was close enough to London. It took until 1817, however, for Wyatt to persuade Wellington to view the property and with his usual decisiveness, by the end of the year the house was his, a present from the nation, for £263,000 (approximately £16 million today), less than half the sum he had been voted by Parliament, which probably prompted him to also purchase Ewhurst a number of years later.

The main part of the house was built by William Pitt in 1630, but little more was done to it until Lord Rivers inherited it in 1745, who had made a few questionable improvements to the house, but certainly beautified the grounds beyond all measure. His brother inherited it on his death, but he had no wish to keep it and was happy to sell it as a 'job lot' when Wyatt persuaded Arthur to purchase it, including

Two of the potential designs for the Grand Palace at Stratfield Saye.

fittings and furniture. Arthur therefore had little to do to the house and had even less compunction to spend any money on it because of the plans to demolish it and build a Grand Palace in its place.

Designs were sought for the Grand Palace, to be named Waterloo Palace, but thankfully they never came to fruition, as the designs were too heavy and monolithic for such a beautiful landscape. The plans proved too expensive and were abandoned in 1821.

Kitty fell in love with Stratfield Saye and delighted in its simplicity and lack of grandeur and she spent much of her time there, even though when the couple were both in residence they inhabited opposite wings of the building, requiring servants to carry messages 200 metres between each other. This is almost certainly another reason why Arthur did little to the house until after Kitty's death. Visitors were not generally impressed, one who seems to have been affected by the cold atmosphere recording that

'The house is not very comfortable, the park ugly, the living mediocre, the whole indeed indicating the lack of sympathy existing between the Duke and his Duchess.'

Stratfield Saye front aspect.

Entrance hall of Stratfield Saye.

Arthur had the house extended later, by adding the outer wings, although built to the same design to match the original house, and added a portico and a large conservatory. He also added central heating radiators and water closets, with soundproofing, in almost all of the bedrooms.

Queen Victoria and her entire entourage visited Stratfield Saye in 1845, and described it as 'very comfortable' and was very struck by the central heating Arthur had installed. He had done everything possible to put the queen off and avoided any mention of Stratfield in her presence, but the queen eventually confronted him and Arthur could only meekly bow and immediately make all of the preparations

necessary. Even his longstanding housekeeper was horrified, being fully aware that the house was 'not fit for the reception of the queen and her court'. The queen and her entourage squeezed in and all found it a delightful place, if only a little too hot, as Arthur always felt the cold and had the heating on and up high throughout.

Stratfield Saye was in a poor condition after the Second World War, having been left empty for many years, but has been lovingly brought back to life by Gerald Wellesley the 7th Duke of Wellington. It can be visited on a guided tour only and is open to the general public a few weekends in the year, at Easter and throughout August.

79: The Duke of Wellington's Annual Rent Flag

Following a tradition begun by Parliament when they granted the funds for Blenheim Palace to the Duke of Marlborough, when Arthur received funds to purchase Stratfield Saye in 1817, a 'rent' was to be paid each year or the estate would be forfeited.

To this very day, the Duke of Marlborough is required to present to Her Majesty the Queen in a private ceremony a flag emblazoned with a fleur de lys on 13 August, the anniversary of the Battle of Blenheim, each year. This then remains displayed on a seventeenth-century writing table at Windsor Castle until replaced the following year. This is his 'rent' for Blenheim Palace.

When Arthur received his funds in 1817, he was therefore similarly required to provide a peppercorn rent each year on the anniversary of 18 June, Waterloo Day. Parliament formally charged him with producing 'one tri-coloured flag for all manner of rents, services, exactions and demands whatever'. It is an absolute requirement and if it ever fails to happen, then by law the estate of Stratfield would revert to Parliament on 19 June. A new tricolour is therefore produced every year with the year stated and is presented to the reigning monarch in a private ceremony by midday at Windsor Castle where it is hung in the Waterloo Room in the castle until replaced the following year. Arthur ensured that there were always two flags made each year, just in case anything ever happened to the first on its way to the monarch. To our knowledge none of the spares were actually ever called on and today only one is produced each year.

The ceremony is seen as sacrosanct and when the 4th Duke of Wellington actually died on Waterloo Day in 1934, the flag still had to be at Windsor by midday, which it was.

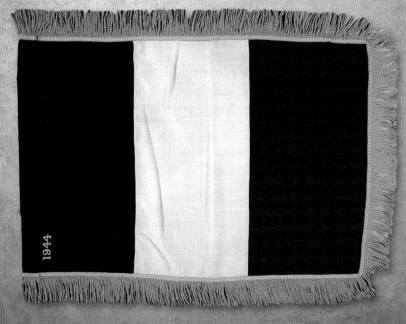

80: The Waterloo Shield

When the Allies captured Paris and Napoleon was forced to abdicate in April 1814, Wellington and his troops were still fighting in southern France, but Arthur was not forgotten.

The Prince Regent gave away a great number of titles and awards to senior officers of the British Army and Arthur was no different, receiving the title of Duke of Wellington, this being the highest rank of nobility available to those not in the Royal Family.

He was also feted by the Allied sovereigns as one of the chief architects of the final defeat of Napoleon, recognising that although the success was due in part to the combined armies of Prussia, Austria and Russia, Wellington's successes in the Peninsula had given Europe hope when all seemed lost.

Arthur was ordered home in May, but went via Paris for five days and then Madrid to see the king, before arriving in England on 23 June

Candelabra.

1814. He immediately made his way to London to join the Allied sovereigns who had all come to London as the guests of the Prince Regent in celebration of the final victory after 21 years of almost continuous war. His carriage was mobbed at Dover and crowds of cheering people lined his route to London, whilst Arthur sat bolt upright and unmoving within. As he always said, 'if you encouraged the mob to give tongue, they might hiss you the next time'. Arriving at Westminster Bridge, the crowd looked to unhitch his horses so that they could pull their hero home themselves, but he was too quick for them, mounting a horse and galloping home ahead of them.

On 28 June Arthur took his seat in the House of Lords for the first time and was thanked by the Speaker of the House of Commons for 'serving at once to adorn, defend and perpetuate the existence of this country among the ruling nations of the world'. The opposition in parliament, who had long predicted a disaster in Spain, now protested that Parliament's grant to the Duke of Wellington set at £300,000 (£14 million today) was not enough and succeeded in raising it to £400,000 (£19 million) in addition to the Parliamentary grant made in December 1812 for another £100,000 (£4.8 million) and an annuity of £13,000 (£620,000) for life or £400,000 in one sum (£19 million). They had awarded him no less than £44 million in today's terms within two years.

This was not the end: the Common Council of London presented him with a fine sword, whilst the merchants and bankers of the City of London commissioned a magnificent silver-gilt shield and two Standard Candelabra, which were not finished and presented to Wellington until 1822 and as such the shield is now referred to as the 'Waterloo Shield' despite depicting ten scenes from Wellington's victories in the Peninsular War.

The crest of the Duke of Wellington.

81: Cartoon of the Duke of Wellington as Master General of the Ordnance

The Ordnance was effectively a separate department of government, with the role of supplying weapons to both the Army and the Navy and also training and overseeing the artillery and engineers and surveyors, even having their own transport and medical staff. It also ran the naval dockyards, barracks and all depot facilities including gunpowder storage both home and abroad. Head of the entire structure was the Master General of the Ordnance. Arthur was given this title in 1819 and retained it until 1827, which also gave him a seat in government, in fact it was the only military appointment with a seat in the Cabinet. It was the ideal post with which Arthur the ex-soldier could reposition himself as a statesman.

His appointment did, however, ruffle many feathers within the Ordnance department because at times Wellington had been a harsh critic of the artillery and particularly at the Battle of Waterloo. Indeed, the officers of the Royal Artillery claimed that Wellington's praise in his Waterloo Despatch of their exertions during the battle was at best lukewarm and that their efforts had not been properly recognised.

The Master General of the Ordnance.

The Duke of Wellington wrote to the Earl Mulgrave, his predecessor as Master General of the Ordnance, on 21 December 1815, explaining the cause of his displeasure:

'... I had a right to expect that the officers and men of the Artillery would do as I did, and as all the staff did, that is to shelter in the squares of the Infantry till the French Cavalry should be driven off the ground, either by our Cavalry or Infantry. But they did no such thing; they ran off the field entirely, taking with them limbers, ammunition, and everything: and when, in a few minutes, we had driven off the French cavalry, and had regained our ground and our guns, and could have made good use of our artillery, we had no artillerymen to fire them; and, in this point of fact, I should have had no artillery during the whole of the latter part of the action if I had not kept a reserve in the commencement.'

Wellington had never been easily convinced of changes to arms and equipment and was certainly very unhappy with the king's alterations to the uniforms of the army, Frenchifying them. Progress in arms development was also slow in this period, but was as much to do with the continued parsimony of government which Arthur, as a Cabinet minister, had to support.

Arthur also took up the role of Master General at a time when British governments traditionally looked to gain a 'peace dividend' by rapidly demobilising a huge part of the war establishment and instigating the strictest economy. Championing such a policy, as his job now was as a member of the Cabinet obviously did not enamour him to the officers and men of the ordnance department.

Following the war, a mixture of poor harvests and high unemployment as the war machine ground to a halt, rapidly gave way to discontent in the country, culminating in the Peterloo Massacre. That terrible event, added to renewed unhappiness amongst Irish Catholics resurfacing, made the government's job particularly difficult. Their overall response was to close ranks and support the authorities come what may, including Arthur, whose public reputation suffered for this. He saw revolution just around the corner and supported the government's imposition of the Six Acts, to restrict the press and banning 'seditious' public meetings.

News of the Cato Street Conspiracy showed how far things had deteriorated, when informants had revealed a plot to seize the entire Cabinet at dinner and murder them. Arthur suggested that they continued with the dinner armed with pistols to flush the conspirators out, but his colleagues preferred safer options. Arthur later admitted 'perhaps they were right'. The lair of this

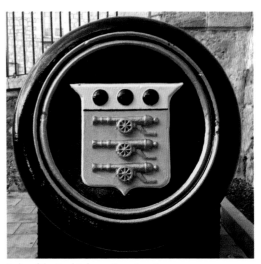

Badge of the Royal Ordnance Department.

group in Cato Street was raided and many were arrested, although some initially fled but were picked up within a day or two. The five ringleaders were convicted of treason and executed. Arthur often stated later that the plan was to behead Castlereagh and himself and to put their heads on spikes, but recent evidence shows that although one or two of the conspirators had a hatred of Wellington, the two they planned to decapitate were Castlereagh and Lord Sidmouth.

The unfortunate death of Lord Castlereagh (he committed suicide) led to a constitutional crisis as the Cabinet wished to replace him with Canning but the king was against it. Arthur refused to be tied to party and chose his own ground, he cajoled the king into accepting Canning, seeing him as the best option at the time. Wellington would effectively rule alongside the unruly Canning, although a remedy for an ear problem using caustic soda, left him permanently deaf in his left ear making his ability to follow conversations notably worse.

Execution of the Cato Street Conspirators.

82: The Wellington Tower, Kilcooney Abbey

Arthur Wellesley, the Duke of Wellington, we know was born in Ireland, at either Trim or Dublin, depending on which version you believe. His family were very much part of the Protestant Ascendancy who had moved to Ireland a century or so before, to oversee the assimilation of Ireland into Britain, culminating with the Act of Union in 1801.

It is often said that when someone called him Irish once, he refuted the assertion with the well known quote 'Just because you are born in a stable does not make you a horse.' This has often been used to castigate him as anti-Irish and ashamed of his birth, the problem is that he never said it. In fact it was said about him by Daniel O'Connell the Irish politician and fervent campaigner for Catholic Emancipation who at his trial in 1844 stated 'The poor old Duke! What shall I say of him? To be sure he was born in Ireland, but being born in a stable does not make a man a horse. No he is not an Irishman.'

In fact, there is no quote from Wellington denying his heritage, but as he was 'British' first and very much a defender of the monarchy

and the established order and church, he was troubled by Irish nationalism and calls for Catholic Emancipation. He was a reactionary, believing that such radical changes would alter the status quo and none for the good.

As early as 1807, he wrote to Lord Hawkesbury that

'I am positively convinced that no political measure which you could adopt would alter the temper of the people of this country. They are disaffected to the British government; they don't feel the benefits of their situation; attempts to render it better either do not reach their minds, or they are represented to them as additional injuries; and in fact we have no strength here but our army. Surely it is incumbent upon us to adopt every means which can secure the position and add to the strength of our army.'

The Wellington Memorial, Trim.

But this was his view of the politics of Ireland, not of the people.

At a time when the population of Ireland was nearly 40 per cent of the total British population (at 6 million inhabitants, the same as it is now) and when there was great agrarian change, many young Irishmen enlisted and fought under Wellington in the Peninsula and at Waterloo. They were renowned for hard drinking and hard fighting and in 1828 he was gracious enough to state in the House of Lords that it was to Irish Catholic soldiers 'we all owe our proud pre-eminence in our military careers'.

Wellington was originally bitterly opposed to Catholic emancipation simply because the king was vehemently against it and for fear of a subsequent attempt to revoke the Act of Union, but by 1829, with Ireland on the verge of an armed rebellion, in agreement with Robert Peel he changed tack. Their view was, that it was better to remove the disabilities imposed on Catholics than to see another bloody rebellion. Together

The Wellington Obelisk, Phoenix Park, Dublin.

they persuaded Parliament and the bill was passed; as always Arthur was ever the pragmatist. He gained much credit in Ireland for seeing this major reform through, although the freeholder threshold ensuring an entitlement to vote was increased, because Catholic reformers had abused the system by converting their tenants (who owed them allegiance) into freeholders to gain votes.

Therefore, Ireland has retained an affinity for Wellington, despite the words inappropriately attached to him, but he would never have thought of himself as an Irishman. Despite this conundrum, Ireland possesses three memorials to the Duke of Wellington. The 70-metre obelisk which dominates Phoenix Park was virtually completed in 1822 although it was not finished until 1861.

The monument at Trim with a figure of Wellington on top was also built in 1817. It is inscribed 'In honour of the illustrious Duke of Wellington, by the grateful contributions of the County Meath'.

The third monument is a folly, a tower also built in 1817 on the estates of Sir William Barker at Kilcooley in County Tipperary. The attached plaque reads, 'Dedicated to HIS GRACE THE DUKE OF WELLINGTON in commemoration of his glorious victory over the FRENCH at WATERLOO on June the 18th An Domi 1815'.

Having left Ireland in 1809, Wellington never set foot on the island ever again and never saw any of the three monuments.

It is perhaps significant, that during the troubles in Ireland these monuments were not destroyed or even defaced. It is probably because he is looked on in Ireland with the pride, that despite everything, he was a great Irishman.

83: A Pair of Arthur's Original Leather 'Wellington' Boots

If anything has come down to posterity from the Duke of Wellington, it has to be the iconic 'Wellington Boot', designed and first worn by himself.

The boot to wear in fashionable London had previously been the 'Hessian boot', which had first appeared in the seventeenth century as a military riding boot in Germany and often included an ostentatious tassle hanging on the front, but these were inadequate for riding, for which you required a proper riding boot with its more rigid leather and bulky 'trim or turndown' which better protected from the wet and mud splashes.

Ever the practical man, Arthur wanted a calf-length boot made in a soft leather, which was ideal for riding, but also suitable for informal dress when in polite society. In 1817 he instructed his shoemaker, George Hoby of St James's Street, to produce the boot in soft calfskin, without a trim, reaching to the middle of the calf and cut quite fitting to the calf, with a small heel. The leather was heavily waxed to make it soft and also to waterproof it. Being tight fitting, they could even be worn under the new 'trousers' which were beginning to be worn.

George Hoby was proud of his association with Wellington and after his victory at the Battle of Vitoria in 1813 he is reported as saying

'If Lord Wellington had any other bootmaker than myself, he never would have had his great and constant successes; for my boots and prayers bring his lordship out of all his difficulties.'

These utilitarian boots soon caught on and they quickly became the height of fashion in London around 1820 and remained so until the 1840s. The name 'Wellington Boot' caught on as everyone wanted to emulate the great war hero.

In 1852 Hiram Hutchinson got the idea to produce a waterproof boot made from vulcanised

A contemporary cartoon.

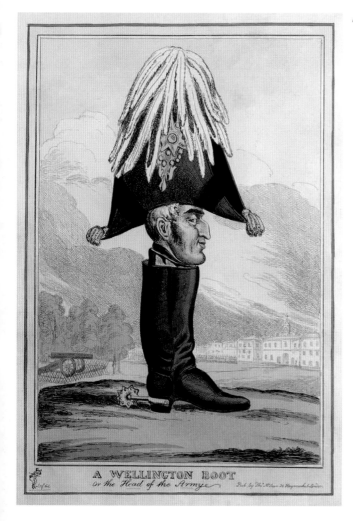

A WELLINGTON BOOT
Or the Head of the Army

rubber from Charles Goodyear and these took off, especially in France and the Low Countries as a cheap alternative to wooden sabots, allowing farmers to keep their feet dry for the first time. The first factory was set up in France named A l'Aigle (Homage to the Eagle). Despite other names being used, the name Wellington boot became synonymous with the rubber footwear. They became an essential item in the trenches of the First World War, the North British Rubber Company (later known as Hunter & Company) producing nearly two million pairs during the war.

Marshal Blücher also had the honour of having a boot named after him. The Blücher was virtually an ankle boot which he felt would be a better design for his soldiers. As you might expect, the British did not take to this new design, one correspondent calling them 'shocking imposters' and they were never taken up.

Later satirical prints showing the Duke of Wellington played heavily on portraying him as his own boot. At his funeral, his favourite horse followed the coffin and his groom placed a pair of his boots facing backwards in the stirrups.

84: A Print of Harriet Wilson

Harriet Dubouchet, who later assumed the name of Wilson, was only 15 years old when introduced to sex, when she soon came to realise that a combination of her looks and her ability to make men lust after her, allowed her to choose a career as a courtesan to the rich and famous, her sister Fanny also taking a similar course. She had a very modern approach to her work, enjoying male company and the fine lifestyle it brought with it, but she could afford to be choosy with whom she cavorted, later writing 'I will be the mere instrument of pleasure to no man. He must make a friend and companion of me, or he will lose me.' The only man Harriet ever claimed to have loved was Lord Ponsonby, but he was already married.

The list of the rich and famous who are linked with Harriet is long, and Arthur Wellesley, who regularly remained in London away from his wife and children, was undoubtedly one. However, as her beauty faded in her late thirties and promises of financial support failed, Harriet notoriously turned to publishing her memoirs, entitled *The Courtesan's Revenge*, in which she was not afraid to name and shame those who refused to succumb to this blatant attempt at blackmail. Publishing the memoirs in instalments caused a sensation, with queues forming outside the

Engraved by Cooper, from an Original Drawing by Birch.

publishers for each edition and continued to threaten her former lovers by stages, causing many to finally capitulate and pay up. The going rate was a £20 per year annuity, or a one-off payment of £200. The publisher wrote to Arthur in December 1824 on Harriet's behalf:

'My Lord Duke, in Harriette Wilson's Memoirs, which I am about to publish, are various anecdotes of Your Grace which it would be most desirable to withhold, at least such is my opinion. I have stopped the Press for the moment, but as the publication will take place next week, little delay can necessarily take place.'

To such a blatant letter, offering to omit his name from her memoirs in return for much-needed funds, Arthur reputedly famously replied 'publish and be damned', although there is some doubt about this claim. Others known to have been close with Harriet are the future George IV, Canning and Palmerston (who both paid to be left out of her memoirs), Lord Stuart and Henry Brougham.

Arthur Wellesley was therefore mentioned in her memoirs, but although there is irrefutable evidence that they were linked in some way, there is also clear evidence that some of Harriet's claims could not and did not happen, including a purported sneak visit from Arthur whilst away in Portugal, which certainly is an invention. She claimed that they had become lovers in 1805, not long after he returned from India and that they maintained a passing relationship for some years, interrupted by the Peninsular War and then eventually drifted apart. She claimed that there

was one last meeting, in Paris in 1814, when they swapped memories and he stopped her laughter by 'kissing me by main force'. She wrote that Arthur was her 'faithful lover, whose love survived six winters'. He was 'my own Wellington, who sighed over me and groaned over me by the hour, talked of my wonderful beauty, ran after me ...' and was 'my constant visitor', 'my old beau'. The truth of her claims are difficult to establish with certainty, but there is some proof that Arthur knew her well and that he was kind to her, offering to supply her funds if she ever needed them, all she had to do was write to him in Spain.

The memoirs were such a success that they went through thirty-one editions in one year and French, German and Spanish editions soon followed, but Harriet was forced to reside in Paris to avoid a nasty and expensive court case. Indeed, her publisher Stockdale was reputed to have made £10,000 from the book, but was ruined by a string of libel suits.

LE COTERIE DEBOUCHE. — Intended as a Frontispiece to Harriette Wilson's Memoirs

Arthur amongst Harriet's many suitors, waiting for the next instalment.

In later life, the newspapers were very unkind to Harriet, often referring to her 'very' faded beauty and mocking her for belatedly discovering the Catholic Church and brandy. On her death in 1845, she was buried in Brompton Cemetery and even now one newspaper commented 'We have now done with this woman, and we hope no stone will be erected to commemorate her memory and disgrace the place of her burial'. Thankfully such mean-spirited comments were ignored and her headstone can still be seen there today.

Arthur ignored her claims and society either disbelieved them or ignored them, as it certainly did not seriously hamper his political career.

85: The Great Reform Act of 1832

When Canning died, Lord Goderich became Prime Minister, but after only six months in office, he resigned. Arthur was approached to become Prime Minister and despite the realisation that the office was one for which he was thoroughly unsuited and unprepared, he finally accepted, viewing it as one more service that the country required of him, rather than out of any personal ambition.

Wellington attempted to construct a cross-party government as he had seen Lord Liverpool achieve so many years ago, but the Canningites resigned and he was forced to form an exclusively Tory government, with Robert Peel leading the government in the House of Commons, whilst Arthur controlled the House of Lords as Prime Minister. Arthur resigned as Commander-in-

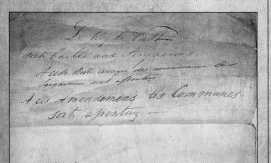

Chief of the Army so that he did not hold two of the great offices of state at the same time.

It was a difficult period in which to be Prime Minister, with agitation throughout the country for both Catholic Emancipation and electoral reform. As has been seen elsewhere, Arthur was naturally averse to change systems that had worked (at least to some extent) for centuries, fearing that major changes demanded by the mob could soon turn into revolution and the entire destruction of the system. Having seen the results of revolution in France Arthur undoubtedly sought to avoid it in Britain at all costs, making him very much a reactionary. However, he was also very much a pragmatist and when the pressure for change became too great, he would give ground, recognising that by doing so he reduced the threat of revolution, his sole purpose.

Arthur had previously been against William Huskisson's proposed sliding scale of taxation as a substitute for the hated Corn Laws of 1815, but he did eventually enact a very similar scheme when it became obvious the harm the Corn Laws were doing. He also aided the enactment of the Catholic Emancipation Bill, recognising that implementing the changes, against the king's will, would be preferable to Civil War in Ireland.

Arthur however maintained a very different attitude regarding electoral reform. The boroughs had been returning Members of Parliament for centuries, but as the towns and cities had grown or declined with the changing shape of Britain following the agrarian revolution and was now changing again as the Industrial Revolution took a firm hold on the country. Population centres had therefore grown or shrunk with time, but their representation in parliament had remained

The Parliament of 1833, following the Reform Bill.

the same. A further set of 'pocket boroughs' had grown over time as the various monarchs had invented boroughs which were unrelated to the centres of population, and were specifically designed by the Crown to be under the control of the king, but soon local magnates had gained control of them. The system of local magnates, who sat in the Lords, having great influence over the members elected for the Commons did lead to a great deal of harmony between both chambers and Arthur did not want to be the man that broke this bond. Eventually he was forced to call a vote of no confidence which he lost and the Whigs under Earl Grey were elected, who sought to pass the Reform Bill.

The Reform Bill was designed to eradicate boroughs with less than 2,000 inhabitants and those with less than 4,000 would only have one seat. This would abolish 170 of the current seats, which it was planned to allocate to the new burgeoning cities, which were often without any

Daguerreotype of the Duke of Wellington circa 1844.

representation at all. It did not, however, go as far as universal suffrage. Earl Grey managed to get it through the Commons, but it was defeated in the Lords and the Whig government resigned. The king recalled Arthur and asked him to form a government, he was personally against the bill, but he felt it was his duty to do the king's will and he tried to form a government but Peel refused to agree to see the bill through. Grey was recalled and Wellington persuaded 100 members of the Lords to withdraw their opposition, allowing the bill to pass. Arthur had agreed to this to avoid the king creating fifty or more new peers simply to see the bill through with a majority. Again Arthur had been pragmatic. The Reform Bill was therefore passed with Arthur's help and the centre of gravity of British politics changed dramatically, with the middle class now holding sway. The working class were not to get their say until much later yet.

It is often claimed that the nickname 'The Iron Duke' was given to Wellington after he fitted iron shutters, following his windows being broken in the Reform Bill riots of 1832. However, the newspapers actually began referring to him as the 'Iron Duke' in June 1830, before the riots occurred. This therefore would appear to refer to his iron will, or determination not to bend, rather than the shutters, which were installed in June 1832.

Arthur eventually retired from public life in 1846, although he remained as Commander-in-Chief, at Queen Victoria's request.

86: The Catholic Emancipation Act

The campaign for Catholic emancipation in Ireland was led by Daniel O'Connell, organiser of the Catholic Association. Richard was Lord Lieutenant of Ireland from 1822 to 1828, and he played a critical role in setting the stage for the Catholic Emancipation Bill. His policy was one of reconciliation, seeking civil rights for Catholics while preserving the rights of Protestants. He used force in maintaining law and order when riots threatened the peace, whilst he discouraged agitation by both the Protestant Orange Order and the Catholic Society of Ribbonmen.

In April 1825 Sir Francis Burdett managed to persuade the House of Commons to pass the Catholic Relief Bill. Both Lord Liverpool, the Prime Minister, and the Home Secretary Robert Peel threatened to resign over the issue, but Wellington worked hard behind the scenes to stop this happening. Although he disliked Burdett's bill, he believed that the time had come to settle things and he produced a plan of his own for legalising the Roman Church in Ireland by means of a concordat with the Pope. The Cabinet crisis ended in May, however, with the defeat of Burdett's bill in the House of Lords. George Canning died in 1827 and he was replaced by Lord Goderich as Prime Minister. Having refused to serve under Canning, Wellington now agreed to resume command of the army. However, Goderich's government collapsed in January 1828, and Wellington agreed to form an administration. Although Wellington and Robert Peel, had previously opposed Catholic emancipation they began to reconsider their views. They had received very disturbing information on the possibility of an Irish civil war. As Peel said

later to Wellington 'though emancipation was a great danger, civil strife was a greater danger'. King George IV was violently opposed to Catholic emancipation but after Arthur threatened to resign, the king reluctantly agreed to a change in the law. Wellington wanted to avoid bloodshed. He knew the majority of MPs favoured emancipation and that they were against the use of force in Ireland. Only a Tory ministry could get the Bill through the Lords and force George IV to give his consent. Although not a supporter of the act initially, Arthur was certainly a pragmatist and saw that reform was better than insurrection. In 1828 the Sacramental Test Act removed the barrier that required certain public officials to be members of the established Protestant church.

This was soon followed by the passing of the Roman Catholic Relief Act on 13 April 1829. This removed many of the still remaining restrictions on Roman Catholics throughout the United Kingdom of Great Britain and Ireland. Catholics could sit as MPs at Westminster and were eligible for all public offices except those of Monarch, Regent, Lord Chancellor, Lord Lieutenant of Ireland and any judicial appointment in any ecclesiastical court. However, at the same time the minimum property qualification for voters was increased, rising from a rental value of 40 shillings per annum to £10 per annum, thereby substantially reducing the number of those entitled to vote. The act also forbade the use of the episcopal titles already used by the Church of England.

It imposed a penalty of £100 on 'any person, not authorised by law, who should assume the title of any archbishop, bishop or dean'. The major beneficiaries were the Roman Catholic middle classes, who could now enter careers in the higher civil service and in the judiciary. The obligation, however, to pay tithes to the established Anglican church in Ireland remained, resulting in the Tithe War of the 1830s, and many other minor disabilities remained. A series of further reforms were introduced to eradicate these issues over time.

O'Connell accepted the act as the majority of members of the Catholic Association were still eligible to vote. It was political reality. He had achieved his aim, but he was seen as a traitor by the Irish peasants.

DOING HOMAGE

Wellington and Peel take turns to kiss the Pope's foot.

87: Contemporary Print of the Duke of Wellington's Duel with Earl Winchelsea

At 8am on 21 March 1829, the Duke of Wellington and Earl of Winchelsea fought a duel at Battersea Fields in South London. Wellington was Prime Minster and his Tory government was in the act of passing the Catholic Relief Bill. The Earl of Winchelsea was a staunch Protestant, and he accused Arthur in a letter of having 'under the cloak of some coloured show of zeal for the Protestant religion, carried on an insidious design for the infringement of our liberties and the introduction of popery into every department of the state'. Insulted by this slur on his integrity, Wellington challenged Winchelsea to a duel, which he readily accepted.

The Duke fired and missed; he claimed he did so on purpose, but Arthur was known to be a poor shot and accounts differ as to whether he missed on purpose. Winchelsea kept his arm by his side at the command to 'fire' then quite deliberately raised his arm and fired into the air. He then apologised for the language contained in his letter. It is almost certain that Winchelsea previously planned his course of action, as the letter of apology was already prepared.

The philosopher Jeremy Bentham was moved to write to the Duke the following day:

'Ill advised man! Think of the confusion into which the whole fabric of the government would have been thrown had you been killed, or had the trial of you for the murder of another man been substituted in the House of Lords to the passing of the emancipation bill!'

88: Portrait of Kitty Wellesley in 1815

After six years of separation, whilst Wellington had been fighting the Peninsular War, he finally returned to Kitty and his two sons who had not seen him since they were aged one and two respectively and could have no memory of their father. Their meeting again in June 1814 was amicable enough, although any feelings of desire had left Arthur many years before, the marriage was simply another duty for him.

Called to serve in Paris as Ambassador Kitty was invited to go with him, as has always been expected for married ambassadors, but once there, Kitty soon found that Arthur had little time for her and even took others, particularly Madame Grassini, on his arm to many of the functions he was invited to, causing a scandal, leaving poor Kitty pining for her boys who were now at boarding school and only came over in the holidays. Remaining in France in command of the Army of Occupation until 1818, Kitty remained at his headquarters, but as time went on Arthur became more and more irritated by his shrew of a wife and her constant quizzing of the officers of his 'family' to find out what he was doing – because he never told her what he was up to.

On their return to England in 1818, they settled at Stratfield Saye, which Kitty particularly loved, but living separately in the two wings, often communicating only by messages carried back and forth by the staff. Arthur, with his work, spent much of his time away, rarely seeing Kitty and was regularly seen offering his arm to many of the finest ladies in society and rumours of affairs abounded, to which Arthur seemed to be oblivious. In reality, he was fully aware but did not care what idle tongues said and sometimes

he even courted controversy and scandalous talk in society, with an impish grin.

Kitty slowly became more of a recluse and rarely attended state functions with Arthur, feeling inadequate and lacking in confidence, and this awkwardness was constantly picked up by those who saw her at these events. Even at Stratfield Saye, she did not like to engage with 'the Duke's company' and did not stay up entertaining his guests or playing cards, but retired early leaving Arthur and his guests, to his great irritation. Many who saw her there describe a woman wholly dedicated to her own two boys and Gerald Valerian, Arthur's brother Henry's son, whom Kitty and Arthur readily adopted and treated as their own son following the failure of Henry's first marriage.

She also happily became a guardian to Arthur's nephew, 'Wicked William's' three children along

Kitty as a young lady.

A rare portrayal of Arthur and Kitty together at a ball in Brighton in 1823.

with Arthur, following the death of their mother who was in despair over William's constant affairs. Despite his nephew's fury (although William did manage to kidnap his youngest son, James, and use him to try to turn the others against Kitty). Kitty was, however, at her very best when required to care for a damaged child.

In 1831, Kitty became seriously ill and at this point the marriage was transformed. Arthur suddenly became the dutiful husband, caring for Kitty tenderly and they finally became reconciled. On one occasion, Kitty ran her fingers up Arthur's arm and found there the armlet she had given him many years before, 'She found it' Arthur reported 'as she would have found it any time these twenty years, had she cared to look for it.' Just before she died, Arthur showed a great deal of emotion and he recalled the tragedy of his marriage and what could have been to a friend with real feeling:

'It is a strange thing, that two people can live together for half a lifetime and only understand one another at the very end.'

Kitty died at 10:30 on Sunday 23 April 1831 at Apsley House, with Arthur and their son Douro at the bedside. When she ceased to breath, Arthur reportedly 'evinced great emotion'. Kitty was the first member of the Wellesley family to be buried in the small crypt of the estate church at Stratfield Saye, Arthur followed the coffin into the vault and stayed alone with her for some time.

Could any woman have really coped with Arthur and kept him happy for all those years? I doubt it, he was too independently minded, as Arthur once admitted to his brother 'I like to walk alone.'

89: Photograph of Ewhurst Park, near Basingstoke circa 1908

The estate of Ewhurst is mentioned in the Domesday Book and was recorded as part of Earl Godwin's estates. It was inherited in 1761 by James Plowden and promptly sold to Robert Mackreth who built the Georgian house, chapel and stable block, while the 902 acres of grounds were established in imitation of the natural style of 'Capability' Brown who was all the rage at the time, although it also had an enclosed formal garden and kitchen garden.

Warner gives the following description of the estate in 1795:

'Here is a winding road amongst well-growing plantations, and by the side of a considerable sheet of water. The ground gradually rises from hence towards the house, and the gentle swells and inequalities are pleasingly interspersed with groups and single trees which we continued amongst till we approached the front of the house. The building is certainly not equal to these outward ornaments, as it consists of no particular style of architecture, being evidently built at

Ewhurst Park, Basingstoke

different periods and very low, but within it contains a most excellent dining-room. The small parish church, which he (Robert Mackreth) has much improved, stands very near it upon the same eminence, so that together with the surrounding foliage they form a picturesque assemblage. But a retrospect upon the water and scenes we had just left was by far the most pleasing. The grounds yet unfinished in the back part of the house also deserve commendation, particularly a terrace, which, though thickly shaded with shrubs and evergreens, affords at intervals much fine prospect of the hills in Berkshire and the surrounding country.'

On 20 January 1832 Arthur wrote to the trustees of the monies granted to him to buy an estate, requesting the issue of a warrant for £150,460 to buy the Wolverton Estate. It is unclear why he bought it, but it is likely that having decided to retain Stratfield Saye as it was, he may simply have wanted to take advantage of the rest of the money granted to him to expand his holdings. This figure was only a part payment, the final cost was to be £178,868 when agreement on reductions, due to the state of certain parts, was made. The cost was broken down as follows – Wolverton Park £52,500, timber £15,500, freehold £38,200 (settled), timber £14,000 (settled), copyhold of inheritance £1,600, timber growing £1,200, copyhold for lives £140, leasehold for 1,000 years £65, Ewhurst freehold £25,000, timber on estate £21,500, copyhold for lives £3,000, leasehold for 21 years £62, furniture, fixtures, underwood, deer, ploughing, etc. £5,900. Regarding the last item, the count of the deer in Wolverton Park in June 1829 was 103 head excluding fawns (65 bucks and 38 does). Twelve bucks were scheduled to be killed that year and probably every year, at 6 years of age or older. William Ruddle of Kingsclere and Joseph Brooks of Wolverton were among those who identified the parts of the estate and whether freehold or copyhold. There were three lodges on the estate occupied by estate workers. The first was Spicer's Lodge on Crabb's Hill, Middle Lodge and Town's End (or Coachman's) Lodge.

Ewhurst Park House was described by White in 1859 as 'a commodious mansion in a large and well-wooded park' was let to various tenants during the nineteenth century (including Alexander Lord Russell, 7th son of the 6th Duke of Bedford, who lived there 1880–1905).

In 1910, *Country Life* described the estate as containing 'a fine artificial lake of 18 acres surrounded by beech trees. The pleasure gardens at that time contained: A fine collection of mature coniferous trees. A formal garden with ornamental pool & retaining walls and a walled kitchen garden …'.

Although the family seat was at Stratfield Saye, thereafter it seems to have been the preferred country residence of the 4th Duke of Wellington, who preferred to stay at Ewhurst and from 1921 he rented Stratfield Saye to his son, until his death in 1934.

In 1943 the Ewhurst and Wolverton estates were sold by auction to cover huge death duties, and during the Second World War, it was taken over by the Canadian Military. Left empty and neglected it was bought in the mid-1950s, and the mansion reduced to a single wing. The original eighteenth-century stables were retained, and in the 1970s the Church of St Mary was declared redundant and is now used as part of the house amenities. Of the extensive woods and walks around the ornamental pool, the bridge, lily lake, Park Copse, Boathouse Copse, Lloyd Copse, Wood Walk all remain today, maintaining the strong structural features typical of an eighteenth-century park. Two ice houses can still be found on the estate.

St Mary's Church.

90: Medal Commemorating Wellington becoming Chancellor of Oxford University

The University of Oxford had made Arthur an honorary doctor on 14 June 1814, which had delighted him. Lord Grenville, Chancellor of Oxford, had become gravely ill in 1833 and Arthur had been informed that moves were afoot to make him his replacement in time. Arthur was genuinely overwhelmed by this, as he reflected on his own poor record in academic pursuits and the knowledge that he had pulled both of his sons out of Oxford and sent them to Cambridge. He could not resist a dig at his brother Richard, who had been forced to abandon his university on the death of their father, writing 'What will Lord Wellesley say?' Arthur wrote honestly pressing the reasons why he should be disqualified, but he was duly elected Chancellor on 29 January 1834, and he was received with the wildest enthusiasm when he went there to be installed on 9–11 June. The Duke, robed in black and gold,

stood outwardly unmoved by the shouting and stamping of feet by the students to show their approval, the noise only abating when he raised his hand. Arthur had to give his acceptance in Latin and although some academics inwardly cringed at the two errors of pronunciation, he got through it and vowed never to speak in Latin again. The enthusiasm of the students led him to declare 'let those boys loose in the state in which I saw them, and give them a political object to carry, and they would revolutionise any nation under the sun'.

His election helped to cause a temporary coolness between him and Peel, who had declined an invitation to stand, but was nevertheless sore on the subject. The Wellington Medal was minted to commemorate his induction as Chancellor of Oxford University in 1834. He had enjoyed being elected by acclaim (one of only two non-Oxonians since Oliver Cromwell ever to occupy

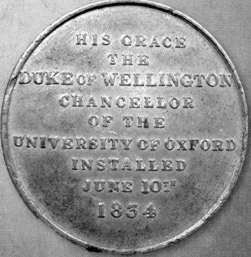

this office), and his enjoyment, even as the most loyal of subjects, was not diminished when, on a fraternal visit to Cambridge to see Prince Albert installed as Chancellor there, he was greeted with more enthusiasm than his royal counterpart, and even more than the Queen herself.

Oxford was then a very different place, with almost the entire staff then in holy orders. Arthur saw himself as an upholder of the established Church and was afraid to become embroiled in the wind of challenge to the status quo that blew constantly through the university. He guided with a strong hand, but bent a little when pragmatism was needed to reach compromise. He took his role as Chancellor very seriously indeed.

His greatest challenge came in 1850 with the Royal Commission on Universities. He forged a path between his own colleges who demanded the continued bar on Nonconformists, whilst recognising himself that the university needed to modernise and embrace modern literature, physics and chemistry. The Commission report arrived just before his death, but he read it thoroughly and suggested that the university should take on many of the improvements contained within. Despite his death, the university readily embarked on the changes he would have wished to see as Oxford thoroughly modernised itself. Arthur must gain much of the credit for the end of the intransigence all so evident at Oxford, spending eighteen years at the helm diligently working for sensible change.

Arthur as Chancellor of Oxford University circa 1850.

91: Replica of the Original Rocket

As we have already seen in his home life, Wellington was generally a supporter of industrial development and he therefore showed a great interest in the new steam locomotion on rail tracks. He therefore accepted the invitation as Prime Minister, to be the guest of honour at the grand opening of the Liverpool and Manchester Railway on 15 September 1830, which was a first in so many ways. It was the first wholly steam-operated railway offering intercity travel, it also introduced dual tracks allowing trains to travel in each direction at the same time and it used a signal system for safety. The company also introduced the first railway timetable and it was the first use of delivering mail by train. The 50-kilometre long railway had been designed by George Stephenson and it took four years to build, its main problem being the section crossing Chat Moss, a huge bog, and the construction of sixty-four bridges and viaducts. Primarily, it had been built to ease the bulk movement from Liverpool of raw materials to the Manchester cotton mills and to transport the finished goods back to the port of Liverpool where they could be exported, but could also accommodate passenger trains as well, all of this detail and great usefulness would have fascinated Arthur.

On the day of the opening, the southern track was reserved for a special train pulled by the locomotive *Northumberland*, then the most advanced locomotive in the world with a 14-horsepower engine. There were three ornamental carriages for the Duke of Wellington and many distinguished guests including a number of ambassadors, a fourth housing a band

The Duke's carriage in red at the opening ceremony.

which played throughout the journey. These were covered carriages with cushioned seating and cloth linings, each carriage designed to take up to twenty-four people in the same luxury as the finest road coaches. The special carriage for the Duke was described as:

32 feet long by 8 feet wide, supported by eight wheels, partly concealed by a basement, ornamented with bold gold mouldings and laurel wreaths on a ground of crimson cloth. A lofty canopy of crimson cloth, 24 feet in length, rested upon eight carved and gilt pillars, the cornice enriched with gold ornaments and pendant tassels, the cloth fluted to two centres, surmounted with two ducal coronets. An ornamental gilt balustrade extended round each end of the carriage, and united with one of the pillars which supported the roof. Handsome scrolls filled up the next compartments, on each side of the doorway, which was in the centre.

On the Duke's arrival, the now-traditional welcome of 'See the Conquering Hero Comes' was played by the band, starting a tradition of opening almost every railway station thereafter

William Huskisson.

with the tune. When the train stopped at Parkside to refill the water tanks, it was intended that the passengers would remain in their carriages, whilst seven other steam locomotives, led by *Rocket*, would pass them on the other track. Despite warnings, a number of passengers alighted, one of whom was William Huskisson, a Liverpool MP, who was travelling with his wife Emily, who sought to hold a conversation with Arthur and shook his hand, as they had previously had a disagreement in Parliament. Suddenly warning shouts that the locomotives were approaching caused those on the tracks to hastily vacate them, including the Austrian ambassador who was saved.

However, it appears Huskisson panicked and tried to enter the Duke's carriage, but grasping the door rather than the solid carriage, it swung open and *Rocket* struck the open door, throwing him to the ground between the two tracks, but unfortunately his leg lay across the track and it severely mangled his leg. The locomotive was removed from the carriages and he was rushed to Eccles, but died there a few hours later, one of the first rail passenger deaths (but <u>not</u> the first).

Arthur wanted to end the day here, but the trains could only run in one direction on the track and were turned around at the end. The Duke was persuaded to continue the journey to Manchester where huge expectant crowds were now spilling onto the tracks. They therefore proceeded and finally arrived at Manchester, the large crowd containing many weavers who were unhappy with the government, held up placards and threw vegetables at the carriage and Wellington refused to get out. They did not alight and finally returned to Liverpool, without partaking of the grand banquet prepared for them at the Adelphi Hotel in Liverpool.

The news of Huskisson's death went around the world and it actually brought the idea of rail transport for passengers to many and gave the railways a huge boost, it did not hurt that the railways was also very financially successful. Soon railways were springing up everywhere, in fact within twenty years 10,000 kilometres of rail track had been laid in Britain.

Arthur avoided the railways completely for over ten years but was eventually persuaded to accompany Queen Victoria on a railway journey in 1843, but that is his only recorded railway journey afterwards.

Memorial stone to Huskisson.

92: Painting of the Waterloo Gallery at Apsley House as it looked in 1852

As part of the major refurbishments of Apsley House in 1829, Arthur had a two-storey gallery measuring over 28 metres long, for his magnificent collection of paintings. It also served as an impressive space in which to accommodate the Waterloo Banquet with ease. The room evokes the style of Louis XIV. The windows had sliding shutters with mirrors allowing them to be closed off at night, which then reflected the light off the candelabras.

The annual Waterloo Banquet, which had started in 1820, had previously been hosted in the dining room which could only seat thirty-five and was therefore a select meeting of his old general officers and some honoured guests, such as King George IV in 1821 (who after a visit to the battlefield with Arthur told everyone he had been at the battle!).

The centrepiece of the table, known as the Baixela da Victoria (the Victory Table Service) was a gift from the Portuguese people. Begun in 1813 and delivered in 1816 in fifty-five crates aboard HMS *Pearl*, it was accompanied by three Portuguese silversmiths in case of damage (luckily they were not needed). It cost £27,000 to make (£1.6 million today).

However, rather than see the numbers dwindle each year with the passing of time, the dinner

The Waterloo Banquet
1836.

was expanded to include more junior officers present at the battle. The table set out in the Waterloo Gallery could seat eighty-five people and King William IV was guest of honour in 1830, the first year that the new Waterloo Gallery was used.

The dinner was an annual event until Arthur's death. It was never cancelled, but Arthur did propose to do so in 1837 when King William IV was on his death bed, but he was told to continue, although apparently it was a sombre evening. The king died two days later.

Wellington had the walls draped with yellow damask as shown in the painting dated 1852,

however soon after his father's death the 2nd Duke had the wall covering changed to red, as it remains to this day.

The painting of the Waterloo Banquet in 1836 by Salter gives some idea of the sumptuous dinner.

The banquet has not been held since Arthur's death in 1852, except for a one-off event in 2015 to mark the bicentennial of the Battle of Waterloo. This recreated the original menu of 1839, which consisted of two soups, thick and clear, fish, beef, venison and game pies, savoury jellies, grouse, snipe and woodcock, sweet puddings and preserved fruit, ices and nuts.

The room set as if ready
for the banquet today.

93: Cartoon Depicting Arthur Acting in All the Posts of Government

Arthur had been superseded as leader of the Tories by Sir Robert Peel and when the Tories returned to government in 1834, the king asked Wellington to form a government, but he declined, believing that it was necessary for the Prime Minister to then sit in the House of Commons and not the Lords. King William IV was therefore reluctantly persuaded to offer the office to Robert Peel, but he was on the Grand Tour in Italy and he would therefore not be able to take up the position within a month, by the time a letter got to him and he could return.

Arthur therefore agreed to stand in as 'Interim Leader', but he refused to make any appointments as ministers, as that would make things complicated for Peel on his return and embarrassing if he wished to remove anyone. Wellington therefore decided that he would temporarily keep all of the offices going himself until Peel returned.

For three weeks in November and December 1834, he was de facto Prime Minister, First Lord of the Treasury, Secretary of State at the Home Office, Foreign Secretary and Minister for War. He held five major Cabinet posts and three lower posts. He set up his headquarters in the Home Office and each day he toured around No.10 Downing Street, the Foreign Office, Horse Guards and the Colonial Office before returning to the Home Office. No appointments were made, no decisions made beyond those that were vital, no policies announced and no legislation introduced, but he ensured that all the minutiae of day-to-day correspondence, which kept the wheels turning was completed. The only role he did give to another, was that of Lord Chancellor temporarily given to Lyndhurst.

As can be imagined, the Opposition, who had been driven out of government by the king, denounced Wellington, not as a caretaker, but as 'His Highness the Dictator!' They argued that the situation was neither constitutional nor legal.

The general public, however, showed great confidence in Wellington, confident that he would not abuse the power he held temporarily. In fact, the situation was turned against the Commons, with comments like 'At last we have a united government' or 'the ministers are of one mind'. Later in life Arthur often laughed at his brief period of dictatorship.

Robert Peel landed at Dover on 9 December and the Duke's 'Dictatorship' was over and he was given the role of Foreign Secretary in the new Cabinet. The most astonishing part in the whole episode, is that no one, not even Arthur himself, would have believed him capable of taking control of the government permanently and making himself sovereign. Arthur was entirely a servant of the Crown and the country.

ACTOR OF ALL WORK

94: Piece of Cake from Queen Victoria's Wedding, 10 February 1840

What Arthur's initial views of having a young woman become the monarch were, are unknown as he was too discreet to say anything. However, Wellington was actually impressed by Victoria's demeanour at the Coronation on 28 June 1838 and the formal receptions that would follow and he rapidly became an enthusiast. After her first Privy Council meeting following her coronation Arthur commented that 'if she had been his own daughter he could not have desired to see her perform her part better'.

The young queen soon showed her determination to do things her way and wished to review the troops on horseback rather than from a carriage, but Arthur discouraged the notion, believing her pictured between the two 'youths' Wellington and Hill, would be a gift for the

Queen Victoria and Prince Albert at a hunt at Windsor. Arthur is in the grey coat in the background.

Victoria's Coronation with Arthur watching.

Wellington and [Peel?] carrying the young Queen.

Prince Arthur.

caricaturists, but she got her own way eventually. Initially Victoria leant heavily on the Whig Lord Melbourne, but by 1840 Arthur, despite being conservative-leaning, was becoming a favourite of the queen. He often sat next to her at dinners and stood proxy for the queen's father-in-law at the Princess Royal's christening.

The queen even asked Arthur if he would lend her Walmer Castle for a spell, which of course he gracefully agreed to. Victoria was delighted

The Crystal Palace.

by its simplicity, but her staff were not so keen describing it as 'a heap of comical rooms ... doors and windows all chatter and sing at once and hardly keep out the dark storm of wind and rain which is howling round'. The royal party stayed a month and Victoria had caught a cold, but she had loved being able to stroll along the beach unattended and unobserved.

When Peel formed a government in 1841 Arthur accepted a post stating that 'The truth is that all that I desire is to be as useful as possible to the queen's service'. Victoria encouraged him to remain in his post as Commander-in-Chief of the Army, even beyond the period that Arthur felt capable of performing the role well.

The queen announced in 1845 that she meant to visit Stratfield Saye, Arthur avoided the subject and hoped that she would forget about it, but he was finally confronted and had to give in gracefully. The weekend actually went very well, Victoria wrote in her journal

'Stratfieldsaye is a low & not very large house, but warm & comfortable & with a good deal of room in it.'

When Victoria's seventh child was born on 1 May 1850, the queen even named her new son Arthur, Duke of Connaught and Strathearn, after Arthur Duke of Wellington as they shared the same birthday and he was made a godparent.

When the Crystal Palace was complete just before the Great Exhibition of 1851, it was found that hundreds of sparrows had got in and were flying around inside leaving a mess. Victoria asked Wellington if he could suggest a remedy, to which he replied without emotion

'Try sparrow-hawks, Ma'am', which apparently worked a treat!

Victoria evinced great sorrow on the death of her 'dear & great old Duke of Wellington' and referring to him as 'our immortal hero'. The queen watched his funeral procession going past and openly wept when his horse was led past by his groom with his boots inverted in the stirrups. She had lost a close and dear friend.

In 1853 Queen Victoria founded Wellington College as a national monument to the Duke of Wellington and it began to take in pupils in 1859, with the queen performing the opening ceremony. It was set up as a charitable educational institution to educate 'foundationers' (the orphan sons of army officers). The first seventy-six boys aged 11 to 15, consisted of forty-nine foundationers paying between £10 and £20 per year and twenty-seven sons of serving officers or civilians paying £70 to £100 per annum. In 1952 the foundationers was extended to the sons of Royal Navy and RAF officers and in 2005 it became co-educational. In 2006 it was opened further to the orphaned children of all service personnel of any rank.

Wellington College, Berkshire.

95: Colza Lamp at Stratfield Saye

As he became older, Arthur was seen as very much a reactionary, who generally sought to avoid change, which he thought might threaten the very fabric of established society, but he was not so backward in accepting modern improvements to living and to some extent travel.

Having purchased both Apsley House and Stratfield Saye, Arthur was not slow in making improvements to living conditions and in fact he was somewhat of a leader in new technologies.

In February 1826, Wellington attended the funeral of Tsar Alexander I of Russia as the official representative of the British government. He was fascinated with Russian secondary glazing, which of course was vital in such a cold climate. Although the weather was freezing, Wellington noted in his letters home how warm Russian apartments were, sometimes too warm for him. He was intrigued by the secondary glazing, and when he returned to Apsley House he asked for it to be installed. Unfortunately, this improvement was later removed, possibly because of changes to the windows or shutters, but it can be seen in the Thomas Shotter Boys watercolour of the Red Striped Drawing Room of 1853.

At Stratfield Saye he made a number of practical innovations, including the heating system in the house. In January 1834 Lord Mahon noted that 'The Duke showed me over his new apparatus for warming the house by tubes of hot water, and told me that including the expense of setting it up, it had cost £ 219 [about £15,000 in modern terms].'

According to Lady Salisbury this heating system almost lead to disaster when Queen Adelaide visited Stratfield Saye in the following

year: 'In the night, the furnace that heats the pipes for warming the house, communicated it to a beam, but the fire was soon put out. Lord Salisbury and I were the only people disturbed, as we slept in that part of the house.'

Queen Victoria and Prince Albert visited Stratfield Saye in 1845 and she was also taken by the central heating system. She promptly returned to London and had a system fitted at Buckingham Palace and soon everybody was copying her.

Arthur also installed a system of Colza oil lamps rather than the dirty candles, which

Apsley House with secondary glazing.

blackened the walls and ceilings. Colza oil is a non-drying oil extracted from rapeseed and is widely used for lubrication of machinery and was used by Arthur as a precursor to the later innovation of gas lighting. Colza oil has some disadvantages, being thick and viscous it needs to be held in a reservoir above the light and fed in by gravity, but it glowed with a cleaner, whiter light of greater intensity than simple tallow candles and was certainly less dirty. The Colza lamps at Stratfield Saye are still present in parts of the house, but many preferred paraffin and gas lighting when these technologies were perfected.

Wellington was also a fan of 'water closets' or flushing toilets and almost every bedroom at both Stratfield Saye and Apsley House was provided with their own, very small ensuite room provided with a sink basin and water closet. In fact he became an early exponent as this advert in the 1839 *Gentleman's Magazine* shows:

Patent Improved Water Closets.

J. Body begs to inform the Public that his improved Patent Water Closets continue to give the most decided satisfaction, and remain free from any unpleasant effluvia. As a proof of which, they receive the recommendation of the most eminent Architects, by whom they have been introduced into the following establishments:

The Duke of Wellington's, Stratfield Say; The Duke of Grafton's, Clarges Street; The Duke of Newcastle, Clumber; The Earl of Lonsdale, Cottismore; The Earl of Kenmare, Killarney; Earl Howe's, Gospall Hall; The Duke of Buckingham, Stowe; Lord Templetown, Berkeley-Square; Lord O'Niell, Donaghheadie; _ Dowdeswell, Esq. Pull-Court near Tewkesbury; The College of Surgeons, London; The New Grammar School, Birmingham; Messrs Coutts and Co. Bankers, London; Messrs Barnett, Hoare and Co. Bankers, London; Messrs Twinings, Bankers, London.

N.B. Premises surveyed, and an accurate estimate given of the expense.

Orders received at SALMON, ODY, & CO's. Patent Truss Manufactory, 292, Strand, London

Wellington was, however, less enamoured with steam power, particularly when in regards to transport, retaining a dislike of the railways throughout his life, although he had good reason for that (see the article on Huskisson).

96: Arthur with Four of his Grandchildren at Stratfield Saye

Arthur's relationship with his two sons was not a good one, Douro actually goes as far as to state that 'My father never showed the least affection for any of us.' Wellington was undoubtedly a busy man, with much correspondence to get through each day and he allowed his duties to entirely take over his life. As Douro explained, 'Charles, Jerry (their cousin Gerald) and I, were taught to go to his room the first thing every morning after we were dressed; and without interrupting his correspondence, for we always found him writing, he would look up for a moment and say, "Good morning", and that was positively all the loving intercourse that passed between us during the entire day.' His strictness towards his two boys remained throughout his life, always pointing out their faults. But for all of this, Arthur always admired his father and sought to be more like him, probably in an attempt to gain his approval. He even dedicated his later life to honouring his father and he singlehandedly produced the nine-volume *Supplementary Despatches* of his father's correspondence. Afraid of being judged against their illustrious father, the boys, intentionally or not, strove to excel at more unusual pursuits, where comparison was not an issue.

The boys had been only two and one year old respectively when Arthur had sailed for Portugal and the boys only knew their father for the next seven years from stories their mother told them and his image in the numerous paintings and

busts of him in their home. Young Arthur looked quite like his father, but he longed for a nose as big as his father's and every day he would check his nose against the bust, eventually exclaiming in frustration 'My nose is such a time a-growing!' When Arthur returned home from Spain, the boys were already at boarding school and only saw their father in the holidays. The relationship never really improved, they effectively led separate lives, the boys when in the Army, using Apsley House like their regimental mess, flitting in purely for meals and a bed.

This, however, sits awkwardly with what we know of Arthur and children later in life. Perhaps because they were not his and therefore no longer his responsibility to bring up, or that he simply learnt as he grew older to give more time to further generations of family, but he is certainly portrayed by many in later life as having a wonderful relationship with children.

Particularly at Walmer Castle from 1830, Arthur could relax and be both a grandfather and have the relationship with young children that perhaps he had wanted to have with his own sons, but never had, largely because he let his work overtake family life. He is often recorded being found under the table at parties messing around with the children, or holding the little hands of little children who fell sick whilst their parents were abroad and meticulously reporting their well-being to their parents.

In 1835 Lady Salisbury recorded that :

Wellington presents a gift to his godchild Prince Arthur.

'He is so fond of children and good-natured to them. He is to go with us some night to see *King Arthur* but regrets he was not able to go on the same night with the children to see their delight in it. "That is what I should have liked."'

Lord Mahon wrote two years later, that 'The Duke has now staying with him, [the] two little children of Lord and Lady Robert Grosvenor, who are gone abroad, and his conduct to these chicks displays a kind-heartedness and warmth of feeling such as their own parents could not surpass, but such as the Duke displays to all'. Lord Stanhope was also told that ' ... the children having expressed their desire to receive letters by the post, the Duke every morning writes a little letter to each of them, containing good advice for the day, which is regularly delivered to them when the post comes in. It also appears that the Duke gratifies *Bo*, as they call little Robert, by playing almost every morning with him at football on the ramparts. We saw him playing with them with cushions in the drawing-room before dinner.'

On another occasion, Wellington, while on one of his country walks, reputedly found a little boy lying on the ground bending his head over a tame toad and crying as if his heart would break. On being asked what was the matter, the child explained that he was crying 'for his poor toad'. He brought it something to eat every morning, but he was now to be sent away to school a long way away, and he was afraid that nobody else would give it anything to eat and that it would die. Arthur however, consoled him by saying that he would himself see to it that the toad was well fed, and further promised to let the boy hear of its welfare. During the boy's time at school he received the following letter: 'Strathfleldsaye, July 1837. Field Marshal the Duke of Wellington is happy to inform Master William Harries that his toad is alive and well.'

97: Wellington's Breguet Pocket Watch with a Portrait of Marianne Patterson Within

Arthur's marriage had soon lost its excitement and he had spent much of his time apart from Kitty. Wellington was however required to attend a huge number of functions wherever he went and he chose to attend them with one of the many young beauties that he seemed to attract, like moths to a flame. Society was often shocked by the attention that Arthur gave these young ladies and rumours abounded regarding his fidelity. There are occasional signs throughout his life that Arthur had a high sex drive, but owing to the discretion of all parties, it is often difficult to know whether the flirtatious behaviour, so disapproved of by society actually went as far as a sexual relationship and a full-blown affair. These constant rumours led many in society to pity Kitty, but there were also many that felt her coldness had driven him to it.

We have already covered his time in Spain, where he may well have had a dalliance when in Madrid and his close connections with two of Napoleon's ex-lovers when in Paris, one of which (Madame Georges) certainly claimed that they had a sexual relationship. We also have the claims of Harriet Wilson, who certainly claimed an intimate relationship with Wellington, which he did not refute.

Beyond these however, it is very difficult to be sure how far things went with many of the other women who came very close to him in his life. Anne Louise Germaine Necker, more commonly known as Madame de Staël, was a close associate from 1814–17, but this relationship was born of two political minds sparring rather than of lust and there is no evidence that their relationship ever got that close.

Lady Charlotte Greville.

Arthur had also met Lady Frances Shelley in 1814 and instantly took a shine to her, much to the delight of the star-struck young lady and her husband. It is clear from her letters and later writings that the relationship was platonic, but was a close friendship in which they could confide their innermost secrets to each other.

Lady Charlotte Greville also met Arthur in 1814 and she was seen with him almost continuously during 1815 and during the years of the Army of Occupation in France. It is clear that both her husband and her son believed that she was way too close to the Duke and were worried about their reputation. We cannot be certain how close this relationship was, but both of them fought hard to maintain their very close relationship despite the views of society.

Lady Frances Wedderburn-Webster was another lady Arthur saw regularly in 1815 and beyond, some describing her at this period as the 'queen regnant'. This dalliance hit the newspapers and caused Arthur a lot of worry, as her husband was reported to be considering bringing a case of 'Criminal Conversation', the term then for adultery. In fact in 1816 the Wedderburn-Websters took the newspaper to court, pointing out that she had been 7 months pregnant at the time of Waterloo and in no condition to carry on such an affair. They received damages totalling £2,000 (around £115,000 today).

Arthur had known Charles Arbuthnot since 1809 and they were close personal friends. When Charles married Harriet Fane in January 1814, she did not come between them, the trio making a very strong friendship and between 1811 and her death in 1834, Arthur wrote well over 1,500 letters to her. Harriet Arbuthnot was sharp witted and politically astute and she proved an excellent sparring partner for Arthur and a close confidante who was not afraid to tell him when she did not approve of his conduct or policies. She certainly did not approve of or

Lady Frances Wedderburn-Webster.

Mrs Harriet Arbuthnot.

like Kitty. Harriet was undoubtedly jealous of his other lady friends, but there is no evidence in any of their voluminous correspondence of a sexual relationship.

Princess Lieven, who came to London to infiltrate British society and to report all that she could learn to Tsar Alexander, made friendly moves towards Arthur and he readily accepted her friendship, but he always remained fully aware of her master. Their relationship certainly never became that close. Lady Salisbury, Lady Wilton, Lady Caroline Lamb and Lady Sarah Jersey were also close later in his life but none of these relationships were overly close.

After 1834, Arthur began rather a strange correspondence of nearly 400 letters with a spiritualist named Miss Jenkins, which some historians have questioned, but they appear to be perfectly genuine. She was a beautiful 20-year-old when she began writing to Arthur when he was 62. They met but Miss Jenkins wanted little more than a spiritual relationship and the correspondence continued, sometimes warmly, sometimes very tartly indeed, but it never progressed further.

Angela Burdett-Coutts, heiress to the Coutts Bank, lived very close to Apsley House in 1837. She was of course the target of scores of hopeful adventurers interested only in her fortune. She maintained a chatty correspondence of some 900 letters with Arthur and on 7 February 1847, when she was 33 and Arthur was 78, she sent him a proposal of marriage! Arthur politely declined, explaining that he could not burden her with his care as he grew old. Their friendship however continued unabated and the exchange of small gifts was never ending. However, near the end, they broke apart and Angela threatened to sue him for breach of promise to marry. Rumours abounded that they did secretly marry, although no evidence has ever been found, but Angela was treated almost as a widow when Arthur died.

Two further images of the Breguet watch.

Arthur is recorded as saying that he had never really loved a woman. If he said it, it was not true, for at times he was infatuated and on one occasion deeply in love. The three American Caton sisters had arrived in Europe in 1814 and they captivated society and were known as the 'Three Graces of Baltimore'. Betsy had been married for a period to Jérôme Bonaparte, but Napoleon had forced his brother to annul the marriage and she soon married Colonel Felton Hervey, one of Arthur's aides-de-camp. However, Arthur's eyes were only for Mary Anne (later she called herself Marianne), who had married a Mr Robert Patterson, a wealthy Baltimore businessman. It would seem that Arthur felt deeply for Marianne, but their relationship was platonic, as neither would sully their reputations whilst their spouses lived. Arthur commissioned Sir Thomas Lawrence to paint portraits of himself and Marianne and he sent the one of him to her. According to society gossip Marianne had now completely eclipsed Madame Grassini in his affections. The romance, or infatuation continued, but in 1821 Marianne returned briefly to America with her ailing husband. Her husband died that Christmas and she returned to Europe as guests of the Duke at Stratfield Saye. Arthur was clearly distraught at the fact that Marianne was now able to marry, but he was not and the relationship remained in limbo. In 1825 Marianne went to Dublin with her sister, where she found Richard serving as Lord Lieutenant of Ireland, who was now a widow. Within months they were seen together, but still the note that arrived at Stratfield Saye on 26 October of that year, bringing Richard's account of his forthcoming marriage to Marianne was like a bombshell. Arthur was furious and this event undoubtedly marred his relationship with his brother for many years. Marianne was Arthur's great love lost and it is certain that he retained a torch for her all of his life, she dying 18 months after him. Arthur kept her portrait in his study and had a 'secret' miniature portrait of Marianne set into his Breguet watch which he kept close at all times. If Arthur ever truly loved, it was Marianne.

98: Death Mask of Arthur Wellesley, Duke of Wellington

Arthur was 83 years old in 1852 but his health, although never perfect, was still pretty good. Only deafness and his habit of falling asleep in the saddle, when his horse would intuitively halt until he woke, told his age, and indeed his death when it came was completely unexpected.

He still spent hours every day reading or dealing with his voluminous correspondence. On the 12 September, he wrote to Lady Salisbury, mentioning with amusement that a handwritten note had arrived that morning 'from a madman who announces that he is a messenger from the Lord, and will deliver his message tomorrow morning, Monday at Walmer Castle!'

Wellington survived the 13th. He had been up at 5:30, strolling in his garden and looking forward to the day ahead. His son Charles had

Arthur's room at Walmer, retained exactly as it was when he died.

arrived with his family and he had enjoyed playing with the grandchildren, had mock turtle soup, turbot and venison for dinner and he took himself to his camp bed late at around midnight, having chatted away with Charles and Sophia, his daughter-in-law.

His valet Kendall knocked his door as usual at 6:30, but an hour later a maid came running to say his Grace was 'making a great noise'. Kendall rushed to the room to find Arthur still lying in bed.

'It is half-past seven o'clock, your Grace'

Arthur replied feebly 'Thank you, where does the Apothecary live?'

'At Deal, your Grace'

'Send for him, I wish to speak to him'.

Dr Hulke was sent for and arrived as quickly as he could. 'I am sorry that your Grace is an invalid. What do you complain of?'

'I think some derangement', was Arthur's reply, passing his hand across his chest.

Hulke was not duly alarmed although his pulse was irregular and he left for his other patients, promising to return at noon.

Kendall asked him if he would take some tea, to which Arthur replied 'Yes if you please'.

Having drunk the tea, Arthur suffered a number of violent fits and when Dr Hulke returned at 9:45 he was unconscious. Mustard poultices were applied and calomel administered but Arthur became restless and they lifted him out of his bed into his chair to be comfortable.

Sophia was called to see him one last time and recorded that 'he was then in his armchair, his legs and feet rolled in blankets, very pale, his eyes closed and breathing heavily, but there was no appearance of pain or suffering'.

He slowly slipped away and at 15:25 on 14 September 1852, he breathed his last so quietly and peacefully that no one was sure that he had gone until Charles held a mirror to his mouth. It

Arthur's dentures.

was how he would have wanted to go – quietly and without fuss.

As was traditional, a death mask was taken without his dentures in, which unfortunately gave his face a hollow, sunken look.

His flag flying at half-mast over Walmer Castle told the world the sad news. Queen Victoria received the news in Scotland and she wrote back immediately to Charles:

The death of the Duke of Wellington at Walmer.

'The Queen is so stunned by the awful suddenness of this sad event, that she cannot believe the reality of it & cannot realize the possibility that the Duke of Wellington, the greatest man this country ever produced, is no more!'

Douro was with his family in Frankfurt when he received the news, but the responsibility of bearing the illustrious name of 'Wellington' was, he felt, beyond him and he continued to sign himself Douro for a number of years. The country went into mourning.

Arthur had left no plans regarding his funeral, probably assuming that his wishes for a simple ceremony would undoubtedly be overturned anyway. He was right, as the queen was determined that he would receive an ornate, very public, State funeral and Prince Albert took personal charge of the arrangements. Because of this, Arthur was to lay in his room at Walmer in a coffin placed on a pedestal next to his camp bed and attended round the clock by a guard of honour, for a full eight weeks. During this period, his body lay in state and was viewed by some 9,000 locals, who had seen him regularly in his walks and rides around Walmer for years.

An ode to the Duke.

99: An Invitation for Mrs Passmore to Attend the Duke of Wellington's Funeral at St Paul's

Queen Victoria took great personal interest in the funeral for her 'dear Duke of Wellington' and Prince Albert took control of many of the details to ensure that it was done right. Having had no idea that the end was so near, no preparations had been made and everything had to be done with great speed. Victoria insisted that both Houses of Parliament were fully involved in the arrangements and this caused further delay before their approval was granted. The Duke's body therefore remained at Walmer, constantly guarded, for a full eight weeks before everything was ready.

The queen was determined that Wellington would be buried at St Paul's resting alongside that other national hero, Nelson. On the evening of 10 November his coffin was finally moved to London in a torchlit procession to the railway station and taken by train (despite his life-long aversion to them) to Chelsea Hospital, where he was to lay in state in the Great Hall. The hall ceiling was decked out like a tent and the walls were adorned with black cloth and adorned with weapons and armorial devices. The coffin was guarded by his old generals. The crowd to see the Duke lying in state grew to such numbers that two women were killed in the crush and troops had to be used to control the numbers. Queen Victoria came herself, but having reached the centre of the room, she could go no further and bursting into tears, she returned hastily to her carriage. It is believed that 200,000 people saw him in the six days he lay in state here.

The night before the funeral, there was a terrible storm, 'a good omen' so the Peninsular veterans said, stormy nights often having presaged one of Arthur's great victories. Estimates vary, but it is believed that over one and a half million people lined the streets to witness the funeral procession and good vantage points had been selling for

exorbitant prices. As a single cannon was fired to signal the start of the procession, the sun broke out and the day was beautiful.

The funeral car had been designed and constructed with incredible speed, but was of the highest quality and only completed minutes before it was needed. The six huge wheels and carriage were cast in solid bronze, the frame measuring 8.2 metres long, 3.4 metres wide and 2.1 metres high, the sides adorned with gilt carving listing his greatest battles and the front and rear adorned with real weapons, flags and armour, taken from the armoury at the Tower of London.

On top of the carriage was placed a huge wooden bier which was then draped in black cloth emblazoned with silver motifs, on top of which would sit the coffin draped in crimson velvet. Arthur's wooden coffin, made by his carpenter at Walmer, was placed in a lead lined coffin and that was placed within one made of English oak. This was then placed within the final outer casket made of Spanish mahogany,

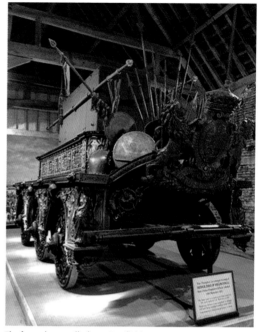

The funeral car on display at Stratfield Saye.

with his coat of arms engraved in the top and an inscription plate added which read:

The most High, Mighty and Most Noble Prince Arthur, Duke and Marquis of Wellington, Marquis of Douro, Earl of Wellington, Viscount Wellington of Talavera and of Wellington, and Baron Douro of Wellesley, Knight of the Most Noble Order of the Garter, Knight Grand Cross of the Most Honourable Order of the Bath, one of her Majesty's Most Honourable Privy Council, and Field Marshal and Commander-in Chief of her Majesty's Forces. Born 1st May 1769. Died 14th September 1852.

Four large halberds stood on the four corners of the bier, which supported a canopy over the coffin, made of worked Indian silver and silk. The halberds made the entire carriage too tall to pass through Temple Bar and therefore a system was installed by which they could be lowered mechanically as it went through. Given the size and mechanical complexity of the car, it is incredible that it was

The carriage fully adorned during the procession.

The procession passes Apsley House.

The service at St Paul's.

Thirteen thousand guests were crammed into St Paul's for the service, on temporary structures, both houses attending in full. Local street urchins apparently dined well on the numberless packed lunches the guests had taken with them, which fell through the boards to the floor below.

Following the service, the coffin was lowered precariously through a hole already cut in the floor into the crypt, as the dean of the Cathedral recorded 'the gradual disappearance of the coffin, as it slowly sank into the vault below, was a sight which will hardly pass from the memory of those who witnessed it.'

The entire funeral cost a staggering £80,000 [£6.5 million today], the funeral car alone costing £11,000 [£900,000]. Victoria wrote to her Uncle Leopold a few days after that 'I cannot say *what* a deep and *wehmtühige* [*sic* – *Wehmutige* – wistful] impression it made on me! It was a beautiful sight. In the Cathedral it was much more touching still!' Not all agreed, many believing such an ostentatious funeral was not in keeping with the plain style of the Duke himself and deploring that there was a huge tawdry trade in funeraria, to commemorate the occasion.

The coffin was set within a massive sarcophagus of Cornish porphyry, as it is to be seen today.

completed in only three weeks, with teams of men working around the clock.

The car was pulled by twelve black horses, draped in black and with giant feathers on their heads, but the weight of the carriage meant that on a few occasions during the procession the car became stuck and had to be freed with the additional effort of dozens of sailors. Ten thousand soldiers, with representatives from every unit in the British Army, formed up in the procession which started at Horse Guards, passed Buckingham Palace on its way past Apsley House, then along Piccadilly, to Pall Mall, past Trafalgar Square to the Strand and from thence to St Paul's.

The procession had started at 8am and Wellington's carriage left at 09:30 and arrived at St Paul's at 12:15. When the carriage finally arrived at St Paul's, the mechanism to turn the coffin failed causing a major delay of over an hour, whilst the crowd within were frozen with the doors propped open for so long.

Arthur's Sarcophagus in the crypt of St Paul's.

100: Pub Sign for The Duke of Wellington

A Wellington secretaire or chest.

Arthur Wellesley became world renowned as the Duke of Wellington and his fame led to many cities towns and villages, mountains and bays being named after him worldwide. There are fifteen places named Wellington in the United States of America, five in Australia, twelve in Canada, two in Chile, four in New Zealand, two in India and one in South Africa. There are also no less than twenty statues or edifices commemorating the Duke around the British Isles and Ireland.

He is also remembered in the boots that he wore, a tall bureau he used on campaign and also a dish (although his association with the naming of Beef Wellington is very obscure). His name was also used on a Second World War British bomber.

In typical British fashion, he is also commemorated with his name above the door of some ninety public houses throughout the British Isles, either as 'The Duke of Wellington', the 'Iron Duke' or simply 'The Wellington'. There is at least one Indian restaurant named 'The Duke of Wellington'.

There are also dozens of Wellington squares, roads, streets and parks. Indeed in every town in Britain there is almost sure to be at least one link to the Great Duke, such was his influence on the first half of the nineteenth century.

Perhaps his greatest accolade, however, was to have six Royal Navy warships named after him. The first was a 74-gun ship launched in 1816, and the second a gigantic 131-gun First Rate launched on 14 September 1852, the very day

The Duke of Wellington, Southampton.

Arthur died. She was powered by both sail and steam and was originally destined to be named HMS *Windsor Castle*. As the first of four of the ultimate development of the 'three-decker' which had ruled the oceans for two centuries, she was twice the size of HMS *Victory*. The ship was renamed in his honour. It was then the most powerful warship in the world, although superseded within three years by the French *Bretagne*. There was also a small sloop named HMS *Wellington* launched in 1934 and after the war was moored at Victoria Embankment on the Thames as a floating livery hall for the Honourable Company of Master Mariners.

The Duke of Wellington, Minehead.

Three other warships have been named *Iron Duke*. The first was a battleship built in 1870, the second built in 1912 was flagship of the fleet at the Battle of Jutland in 1916. The third HMS *Iron Duke*, a Type 23 frigate, was launched in 1991 and is still in service at the time of writing.

Another legacy of Arthur Duke of Wellington is the world-renowned King's College London, which was established in 1829 by King George IV and Arthur and received its royal charter as a university college. It was established in response to the formation of University College London in 1826 as a purely secular institution. Kings was specifically set up 'to imbue the minds of youth with a knowledge of the doctrines and duties of Christianity, as inculcated by the United Church of England and Ireland'. Attendance at chapel and the study of Christianity was a core part of college life.

HMS *Wellington* in 1852.

Index

1st Division, 124
1st Native Cavalry, 35
2nd Division, 104
2nd Native Cavalry, 35
3rd Division, 110, 120, 123
3rd Foot (Buffs), 76
4th Division, 119, 124
4th Madras Native Cavalry, 42
5th Division, 119, 120, 123, 125
5th Madras Native Cavalry, 42
6th Division, 124
6th Line Battalion KGL, 62
7th Division, 100, 124
7th Foot, 104, 203
7th Madras Native Cavalry, 42
9th Légere, 79
12th (Prince of Wales's) Light Dragoons, 14
13th French Dragons, 129
14th Light Dragoons, 77, 149
18th Light Dragoons, 14, 153, 181
19th Light Dragoons, 33–4, 42
22nd Ligne, 125
23rd Foot, 106
23rd Light Dragoons, 79
25th Light Dragoons, 35
29th Foot, 68
30th Foot, 125
31st Foot, 104
33rd Foot, 15, 24, 25–6, 30, 49
40th Foot, 107
41st Foot, 14
43rd Foot, 62
44th Foot, 125
51st Ligne, 129
52nd Foot, 62, 171
57th Foot, 106
58th Foot, 14
62nd Ligne, 125
71st Foot, 99
73rd Highland Regiment, 14
74th Foot, 42
76th Foot, 14

78th Highlanders, 41
79th Foot, 63, 100
80th Foot, 203
81st Foot, 59
87th Foot, 153
88th Foot (Connaught Rangers), 100
92nd Foot, 62–3
94th Foot, 44
95th Foot, 62, 63, 64

Abrantes, 78
Adelaide, Queen, 272
Adour River, 187
Ahmednuggur, 39
Alava, General Miguel de, 123, 179, 208–10
Alba de Tormes, 125, 134
Albuera, Battle of, 103–6
Alcantara, 78
Alexander I, Tsar, 194, 272, 280
Allen, Major, 30
Almada, Lines of, 94
Almaraz, Bridge of, 79, 122
Almeida, 73, 86–8, 98, 102, 103, 109, 122
Anglesey, Marquess of – see Paget
Angouleme, Duc d', 193, 210
Annual Rent, 235
Apsley, Lord, 224
Apsley House, 18, 60, 152, 154, 155–6, 204, 215, 220, 224–7, 256, 265, 272, 273, 276, 280, 287, 288
Arbuthnot, Charles, 279
Arbuthnot, Harriet, 225, 279
Arcangues, 173
Argaum, 43
Arinez, 149
Arthur, Prince, Duke of Connaught & Strathearn, 269, 276
Assaye, Battle of, x, 38–42, 43, 50, 126
Aston, Colonel Henty, 30
Atkins, Tommy, 24
Austria, x, 23, 109, 149, 154, 169, 176, 196, 198, 199, 205, 215, 236, 264
Aveiro, 74–7

Badajoz, 102, 103, 117–21, 122, 135, 208
Bailen, 208
Baird, General Sir David, 31, 36–7
Baji Rao, 38
Balcombe, Elizabeth 'Betsy', 46
Balcombe, Jane, 45
Balcombe, William, 45
Ballesteros, General, 130
Banks, Sir Joseph, 229
Bantry Bay, 54
Barker, Sir William, 243
Baroda, Gaekwad of, 39
Barrosa, Battle of, 103
Barrie, General, 109
Batavia, 36
Bavaria, 215
Bayonne, 170, 172, 173, 175, 176, 187–9
Bedford, Duke of, 258
Beethoven, Ludwig van, 148, 149
Belgium, 23, 97, 199, 201, 205, 214
Benavente, 203
Bentham, Jeremy, 254
Berar, Rajah of, 38
Beresford, Colonel Marcus, 47
Beresford, Marshal William Carr, 95, 98, 103–6, 177, 179, 184
Bilbao, 149
Bishopwearmouth, 57–8
Blake, General, 103, 104
Blenheim, Battle of, 235
Blücher, Marshal, ix, 199, 202–2, 205, 206, 207, 214, 222, 245
Board of Control of India, 18
Boigne, Countess de, 194
Bombay, 36–7
Bonaparte, Jérôme, 281
Bonaparte, King Joseph, 127, 129, 132, 133, 134, 148–9, 155, 156, 161, 218
Bonaparte Pauline, 190
Bonet, General, 124
Bordeaux, 179
Bourbon, Maria Theresa de, 130
Bowes, General, 123
Boxtel, Battle of, 23
Brazil, 55, 66
Briars, The, 45–6

Brissac, Duc de, 13
Brougham, Henry, 247
Brown's Establishment, Chelsea, 10
Brunswick, Duke of, 107
Brussels, 6, 10, 12, 182, 190, 198, 199, 201
Buckingham, Marquis of – see Grenville
Buenos Aires, 55
Burdett, Sir Francis, 252
Burdett-Coutts, Angela, 280
Burgos, 132–5, 145, 146, 148
Burrard, Lt General Sir Harry, 67–9, 70, 71, 72, 73
Burton, Decimus, 227
Busaco, Battle of, 85, 87, 88, 94, 97, 208
Byron, Admiral John, 228

Cadiz, 50, 85, 103, 127
Cadogan, Charlotte, 56, 107
Cadogan, Emily Maud, 56
Campbell, Colin, 44, 114
Campo Maior, 103
Canning, George, 55, 108, 239, 247, 249, 252
Cantillon, Marie Andre, 216, 218–19, 223
Castenschiold, General, 62
Castlereagh, Lord, 67, 108, 193, 196, 198, 239
Cathcart, General Lord, 61–2
Catholic Emancipation Act, xi, 18, 249, 252
Cato Street Conspiracy, 239–40
Caton, Betsy, 281
Caton, Marriane – see Patterson
Cavendish Square, 7
Cecil, Lady Georgina, Marquess of Salisbury, 108
Ceuta, 131
Ceylon (Sri Lanka), 36
Charleroi, 201
Charles IV, King of Spain, 130
Charost, Hotel de, 190
Chelsea Hospital, 285
Christ Church College, Oxford, 16
Cintra, Convention of, 70–1, 74, 83
Ciudad Rodrigo, 86, 87, 102, 103, 109–11, 117, 138, 140, 208
Ciudad Rodrigo, Duque, 115, 116, 130
Cloncurry, Lord, 16
Clausel, General, 124, 129, 132, 157
Clinton, General Henry, 124, 129, 132, 170, 178
Coimbra, 75, 87, 94

Colborne, Sir John, 106
Cole, Colonel Lowry, 47, 106, 157, 177, 178
Colza Oil, 272–3,
Combermere, Lord, 19, 203
Concepcion Fort, 86
Conde, 23
Congreve, William, 89–90, 188
Copenhagen, 50, 53, 60–5, 70, 90, 211
Copenhagen (horse), 211–13, 227
Cork, Ireland, 14, 23
Corn Laws, 249
Cornwallis, Lord, 25, 49
Cortes, 130, 208, 210
Corunna, Battle of, 73, 74, 140, 203
Costa, Jose das Neves, 91
Cotton, Admiral, 70
Cowley, Baron – see Henry Wellesley
Cradock, General 'Beau', 9, 74, 75
Craufurd, General, 86, 110, 111
Creasy, Sir Edward, 11
Crystal Palace, 270
Cuesta, General, 78–80

Dalrymple, Lt General Sir Hew, 67, 69, 70–3
Daly, Nurse, 2
Daly's Club, 8
Dambal Fort, 34
Dangan Castle, 2, 3, 5, 16, 27, 53
Deerfield (Dublin), 53, 55
Delaborde, General Henri, 66–8
Denmark, 61, 211, 215
Denmark, Crown Prince of, 61
d'Erlon, Comte, 157, 160, 206
Dhoondia Wagh (Dhondia Wagh), 33–5, 36, 141
Diocesan School (Trim), 10
Douro, Lord, 59, 84, 256, 275, 284
Douro River, 75, 76, 146
Downing Street, 50–1, 212, 225, 267
Dublin, 1–2, 3, 8, 14, 16, 21, 22, 23, 49, 53–5, 56, 59, 61, 241, 281
Dubouchet, Harriet – see Harriet Wilson
Dubreton, General, 132
Dumouriez, General, 23
Dungannon, Viscount, 5
Dunkirk, 23
Durham Cathedral, 57–8

Eagles, ix, 125, 129, 206
Eardley, Baron, 144
East India Company, 18, 30, 32, 38, 45
Egypt, 30, 36, 37, 55, 222
Elba, 190, 198
Elvas, 73, 103
Elysees Bourbon, 46
Eton, 6, 10–11, 16, 56, 59, 60, 107, 228
Ewhurst, 231, 257–9

Fane, Harriet, 279
Ferdinand VII, King of Spain, 115, 155, 161
Fitzroy, The Honourable Henry, 144
Fletcher, Lt Colonel Sir Richard, 91
Forbes, Admiral, 228
Forbes, Katherine, 228
Fort William College, 18
Fox, Corporal 18th Hussars, 153
Franceschi, General, 75
Francis II, Emperor of Austria, 215
Fraser, Sir William, 11
Frederick August IV, King of Saxony, 215
Frederick William III, King of Prussia, 215
Freese, Miss Isabella, 47
Freineda, 112–13
Freire, General Bernardino, 67
Fremantle, Captain John, 153
Fuentes d'Oñoro, Battle of, 98–101

Gambier, Admiral, 61
Gave d'Oloron, 176
Gawilghur, x, 43–4
George III, King, 73, 83, 229
George IV, King, 229, 247, 252, 265, 291
Georges, Mademoiselle, 194–5, 278
Gleig, Reverend, 2, 10
Goderich, Lord, 249, 252
Godoy, Manuel, 115
Goodyear, Charles, 245
Gordon, Colonel James Willoughby, 138, 211
Governor General of India, x, 18, 31, 38
Goya, 129, 135
Graham, General Sir Thomas, 146, 149, 164, 168
Grassini, Madame Giusseppina, 193, 194, 255, 281
Grattan, Henry, 21
Great Exhibition, 270

Great Reform Act, xi, 249
Green, Private William, 95th Foot, 63
Grenville, George Nugent Temple, Marquis of
    Buckingham, 14, 260
Greville, Lady Charlotte, 279, 269
Grey, Earl, 250-1
Grosvenor Chapel (Mayfair), 7
Grosvenor, General Thomas, 211
Grosvenor, Lord, 277
Grouchy, Marshal, 201
Guards, The, 23, 79, 107, 173, 189

Hague, The, 207, 209
Halifax, 25
Hampton Court Palace, 7, 56, 144
Hanover, 154, 215
Harley Street, No. 11, 59
Harris, General, 31-2
Harrow, 16
Hatfield House, 59
Hawkesbury Lord, 241
Hay, General, 189
Hay, Lady Elizabeth, 59
Hervey, Colonel Felton, 281
Hill, General Rowland, 75, 122, 129, 134, 145, 146,
    157, 173-5, 176-7, 183, 268
Hill-Trevor, Anne, Countess Mornington, 6
Hilsborough, Viscount, 6
Hinuber, General, 189
HMS *Iron Duke*, 291
HMS *Lion*, 228
HMS *Pearl*, 265
HMS *Prometheus*, 61
HMS *Surveilante*, 75
HMS *Wellington*, 290, 292
HMS *Windsor Castle*, 290
Hoby, George (bootmaker), 244
Hoghton, 106
Holkar Yashuant Rao, 38,
Holland, 22, 23-4, 36, 53, 214
Hope, General, 173, 187
Hougoumont, 206
Hulke, Dr, 283
Hulme, Staff Surgeon John, 209
Hunter & Company, 245
Huskisson, William, 249, 264

Hutchinson, Hiram, 244
Hyde Park Corner, 215, 224, 225, 227
Hyder Ali, 29-30, 89

Insurrection Act, 54
Interim Leader, 267
Ireland, Bank of, 22
Irish House of Commons, 16, 21, 22, 226
'Iron Duke', the, 251, 289
Isle de France (Mauritius), 36

Jalna, 40
Jenkins, Miss, 280
Jersey, Lady Sarah, 280
Johnston, Elizabeth, 18
Jourdan, Marshal, 145, 153
Junot, General Andoche, 66-72

Kellerman, General, 70, 71
Kildare Street Club, 8-9
Kilkenny, 14
King's College, London, 291
Kinsale, 14
Kioge, 62-3

La Belle Alliance, 201, 207
La Merced, Fort, 122
La Rhune (mountain), 171-2
La Rochelle, 71
La Torre, 115
Lake, Colonel, 67-8
Lake, General, 38-9, 43
Lamb, Lady Caroline, 280
Laswari, Battle of, 43
Latour-Maubourg, General de La, 106
Lawrence, Sir Thomas, viii, 6, 229, 281
Leach, Captain, 95th Foot, 64
Leipzig, Battle of, 149
Leiria, 75
Lennox, Louisa, 5
Leveson-Gower, Lord Granville, 163
Lieven, Princess, 280
Light Division, the, 86, 99, 110, 119, 171, 173
Ligny, Battle of, 201, 207
Linsingen, Major General, 62, 63
Lisbon, 20, 66, 67, 68, 69, 71, 72, 74, 75, 78, 82, 87,
    91, 92, 94, 95, 107, 144, 151

Liverpool, Lord, 249, 252
Liverpool & Manchester Railway, 262
Long, General, 103
Longford, Lord, 27, 49
Lord Lieutenant of Ireland, 14, 18, 53, 204, 252, 253, 281
Louis Phillipe, King of France, 11
Louis XIV, King of France, 265
Louis XVI, King of France, 22, 23
Louis XVIII, King, 169, 179, 190, 215
Louvre, The, 220
Lyndhurst, John Copley, Lord, 267

Mackenzie, General Alexander, 75, 78
Mackinnon, General, 111
Madras, 29, 42, 144
Madrid, 79, 115, 127–9, 130, 132, 134, 135, 150, 155, 190, 208, 236, 278
Mahon, Lord, 272
Maison du Roi, 207
Malabar Itch, 37, 38
Malcolm, Admiral Sir Pulteney, 46
Mallavelly, 30
Malmesbury, Lord, 107
Maratha Confederacy, 30
Marinet, Monsieur, 216
Marlborough, Duke of, 107, 126, 231, 235
Marmont, Marshal, 109, 111, 122–4, 129
Martello Towers, 54
Maryborough, Baron – see William Wellesley-Pole
Marylebone Cricket Club, 144
Masons, the, 5, 16, 19–20, 22
Massena, Marshal, 86–8, 92, 94, 98–100, 102, 103, 109, 193
Master General of the Ordnance, 238–9
Master of the Mint, 228, 229
Maya Pass, 157, 159, 170
Maynooth College, 55
McHenry, Fort, 90
McGrigor, Doctor, 135
Meath, 4, 16, 20, 243
Medellin, Battle of, 78–9, 208
Merrion Street, 1–2
Metternich, Prince, 198
Moira, Lord, 22, 23
Mondego Bay, 67

Mont St Jean, 202, 206
Montalembert, Charles de, 11
Moore, General Sir John, 59, 68–9, 71, 73, 74, 203
Mornington, Countess – see Anne Hill-Trevor
Mornington, Earl of, 3, 5, 16, 18, 30, 230
Mornington House, 1–2, 16, 53
Mortier, Marshal, 103
Mulgrave, Earl, 238
Murray, Colonel George, 65, 70, 71, 77
Musée Napoleon – see The Louvre
Mysore, 29–30, 33–5, 38, 89–90
Mysore, Sultan of, 33–5
Mysorean rocket men, 89–90

Napier, General Sir William, 59
Napoleon Bonaparte, ix, x, xi, 30, 45–6, 50, 66, 71, 81, 85, 102, 105, 143, 145, 149, 151, 153, 157, 161, 162, 169, 176, 182, 186, 188, 190, 194, 196, 198, 199, 201–2, 205–7, 212, 215, 218, 219, 220, 222–3, 230, 278, 281
Necker, Anne Louise – see Madame de Staël
Nelson, Admiral Horatio, 50–2, 61, 285
Netherlands, the Austrian, 23
Netherlands, The, 154, 190, 198, 199, 201
Ney, Marshal, ix, 20, 78, 193, 201, 218
Nive River, 173
Nivelle River, 172, 201
Nizam of Hyderabad, the, 29, 30, 38–40, 141
Northumberland, Duke of, 16
Northumberland (steam engine), 262

Ocana, Battle of, 85
Occupation, Army of, 194, 214, 215, 255, 279
O'Connell, Daniel, 241, 252, 253
Oporto, Battle of, 74–7, 95, 97, 209
Orange, Prince of, 193
Oropesa, 79
Orthez, 176–8, 179, 209
Ostend, 23
Oxford University, Chancellor of, 260–1

Paget, General Sir Edward, 139
Paget, Lord Henry William, 107, 108, 203–4, 206
Pakenham, Catherine 'Kitty', ix, x, 9, 22, 27–8, 47–9, 56, 59, 84, 193, 194, 232, 255–6, 278, 280
Pakenham Hall, 27, 28, 47, 49

Palencia, 146
Palmerston, Lord, 194, 198
Pamplona, 149, 157, 161, 168
Paris, 16, 46, 102, 108, 190, 193, 209, 216, 218, 220, 236, 247, 255, 278
Paris, Treaty of, 214
Parijskaia, Maria, 194
Parkside, 264
Passajes, 165
Patterson, Marianne, 18, 278, 281
Peel, Sir Robert, 227, 242, 249, 251, 252, 253, 260, 267, 269, 270
Peepulgaon, 39, 41
Peniche, 73
Penrose, Admiral, 188
Pero Negro, 91, 94
Perron, Pierre, 39
Peymann, General, 64
Philippon, General Armand, 117, 120
Pichegru, General, 23–4
Picton, Major General Sir Thomas, 110, 177, 184
Pierrepont, Augusta, 60
Pignerolle, Marquis Marcel de, 12
Pistrucci, Benedetto, 229, 230
Pitt, William, 231
Pitt, William the Younger, 16
Plancenoit, 207
Plasencia, 78
Plowden, James, 257
Poco Velho, 98, 99
Pohlmann, Colonel, 40, 41, 42
Poland, 198
Pole, William, 228
Pole-Tynley-Long-Wellesley, William, 230
Polish lancers, 106
Pollilur, Battle of, 89
Ponsonby, Lord, 246
Poona, Battle of, 38
Popham, Admiral Sir Home, 132
Portland, Prime Minister, 83
Porto – see Oporto
Portugal, x, 18, 20, 67, 70, 71, 73, 74, 75, 78, 80, 81, 85, 86, 87, 88, 90, 91, 92, 94, 95, 98, 102, 103, 108, 122, 123, 143, 145, 146, 151, 154, 175, 203, 208, 247, 275

Portuguese troops, x, 67, 74, 75, 76, 77, 78, 80, 81, 82, 87, 88, 92, 94, 95, 96–7, 98, 103, 106, 109, 114, 120, 123, 131, 160, 169, 173, 199
Powercourt, Lord, 12
Prince Regent, the, 153, 203, 220, 236
Prize Money, 32, 65
Prussia, x, 23, 154, 169, 176, 196, 199, 201, 205, 206, 207, 214, 215, 236

Quatre Bras, 200–01
Queluz Palace, 71

Ramsay, Captain Norman, 100–01
Retiro, The, 127–9
Rey, General, 164, 168
Richelieu, Prime Minister, 215
Richmond, Duchess of, 201
Rifle Corps, the, 59
Rivers, Lord, 231
Robertson, Sergeant David, 92nd Foot, 62
Rochefort, 71
Rocket (steam engine), 264
Rockets, 30, 61, 64, 89–90, 188
Roland, Hyacinthe-Gabrielle, 16
Rolica, Battle of, 67
Roman Catholic Relief Act, 253
Roncesvalles Pass, 157
Royal Academy of Equitation, Angers, 12
Royal Commission on Universities, 261
Royal Hospital Chelsea, 72
Royal Mint Museum, 229
Royal Navy, the, 89, 228, 271, 289
Royal School Armagh, 16
Russell, Lord Alexander, 258
Russia, x, 70, 113, 145, 154, 169, 176, 196, 199, 205, 215, 236, 272
Rutland Square, Dublin, 49
Rye, 49

Sacramental Test Act, 252
Sahagun, 203
Salabat Khan, 35
Salamanca, 109, 122–6, 127, 134, 145, 208, 215
Salisbury, Lady, 182, 272, 276, 280, 282
Samuel Whyte's Academy, Dublin, 10
San Carlos, Duquesa de, 194

San Cayetano, Fort, 122
San Sebastian, 157, 161, 164–8
San Vincente, Fort, 122
Santarem, 94
Sauveterre, 176
Saville Row, 230
Saxony, 198, 215
Schaumann, Commissary, 112
Schwartzenberg, Prince, 199
Scindia, Daulet Rao, 38–40
Seguier, William, 155
Seringapatam (Srirangaptana), 26, 30, 31, 32, 33, 35, 47, 89, 141
Seteais, Palace of, 71–2
Seville, 85, 127
Seville Regiment, 208
Shannon, Bugler Paddy, 153
Shelley, Lady Frances, 163, 279
Sherbrooke ,General Sir John, 24, 26
Sidmouth, Lord, 239
Six Acts, The, 239
Slave Trade, xi, 191, 198
Smith, Lady Anne, 144
Smith, Emily, 144
Smyth, Charles Culling, 144
Somerset, Lt Colonel Fitzroy Lord, 160, 216, 218
Somerset, Henry, Marquess of Worcester, 144
Sorauren, 157
Souham, General, 133
Soult, Marshal, ix, 74–7, 78–9, 95, 103–6, 117, 127–9, 132, 133–4, 138, 149, 157, 160, 165, 168, 169, 170, 171–2, 173–4, 176–7, 179, 183, 186, 187–8, 189, 193
Southampton, Baron, 144
Spain, x, 18, 20, 23, 44, 66, 73, 76, 77, 78, 81, 85, 94, 98, 102, 103, 108, 111, 114, 115, 117, 121, 122, 127, 130, 135, 143, 145, 146, 148, 149, 151, 154, 157, 161, 162, 180, 181, 194, 203, 208, 209, 210, 211, 222, 237, 247, 276
Spanish troops, x, 78, 79–80, 103, 104, 106, 111, 125, 129, 130–1, 145, 157, 161, 169, 170, 176, 184
Sparrow, Olivia, 47
Spencer, General Sir Brent, 67
St George's, Dublin, 48–9
St Helena, xi, 43, 46, 207, 218, 223
St Jean de Luz, 188

St Jean Pied de Port, 169
St Julian Fort, 91
St Luke's Chelsea, 57
St Michael's Sunderland, 57
St Paul's Cathedral, 52, 285, 288
St Peters, Dublin, 1
St Petersburg, 149
Staël, Madame de, 191, 278
Stephenson, George, 262
Stevenson, Colonel, 34, 39, 40, 42
Stockholm, 107
Stratfield Saye, 60, 162, 210, 211–12, 224, 231–4, 256, 258, 270, 273, 274, 281, 286
Stuart, Lord, 247
Stuart, Lt General John, 38
Sultanpettah Tope, 30
Susannah (ship), 37
Sweden, 55

Tagus River, 70, 75, 78, 80, 91, 94, 122,
Talavera, Battle of, 78–80, 81, 83, 95, 115, 208, 286
Talleyrand, Foreign Minister, 198
Temple Grove School, 59
Thouvenot, General, 188–9
Tipu Sultan, 29–32, 89
Toledo, 122
Tordesillas, 146
Toro, 146
Torres Vedras, 91, 94
Toulouse, Battle of, 179, 183–6
Trafalgar, Battle of, 50, 208, 288
Travancore, 30
Trim, 4, 10, 16, 19, 20, 21–2, 228, 241–2, 243
Trinity College Cambridge, 3, 59
Tudela, Battle of, 208
Tuileries, the, 190

Uxbridge, Earl of – see Henry William Paget

Valenciennes, 23
Valladolid, 129, 146
Vane, Sir Charles, 211
Venezuela, 55, 67
Victor, Marshal, 78–9, 95
Victoria, Queen, 11, 26, 225, 234, 251, 264, 268, 269–72, 283, 285, 288

Victory Table Service, 265
Vienna, 198, 215
Vienna, Congress of, xi, 193, 196–7
Vimiero, Battle of, 68, 70, 83
Vinegar Hill, Battle of, 54
Vitoria, Battle of, 145–8, 152, 155, 157, 180, 181, 208–10, 215, 244

Walmer Castle, 269, 276, 282–4, 285, 286
Walsh, Lord, 12
Waterloo, Prince of, 214
Waterloo Banquet, the, 265–6
Waterloo Palace, 232
Wavre, 201
Wedderburn-Webster, Lady Frances, 279
Weimer, Marguerite – see Mademoiselle Georges
Wellesley, Anne, 116, 144
Wellesley, Arthur Richard, Lord Douro (son), 59
Wellesley, Charles (son), 60, 282–3
Wellesley, Francis Seymour, 6
Wellesley, Reverend Gerald, 49, 56
Wellesley, Gerald Valerian, 58
Wellesley, Henry Baron Cowley, 56, 107–8, 203

Wellesley, Mary Elizabeth, 6
Wellesley, Marquess Richard, 3, 4, 6, 16–18, 29, 30, 36, 38, 83
Wellesley, William, 83, 228
Wellesley-Pole, William, 216, 228–30
Wellington College, 271
Wesley, Garret, 3, 19, 228
Westmorland, Lord, 14
Wilberforce, William, 191
William IV, King, 266, 267
William of Orange, King, 199
Wilson, Harriet, 246, 278
Wilton, Lady, 280
Winchelsea, Earl of, 163, 254
Windsor, Dean of, 58
Windsor Castle, 235, 268
Wolfe Tone, Theobald, 21
Wolverton Estate, 258
Wood, Colonel, 211
Württemberg, 215
Wyatt, Benjamin, 224, 231

York, Duke of, 15, 23–4, 180